Surviving Internal School Politics

Practical Strategies for Dealing with the Dynamics

Second Edition

Beverley H. Johns, Mary Z. McGrath,
and Sarup R. Mathur

ROWMAN & LITTLEFIELD EDUCATION
A division of
ROWMAN & LITTLEFIELD PUBLISHERS, INC.
Lanham • New York • Toronto • Plymouth, UK

Published by Rowman & Littlefield Education
A division of Rowman & Littlefield Publishers, Inc.
A wholly owned subsidary of The Rowman & Littlefield Publishing Group, Inc.
4501 Forbes Boulevard, Suite 200, Lanham, Maryland 20706
www.rowman.com

10 Thornbury Road, Plymouth PL6 7PP, United Kingdom

British Library Cataloguing in Publication Information Available

Library of Congress Cataloging-in-Publication Data

Johns, Beverley H. (Beverley Holden) author.
[Surviving internal politics within the school]
Surviving internal school politics : practical strategies for dealing with the dynamics / Beverley H. Johns, Mary Z. McGrath, Sarup R. Mathur.—Second edition.
pages cm
Includes bibliographical references.
ISBN 978-1-4758-0095-1 (pbk. : alk. paper)—ISBN 978-1-4758-0096-8 (electronic)
1. Teachers—Professional relationships. I. McGrath, Mary Z., 1947- author. II. Mathur, Sarup R., author. III. Title.
LB1775.J544 2013
371.1—dc23
2012039169

™ The paper used in this publication meets the minimum requirements of American National Standard for Information Sciences Permanence of Paper for Printed Library Materials, ANSI/NISO Z39.48-1992.

Printed in the United States of America

Contents

Introduction

Educators have a rewarding profession—molding the future generation of our country. What educators teach children can make a positive difference in their lives. They are excited about working with their students.

They learn to see progress in small steps and celebrate their students' successes. At the same time, they pat themselves on the back when they have planned and executed a great lesson. They cherish those moments when a student lets them know that he or she has finally gotten a concept.

Yet, educators have learned early in the year that there are a set of dynamics among their colleagues in the school environment—the internal politics of the school. Whether they learn to understand and live within that group dynamic will determine their success with their students.

If educators are bogged down with gossip, ostracism, and upsetting events, they will not be able to work effectively with their students. These dynamics are illustrated throughout this book through the use of fictitious educators who portray staff dealing with situations to which readers can relate.

In each chapter, readers will find an action plan designed to provide tools that educators should utilize in surviving internal politics.

The newest version of this book provides readers with two new chapters. One gives practical advice for working successfully in the teaching profession at a time when there is so much negative publicity about education and there are many attacks on the work teachers do. Indeed, educators are teaching in troubled times, and the one new chapter provides them with practical strategies on how to maintain a positive attitude.

The second new chapter focuses on strategies for dealing with the expanding world of technology. With the increasing use of social media and texting and with easy access to technology, all educators are presented with new challenges.

This book provides readers with the basic coping strategies of surviving within the political arena of their schools. It was once said, "There is no such thing as staying out of politics; all issues are political."

If educators want to survive, they should read this book and find practical strategies from those who have collectively worked within the school setting for over seventy-five years—the voices of experience share helpful coping skills.

Chapter One

Managing School Politics and Maintaining Personal Integrity

> To me
> Integrity
> Helps to withstand outside pressures
> That don't fit my moral measures
> "They" want me to be untrue
> To what I know I must do
> Character counts wherever I go
> At school I refuse the undertow
> When pulled by an educational trend
> A higher law tells me I cannot bend
> If I am connected to the good and true
> My heart will tell me just what I should do.

Amanda, an experienced teacher, has become aware of the range of methods and texts touted as being the best in the field of math. Amanda has at this point in her career worked with many students who struggled with various aspects of math. Through her training and hard-won hands-on experience, she developed a repertoire of methods that help her to meet the needs of many students. She reached a level of confidence and knew exactly what to do when presented with a particular kind of problem.

To Amanda's satisfaction, her peers began to come to her to troubleshoot when they were stuck and unable to help a student who was struggling. When going to a convention and moving among the booths, she instinctively knew what materials to eliminate as a potential purchase and where to place her attention as she detected what she believed to be legitimate methodology.

Over the years, she has seen trends come and go. She could time the return of the pendulum swing in the popularity of methodology. Despite trends and fads, Amanda continued to successfully teach her students and advise her peers in the process of math instruction.

One year, a particular method of math instruction caught the attention of educators in a really big way. In fact, publishers fell like dominoes to follow the fall fashion on how best to teach math. Amanda began to feel concerned when her district decided to revisit its current program. She believed that she and her peers were doing their best, and she felt skeptical about getting on the latest bandwagon.

She hoped that this trend would pass quickly and that it would not interfere with or obstruct the way she taught. The way that Amanda taught was working! Year after year, students from other districts who arrived in her class with skill deficits found that with her help they began to take off. She filled in their instructional holes and, after detecting what worked best with them, set each one in the direction of success.

Amanda's fear of the winds of change materialized one blustery winter day at her school's weekly faculty meeting. Her principal announced that the district was seeking volunteers to be part of a committee to adopt a new program. The principal asked if anyone was interested in becoming part of that committee. Due to her proven expertise and interest, all heads turned in Amanda's direction.

Thinking that it would be a fascinating experience to view and evaluate a variety of materials, she decided to apply her well-developed skills and finely tuned instincts to this decision-making process. The district administrators presented their mission as one of great importance and high professional value. Various publishers came to meetings of the committee to share their newest offerings. Amanda listened and watched. As each meeting came and went, she began to feel emptier. Red flags went up, and she felt sincere concern for particular students in her class.

She feared that these programs would not work for some of her students. Yes, these books and materials were well packaged. Yes, there were great elements in each, but then after being inundated by these sales presentations, she returned with relief to her classroom to do what she knew how to do best in order to ensure success for her students.

Initially, Amanda shared the interest and enthusiasm of others on her committee. She believed as they all did that they were about to embark on a worthy and interesting venture on behalf of the young people of her district. As the weeks wore on, the other committee members maintained their interest and excitement. Amanda, on the other hand, became more critical and felt grave concerns. Why was she feeling like the Lone Ranger in this group?

Eventually, Amanda could not contain herself, and she began to challenge the publishers' salespeople. Even though they struggled when presented with her direct and clear questions and did not give answers to her satisfaction, the others on the committee maintained their trust in this process. Amanda saw more and more weaknesses and contrasts to the ways that she brought solid instruction to her students.

Word got out that Amanda was separating herself from the cohesiveness that the committee was trying to establish, and members described her to peers in their respective schools as the one who was blocking the process. Rumors flew in her district that she was locked in to math methods that were outdated. She became more and more isolated on the committee. After awhile, she received fewer and fewer requests for feedback and instructional advice from the teachers in her own school.

In spite of it all, she continued to steadily and successfully teach math skills and concepts to the students in her charge. Ultimately, the math committee voted on a program adoption. In her mind, the best one was still not as good as what had been going on in her school. Amanda was the only "nay" vote at the final committee meeting. Despite her public opposition, little was said to her about her concerns. No administrator or committee member took time to ask her why she voted against the committee's recommendation.

The school year ended, and Amanda sent a classroom of students who had developed solid math skills on to the next grade. She packed up her materials and took her summer break. At the fall workshop, she learned that the district required her to use the newly adopted program for all of her students. By consenting to do this, Amanda knew that she would be turning out less successful students the following spring.

What would she do? Go along with the district? Resign in order to avoid violating her principles? Tough it out and seek to build a coalition with others who would eventually become as disturbed about the program as she was? Seek another role in the district, one that did not involve math instruction? These are questions that teachers might ask themselves if they were in a similar situation.

Perhaps the fictitious story of Amanda sounds a bit like an exercise designed to help a student come to terms with personal values. Incidences like what Amanda faced occur, though often on a smaller scale, in the professional lives of teachers all the time. If a teacher does not have a sense of solid values or a bedrock core of justice, honor, integrity, and honesty, he or she will be like the other committee members whom Amanda encountered.

Such teachers go with the flow and follow any Pied Piper who comes down the line. They do not even realize that there is a grain to go against because they have no substance with which to challenge flimsy and questionable teaching methods, nor do they have the gumption to speak out for solid values. They espouse no enduring substantive values. They lack the ability to envision a future that is frightening for youth because they cannot see consequences of change for change's sake. They simply smile, nod, and agree to just go along and get along.

When a teacher has not built an inner core of integrity, political correctness trumps ideology. To know what one believes based on maturity and morality comes with time and openness. Having the instincts to detect direction, apply principles, and follow through with predictability and steadiness in a changing educational world challenges the most respected of teachers. Yet somehow, when the rubber meets the road and daily decisions present themselves, teachers apply right and good values to the teaching task on a continual basis.

They have no problem determining when students are telling the truth. They sense when peers are not being honest or when peers are betraying them and aligning with other coworkers on a regular basis. When the time is right, teachers realize in their spirits how and why they must act. They act and, by being principled in their decisions, build their confidence in their abilities to continue in their directions.

How do they know what to do? Where does this well of values come from? Teachers from various backgrounds, political persuasions, levels of experience, training institutions, and faith walks find their ways through the morass of moral and ethical issues presented to them when they sincerely seek to find the answers that best apply to situations.

They stop; listen to the authenticity within their own beings; and seek spiritual assistance and the help of their friends, families, and faith communities as situations warrant. They know that, sometimes, the way is clear and definite. They realize too that there are times when clarity comes slowly.

Yet, they trust that they will be where they need to be, doing what they need to be doing at the right time. From the truth in their own hearts and the optimal conditions that they have created and experienced from their own teaching backgrounds, they fashion the present to define futures that promise the best for their students and their schools.

They also accept the fact that they will face dead ends, speak and not be understood or supported, and fail when using the best instruction that they know due to factors in the lives of students that are beyond their control. In spite of the ups and downs of education, they also strongly believe that they will have the insights and courage to manage what awaits them in the days ahead. They decide to use defeat as a learning experience to draw from in the future.

Each experience becomes an event to add to their personal information bank to be drawn on if a similar situation occurs in the future. They understand that life is composed of ups and downs, joys and sorrows, victories and defeats. They prepare for these opposites as they present themselves in the arena of the classroom, at an educational committee meeting, on the playground, in the gym, or at the end of an ordinary day as students file onto the bus.

Teachers who apply principles for the benefit of their students, families, and learning communities know who they are and where they have been, and they prepare as best they can for where they are going educationally and professionally. Day after day, they build on their insights and experiences to clearly define their roads toward their professional futures.

They simplify work-world complexities, and they create and influence the unfolding of each moment so that it connects best to the following year. Each knows his or her way and lives it according to educated judgment and integrity.

APPLYING MORAL VALUES AND PROFESSIONAL PHILOSOPHY

Teachers do not reach their personal pinnacle of ethical and moral practice overnight. The give-and-take of teaching creates new questions and presents growth opportunities on a regular basis. Sometimes, situations present the invitation to act and to act with gusto, with vocal or written expression of affirmation or opposition. At other times, prudence suggests that refraining from speech holds a stronger sway in a situation.

Wisdom, knowledge, personal experience, trust of a colleague, the advice of a supportive soul friend all add up and point to the time and place to take action. A teacher's personality, background, working situation, and depth of knowledge mix to create a direction and response to a student need or to a systemic issue that could only happen once and happen rightly as a result of this mix.

Complexities become situations that, with repetition, can change into those of clarity and simplicity. With this repetition comes refined life and professional experience. Yet somehow, once it seems that instructors believe that they have found a plateau and think they know what to do in just about any circumstance, a new student arrives presenting an educational puzzle that is completely out of the range of what has ever occurred in the past.

Just when a teacher settles in with a team and has the belief that the team is working, one member retires and the group dynamics become confusing again. With such change, the remaining team members must regroup, learn to trust, and discover what to say and how to arrange their planning with consideration of the new person among them. They must face the potential of philosophical differences and work together to speak forthrightly and openly to one another to determine their collective direction.

With change and with challenge comes the invitation to any educator to reach for the greatest good in the immediate circumstances, as well as that in the big picture. Without a perfect template, teachers bring the best from their sharpened intellects and seasoned souls to keep their classrooms and colleagues on course. They apply their values to the many challenging and unpredictable circumstances that demand direction during the workdays of any professional educator.

Such teachers develop a professional belief statement drawn from their religious or ethical principles, school situations that they and others have encountered, and life experiences. In order to keep fresh and aware, they review these ideas regularly, changing the statement as they grow in insight, character, and professionalism. They also examine the challenges of each day through the prism of their own growth. Thus such educators continue to process life on a regular basis, with full awareness that life is a gift and they intend to live with full integrity.

Though there is not a formula out there that best fits each unique teacher, any professional educator can develop ways to respond to his or her students' unpredictable learning and emotional concerns, parents' questions and needs, colleagues' interests, and administrators' views. When teachers formulate professional ethics and creeds that become more than intellectual beliefs, they integrate ideals into their teaching personalities.

As their values become natural parts of their professional demeanors and impact their daily exchanges, students and peers benefit. Thus these educators enter their school well prepared to meet the variety of people and situations that come their way each day. (More on this topic can be found in Chapter 3, "Everyday Challenges to Our Educational Values" in *Ethical Dilemmas in Education* by Johns, McGrath, and Mathur, Rowman and Littlefield Education, 2008.)

STANDING AGAINST THE TRENDS AND TIDES OF EDUCATIONAL PRACTICE

During the pre-teaching phase of an educational career, aspiring educators open themselves to the knowledge, perspectives, and experiences of their professors and the teachers whom they are selected to work with in their first school situation. Once in the field and working with their own students in a formal educational setting, new teachers begin to apply what they have learned.

Through the daily interaction with students, teachers in the initial phases of their careers take what they have been given in formation, apply it to their current situations, and try to reconcile what they know with the expectations in the setting. When starting in a school district, a teacher fresh from a college or university arrives with ideals and expectations that may be challenged once he or she begins to work full-time in a school.

Perhaps the school district espouses a philosophy that contradicts earlier training, or maybe this teacher is placed on a team trained in another educational era with completely different ideas on how a curriculum should be applied. If so, new teachers face potential conflict between their own senses of direction and the educational cultures to which they have been assigned. They may believe that they have the upper hand as far as educational methodology goes, given that they have been schooled in the latest in educational thinking and research.

Veteran teachers may not have a strong interest in what a new teacher has learned and could even be threatened by a new teacher's awareness of current educational theory and practice. Over time, through trial and error, application of training, and openness to what has worked for other educators, new teachers learn to share successes and failures on a daily basis. In doing so, they find a growing sense of understanding of what works best for their students.

If wise, they will be alert to effective practice whenever they see it, and they will determine if it is applicable to their current situation. There is always something to be learned from experienced teachers. New professionals, in turn, bring with them growth opportunities for those who have worked for some time in a school setting. A mature give-and-take allows for respectful associations and ongoing professional growth.

Educational opinion and methodological differences do not always exist between teachers trained in various periods. Sometimes, teachers like Amanda find opposition in their peer groups or even in a district that is going in a different direction from what they believe is best for students. Teachers in such circumstances face difficult dialogue and pressure to comply with mandates that go against their professional grain.

When faced with encouragement to move in a direction that seems different or difficult, they must respond from a true sense of belief in what is best for students, not what is familiar and comfortable. Once that aspect is discarded, they must view educational history, not the location of the current pendulum in the swing process, and try the best they can to get to the heart of the matter.

The first step is an honest quest to make a distinction between educational advancement and a package that is simply a part of a trend. If teachers discover that they are resistant simply because they are not comfortable with change, they have an issue of being closed to growth. If that is the case, it is a matter of their edging toward growth, their being willing to become open to new learning, and their trusting in another's ability to add to their educational repertoire.

On the other hand, if teachers are clearly affronted with something imposed on them that they strongly believe is detrimental to students, then they are faced with a completely different issue. It then becomes a matter of deciding why, in concrete as well as philosophical terms, they cannot go in the same direction as that of their district or team. This fork in the road is a time for decision and foresight in terms of what the consequences will be if conflict comes out in the open.

Perhaps it would be a matter of a sincere discussion with an administrator or team leader. With proper understanding between the individuals, a level of latitude could be agreed on to sufficiently satisfy both parties. Maybe it is a matter of serious soul-searching if a teacher believes that she or he cannot work compatibly with a group or within a certain system. Seeking the greatest good, a teacher may decide to risk going solo and taking the fallout.

Perhaps in doing so a teacher may need the support of the union. Departing from the formal philosophy of a school district may mean building a lateral coalition with others who have similar concerns. After discussion that a program is not really working and that this reality is true in several classroom situations, those in the position of decision making may better hear the issue so that change and redirection can come about.

No situations of educational differences resolve themselves without effort and sincerity on the part of all involved. Oftentimes, with courage and skilled communication, educators ably come to agreement and acceptance as they strive to bring balanced and effective instruction to students. Unfortunately, there are times when a resolution cannot be found and the minority party, despite being a prophet that no one chooses to hear or is ready to believe, decides that it is time to depart from the current situation.

Teachers in this position may decide to go into another branch of education in their immediate or different circumstances, or they may take their philosophies and ideas with them and move forward into a more compatible setting. They may even establish their own private business in the form of an institute or entrepreneurial endeavor.

At the time, their conflicts with their current circumstances may seem like dead ends and defeats. Yet that crisis becomes the open door to reaching their professional potential that would have gone unrealized if they had left their concerns unchallenged and remained in their former roles.

LOOKING INTO THE MIRROR

Teachers who choose to speak out and challenge the status quo do not do so lightly. Instead, they come to the realization that they are at great enough odds with their current circumstances and that they must act. In acting, they have to clearly know why they disagree with their situations and fully realize what they believe and desire professionally. To find that sense of personal and professional certitude, teachers muster their courage and begin with themselves.

They view their workplace from the vantage point of a synthesis of the Golden Rule, their spirituality, and social conscience. As these factors blend within the teachers' vision, coloring their background and training, the teachers know what they need to do daily in order to be able to stand before the mirror at night and look into their own eyes. Before that mirror, they should say "yes" to their day and affirm their decisions and responses to the expressions of trust in the eyes of their students.

They breathe a sigh of relief that they stood their ground when confronted by a colleague whose intentions were destructive and negative. Teachers with integrity, looking into their own eyes, see a sparkle and notice deep satisfaction because they know that they are operating within the confines of integrity. When at work or at home, with their friends or with community associates, they are who they are. They present their true selves with full appreciation for the dignity of those with whom they come in contact at all times, whether that be at work or elsewhere.

They can truly maintain a consistent personality whether wearing a professional or parent hat. Because of this, such staff members are not strangers to themselves or to others. Their integrity impels them to be the same when meeting students, colleagues, and families in the classroom, at the conference table, or at the community center for a sports event. Teachers of integrity can also look into the same mirror and admit their errors at the end of each day.

By reviewing a rerun of their day, they recognize where they could have applied more patience, courage, or common sense. Being honest with themselves, they resolve to return to anyone whom they may have offended and to rebuild the relationship with an apology or a gentler manner. They understand that they are constantly reaching for a higher level of professionalism and that the only way to get there is through reflection and application of new understandings to their relationships in the workplace.

WITHSTANDING UNPROFESSIONAL PEER PRESSURE

In spite of their best efforts, some teachers who aspire to act with goodwill and treat their peers with respect do not always experience reciprocal behavior. Among these peers are staff members at school who look in the mirror at night simply to brush their teeth. These teachers base their actions on their needs and concerns at the time. Self-will, an unprincipled view of the world, and an unexamined pattern of behavior keep them from evaluating their own approach to their jobs and the people whom they encounter there.

Consequently, clashes occur between teachers seeking harmony and opportunities for growth and those putting in their time and getting caught up in daily pettiness. Like individuals seem to cluster together. Some groups of teachers decide on a course of action, and when someone on their staff chooses to express opposition to the status quo, that person upsets the apple cart. His or her opinion may challenge peers to take the high road when they prefer to take the easy path.

By acting with integrity, simply by being themselves, teachers on this high road either draw others to follow them or bring out the fears and insecurities of those unable to follow the same course. Whatever the dynamic, teachers who live on principle inevitably come up against opposition in the form of peer pressure.

Underhanded and unprofessional behavior surfaces in a system when those espousing the standard way of operating decide that their patterns are being threatened by someone who, through manners, words, or actions, represents a potential loss of their comfortable or incompetent ways. Thus, they metaphorically twist the arms of those whom they want to pull back in line in order not to lose their own lower standards or familiar ways of carrying out their careers.

Sometimes teachers find themselves alone and up against a group of peers who insist on badgering them or shunning them into compliance with systemic status quo practice. When in this situation, they realize that they have options to survive and counter such unprofessional peer pressure. Educators with firm integrity may choose to revisit their personal belief statement in order to decide if what they are being pressured into is in line with their own professional ethic.

If such teachers have determined that their own stance, opinion, or direction differs from that of their peers, they determine whether they can look into the mirror and live with compliance to others' wishes. If teachers with solid integrity decide that their own direction departs from what peers are pushing, they mentally review the fact that these people are peers and they themselves do not have to be subordinate to equals.

With that in mind, they determine to move forward as before, giving no credence to external pressure. Courage and inner strength help to outlast unrelenting pressure from peers who, without convictions based on principle, cannot outlast secure and professional individuals. Without a strong direction and belief system, those with weak standards will lose steam and give up.

HANDLING UNPROFESSIONAL PRESSURE FROM AN ADMINISTRATOR

Sometimes the building or department administrator places pressure on a teacher to act in a certain way. Technically, they abuse their authority by asking a teacher to break district protocol, state policy, or even the law. Perhaps they will ask for falsified reporting of some kind or pressure a teacher to withhold information that the law requires reported. Here a teacher is caught between two authorities, yet the one in the position of authority, by asking for breach of policy or legal requirements, has moved apart from true authority.

By asking a teacher for unethical or illegal practice, the authority figure has stepped aside from legitimacy in viewpoint and position. Teachers in such circumstances find themselves in a difficult spot that is not one of their own choosing. Nevertheless, if they quietly submit to the administrative request without discussion or challenge, they risk placing themselves in a position of receiving sanction, in addition to facing themselves in the mirror at the end of the day.

Bottom line: If a teacher has to sign off on a form that represents a compromise to the truth, that teacher is taking responsibility for the information that she or he has verified. If teachers withhold information that requires immediate reporting, they are not only jeopardizing a young person but are also risking that the reality of the circumstance in question will be discovered by another staff person or individual outside the school. Ultimately, they will have to face the question of why they chose not to take proper action.

Because the administrators, through unethical behavior, have decided to abdicate their position of trust, a teacher then must move toward another seat of authority. That may be in the form of a principal or a principle. It is a delicate matter to speak to another administrator or director about a fellow peer, yet the whistle must be blown on wrong action. This can be done with delicacy and confidentiality if a teacher trusts and respects another district administrator.

If such a relationship does not exist, a union representative can be approached for confidential consultation to help determine a proper course of action. If a teacher decides it is better to act from principle, that teacher may decide to seek guidance from a trusted outsider, even a lawyer, or keep his or her own counsel on the matter. Each event, whether occurring with peers or administration, requires a unique response from a teacher caught in any ethical quagmire. Taking the road of integrity, though it may appear difficult, remains the only path to true professionalism.

CHANGING DIRECTIONS MIDSTREAM: REVERSING AFTER BEGINNING TO YIELD YOUR VALUES

Fatigue, busyness, or fear may cause teachers to take a direction in their own actions that they eventually regret. Then after reflection, the convergence of actuality and their spirituality, or just plain discomfort, they realize that they have compromised. Backpedaling is harder than taking immediate action. However, an unaddressed action that causes anguish does not disappear until it is addressed.

Because each circumstance differs, the route back to square one, where an act can be rectified and changed, will be unique. Perhaps things can be made right again through an anonymous letter or a private conversation. Professional threads that need to be unraveled and rewoven can be fixed, as well as something that has been broken, with sincere intent and action based on reflection or wise advice. What matters is the objective and effort to rebuild a broken relationship or fix a report that needs to be corrected.

Once teachers in such situations have found the new road, they then need to take credit for arriving at the realization that they need to act and follow through. Once these individuals have changed direction, they must avoid berating themselves for not acting sooner. Admitting a mistake is part of being human, and professionals respect those in their midst who face their actions with honesty.

INTEGRITY THROUGH ADVOCACY FOR STUDENTS WITH SPECIAL NEEDS AND VULNERABILITIES

Does working with students with special needs require a certain kind of sensibility or ethical mind-set? Perhaps knowledge of educational needs leads one to realize that all students learn differently and that each child responds best to a particular kind of instruction. Students with a range of academic, social, and emotional needs can overwhelm even the most skilled on a staff. Some students require more effort on the part of a teacher than others.

Because the knowledge of learning differences has grown, the challenge to recognize and assist students with unique needs presents itself as a hard one. Again, integrity calls on staff members to notice the need and address it properly. Working with a student in a group who varies from the rest of the students requires thought and special skill. Professional development classes and teacher training sessions give teachers the opportunity to hone the skills necessary to not only teach these students effectively but also advocate for them.

Sometimes the word *equality* is one tied closely to *ethics*. After all, everyone wants to be treated fairly and justly. However, when a teacher facing an entire classroom looks at these students and determines that all of these young people should be treated equally, that teacher has just created an impossible task. Giving equal time and effort to each student in a classroom comprised of individuals with varied needs and abilities would be a difficult task indeed. Equality in regard to students has an entirely different and new definition.

Perhaps it is best to say that teaching a class of students and treating them as equals means giving each one the type of instruction and level of effort needed for the student to reach his or her potential. It may require far less time for a teacher to ensure that an average or top student meets and even exceeds his or her capabilities. A child who is emotionally and academically vulnerable needs a great deal of consideration in order to make his or her way through a day in a typical classroom.

Once this redefinition of equality becomes a part of a teacher's mind-set and various practices and accommodations become a normal part of classroom routine, all students benefit. Students with emotional, academic, and social challenges benefit from practical instructional components and educational practices such as the establishment of a routine that is predictable and free of complexity. It is to their advantage when they can begin each day with a ritual that signals that the class is a cohesive group and that all belong.

It is helpful when they have a specific spot where they can turn in their assignments. Use of verbal review of a visual schedule before each day or before a new class begins reorients the students. Students become grounded when they are able to sit in a spot that allows for optimal learning through consideration of lighting, hearing needs, and distractions from peers, door-ways, and windows. Teachers affirm these students when they are aware of student strengths and capitalize on them whenever possible.

It is helpful if teachers read the files of students with special needs for tips on how to assist them best and apply accommodations to ease learning for students whose needs are not met by standard instruction. Teachers can also support students when they foster mutually beneficial relationships among them. Teachers should arrange the bulletin boards and display areas so that everyone can read the postings. It is also beneficial when a classroom is free of excess clutter and objects hanging from the ceiling.

Teachers ultimately support students when they stay connected to parents in a partnership relationship and join professional organizations that offer conventions and networking events where teachers learn strategies to apply to their teaching. It is wise to present a lesson or concept with as many modalities as possible in order to reach all students.

Growing teachers remain open to new alternative instructional strategies and stay alert for signs of academic and emotional difficulty in their students. They work closely with special-ists to address any issues as soon as possible through arranging time for support or the referral process. The features and practices just mentioned may seem like common sense and basic practice, yet sometimes teachers are too busy or too close to their own situation to maintain habits that support and enhance the learning of each student in the classroom.

It may appear to take a lot of time to put certain components into place to assist students with special needs. However, once procedures and routines are established, they become time-savers because students that would otherwise flounder function more capably due to proper instruction and helpful organizational systems. When a teacher sets up a classroom environment and a set of instructional plans with the full range of students in mind, all benefit.

CREATING A POLITICAL CLIMATE THAT FOSTERS THE NEEDS OF ALL STUDENTS, ESPECIALLY THE MOST CHALLENGED

For several years, Gina Benson taught children with special needs. During her teaching experi-ence, she worked with many staff members across academic disciplines. From her point of view, she saw students on her caseload thrive in some classrooms and progress more slowly, if at all, in other environments. She wondered why there was such a range of success when her students worked in a variety of settings. Over time, many teachers directly or indirectly communicated to her the answer to her question.

Their casual conversations and teaching practices told Gina a great deal about why some students thrived or floundered in their classrooms. When Gina ate in the staff lounge, she noticed that staff members spoke in various ways about all of their students. Some teachers referred to Gina's students as "those kids" and blatantly voiced their resentment about the time it took them to stop and give special assistance to one student who did not grasp a concept taught through verbal explanation.

Edith Kingswood, an experienced staff member, spoke with particular venom about a student in her class who had an individualized education plan. She could not understand why this child did not learn social studies through her lecture methods. Gina overheard the concerns of this teacher and after school approached Ms. Kingswood and offered to ease the frustration by coming in and working with that student in order to "translate" the concept presented by the teacher. As days passed, Gina assisted other students who struggled with an overly verbal style of instruction.

Gina's efforts brought down Ms. Kingswood's stress level considerably. A few weeks later, Ms. Kingswood mentioned to Gina how much she appreciated her efforts. She also asked Gina if she would be willing to teach the class the next concept, aiming her instruction at the success of the students that had academic difficulty. Gina took over the class the next day, and to Ms. Kingswood's surprise, the students that she had perceived as being difficult to teach learned more easily.

Because of Gina's lesson, Ms. Kingswood began to change how she presented her lessons and found that she, too, could reach the same level of success with these students as Gina could. Formerly a vocal complainer in the lounge, Edith Kingswood began to speak of her success with students that had formerly caused her great frustration. She now had confidence in her approach to students that had formerly caused her anxiety. She gained a new range of instructional competence that could be applied to situations that had caused her discomfort.

With an increased repertoire, Ms. Kingswood was now open to working with a broader range of students. Further training helped to change her attitude from one of resistance to one of openness. With Ms. Kingswood being more relaxed in the classroom, her students could also relax and learn from a teacher who felt capable of working with them and thus willing to go the extra mile to be of help.

Gina shared her story with her director, Jan Marks, who made a further suggestion. Having special training funds, she stated that she could use them to send Gina and Edith to a daylong training on curriculum modification and alternative instructional strategies. They both found the day to be beneficial and returned to school with enthusiasm. Their excitement transmitted to other staff members and the climate of their building changed on behalf of students with special needs.

Through relationship building and strategic assistance and partnering, teachers can change the attitudes and approaches of their peers. Through time and patience, teachers like Gina and Edith find a means to work together for the greater good of all their students. In doing so, they enhance their own enjoyment of their teaching jobs and spread their influence throughout an entire school building.

Matt Randin, a recent university graduate, arrived at his new school with the attitude that because he had the latest instruction from a nationally noted education professor, the teachers with whom he was about to work would immediately turn to him for an upgrade on their teaching methodologies. However, when he arrived, he noticed that all teachers had their own patterns of success. In addition, they also honestly admitted when they struggled with managing student behavior or deciding on a proper instructional strategy.

Matt was assigned a typical group of middle school students in his social studies class. On the first day of school, he began class only to find that one student, Reese Johnson, refused to cooperate with his directions. Day after day, Matt found that no matter what he said or did, the student would not comply with very routine directions.

Across the hall, Bill Martin spoke quietly and evenly to his science students, placed them in groups for projects, and managed quite well to achieve successful cooperation among all of his students. Matt noticed this and was even more surprised when he saw Reese Johnson, the student that gave him the most difficulty, responding well and behaving within the range of the other students in the class. He decided to swallow his pride and to approach Bill Martin about how he managed to work so well with Reese.

After school, Matt stepped into Bill's classroom to talk about this student with a behavior problem. Bill did not realize that Reese had a "behavior problem" but remained open to all that Matt had to share. Bill treated Matt with dignity and respect. Though he saw this new teacher struggle, he gave him acceptance and tips on how to work with Reese and other students that could be challenging. As weeks passed, Matt became better able to work with Reese, and he and Bill developed a level of trust. Both teachers began to share with one another on a regular basis.

Matt appreciated being able to share what he learned at the university, and he certainly valued Bill's experience and background. By simply doing his job to the best of his ability, Bill worked with integrity and influenced the climate of his own classroom and the room across the hall. Having a can-do attitude, Bill brought Matt on board in a way that helped him to strengthen his skills and gain a trusted colleague at his first job. Bill, by being open, prevented Matt from giving up.

Matt picked up on the rule in his school that it is alright to share concerns and frustrations with peers, and he was thus able to follow the example of other teachers in his building and seek help when he needed it. The successful, professional relationship between Matt and Bill illustrates how one teacher, by doing his work well, sent the message that things could work out with proper methods, classroom organization, and behavioral training.

When Bill responded to Matt, he extended the positive culture of his school, a culture of collective integrity that allowed for the give-and-take of professional exchange and mutual mentoring. Whether teachers of integrity display their character through the ordinary give-and-take of teaching and working with colleagues or by challenging the status quo at the district level, their approach to their work makes a difference.

When students or teachers are affected by the actions and manners of a teacher with integrity, they benefit from the presence and personality of this professional. The personal character of a teacher goes a long way to bring growth and integrity to those that he or she influences in the ordinary circumstances of school life.

ACTION PLAN

1. Educators should take time to step back and gain perspective on professional beliefs and standards about all applicable curricular areas.
2. Educators should access reflection as an ongoing process by noting who they are and paying attention to what comes to mind in terms of how they handled the events of the day.

3. Educators should select role models both inside and outside of education and watch how these people work and relate in order to apply similar behaviors and attitudes to the school environment. They could then list three examples of when they or another educator acted with character while in the educational setting.

4. Educators should pause spontaneously throughout each school day to listen to their own heart and to reflect on their recent work relationships and experiences.

5. Educators should maintain contact with supportive and mature friends, family, mental health professionals, or clergy. They can help maintain direction and offer encouragement and perspective when those in close proximity create various challenges.

6. Educators should seek help from a trusted teacher or administrator to navigate through, beyond, or out of difficult circumstances.

Chapter Two

It's Those Little Things That Build Up in Schools

> You think it's just a little thing
> But for me tension it brings
> You invaded my space
> I saw you make a face
> In meetings you talk fluff
> I want to discuss the big stuff
> You tie up the machine when I want to copy
> At the end of the day your room is so sloppy
> You burned up the laminator
> For me, you are a stress generator.

It is indeed those little things in schools that generate stress for others. Although educators may be unaware that something bothers a fellow staff member, they know that they have done something that has caused an impaired relationship with a colleague but may not be sure what they did.

What appears to be a little thing—using the copy machine when someone else wants it, having a messy room, talking too much in a faculty meeting—can set the stage for a difficult year in a school. Picture this scenario to illustrate the point.

Alicia is new to the school and is looking forward to the first faculty meeting. She arrives at the meeting and finds a seat at the large U-shaped table that has been set up for the meeting. A disapproving glance comes from some of the staff members as they enter the room. Alicia is wondering why. When Ms. Brown arrives, she looks particularly bothered but says nothing and goes to another location, far away from Alicia.

Whispers come from that side of the room. Alicia still can't figure out what has happened. Another new teacher arrives and sits by Alicia, and engages in a conversation with her. The administrator arrives and looks at Alicia with a surprised expression on her face. What has happened?

Introductions are made, and the meeting proceeds for the next two hours. After the meeting is over, Alicia continues to visit with the other new teacher in the building. Alicia then returns to her classroom excited about getting ready for the big day tomorrow.

One of the other teachers who teaches across the hall comes over to see how she is doing. She asks Alicia what she thought about the staff meeting. Alicia confides in her that she picked up some "bad vibes" from Ms. Brown. The teacher then tells her that Ms. Brown has been in that school for over twenty years and has always sat in the seat Alicia occupied; she was really upset that she had the "nerve" to sit in "her seat." Alicia learned an important lesson the hard way.

Educators who have worked in schools for many years know the importance of respecting other people's spaces. Educators get used to sitting in certain seats at faculty meetings and don't want anyone else, especially someone new, sitting in their seats. Some fellow colleagues become so upset when this happens that they can't or won't actively participate in the meeting.

Alicia unknowingly got off on the wrong foot. Although this may seem like a small act, it isn't. She upset the routine of the faculty meeting and made it difficult for herself to gain the respect of Ms. Brown, a senior teacher who carries a lot of weight in the building in which she is working.

What could Alicia, as the new teacher, have done to avoid this unfortunate event in the beginning of her career in the new school building? When she arrived, she could have stood up and visited with fellow teachers as they arrived. She could have seen where they sat and seen what places were left unoccupied right before the beginning of the meeting. She could have asked other teachers which seats were not taken and sat there. It is important to get the lay of the land before jumping in and invading what someone else sees as her or his space.

What appears to be a small thing really isn't and can set the tone for the year. Different personnel in school buildings respond to those actions that may appear to be small stuff to one person but are not small stuff to them. Perhaps a teacher made too many copies on the photocopy machine or used too much laminating film. Individuals can incur the wrath of some staff members by those little things that can snowball and cause alienation with their colleagues.

Let's look at what may appear to be small stuff to other specific personnel but is really what matters to these individuals.

It is critical that teachers value all of the members of the school team. It has often been said that it is the school secretary or the school custodian or some other person other than the building administrator who runs the school. Although this may not be factually true, it is important for educators to recognize the important role that each of the members of the school team plays in the functioning of the school.

At the same time, each educator must learn about the small actions or events that may ruin the educator's relationships with those individuals. The educator should always refrain from perceiving himself or herself as being more important than anyone else. This feeling, if it is exuded by the educator, will quickly be sensed by the individual and can easily break a relationship and set the educator up for failure in the school building.

UNDERSTANDING THE CRITICAL ROLE OF SPECIFIC SCHOOL PERSONNEL

Bus Drivers

Some educators say that they cannot be bothered with how the students behave on the bus—that teachers have enough to do to monitor the behavior of the students within the classroom. This attitude is quickly proven to be problematic. If students have a problem on the bus, it will typically carry over into the classroom.

If the educator could spend a day on the bus route into school, the educator may be convinced that he would not want the driver's job. After all, in what other profession is an individual expected to provide supervision and behavior management with his or her back turned to the students? Educators need to respect the critical role that the bus driver plays in the lives of children.

Bus drivers are entrusted with the physical safety of the children. They are also the first member of the school personnel team that the child sees at the beginning of the day and the last member of the team that the child sees at the end. They hear a lot of critical information on the bus; that information can be valuable to educators, but if the educators have gotten off on the wrong foot by not respecting the driver, then the bus driver will not share the message.

The most common complaints heard from bus drivers include teachers not sending the students out to the bus on time, sending children home with snacks, not following up on a behavior problem that the bus driver has reported, and not providing needed information to the driver.

Bus drivers are on tight schedules and face the pressure of getting everyone home on time, even when the weather conditions may be abysmal. The teacher does not see why it is such a big deal that he or she is running behind schedule and therefore does not get the students out to the bus on time. The driver then cannot stay on schedule and may get reprimanded by a supervisor or have to deal with a parent who is worried or angry that his or her child did not get home on time.

Many bus drivers do not want students to eat on the bus, and many have rules that students cannot eat on the bus. However, the teacher may have given the students candy before the students got on the bus. The students do not keep the food in their book bags and get the candy out on the bus with the bus driver either seeing it or not seeing it. The bus driver finds out about the candy when he or she finds candy wrappers on the floor of the bus. The bus driver is not happy.

If the teacher is going to give the student candy, he or she should check with the driver to see whether this is acceptable or whether the student needs to eat the candy before he or she gets on the bus.

Another idea that can be effective is for the teacher to give any food to the student in a sack and for the teacher or student to give that sack to the bus driver to keep in the front of the bus. Be aware, however, that some bus drivers don't like sacks at the front of the bus because of the space that the sacks occupy. Working with the bus driver to see what he or she permits goes a long way in building rapport.

The educator should be empathetic to the concerns of the bus driver when the driver is having behavioral concerns with a student. A simple statement such as "How can I help you with this problem?" goes far in establishing a positive relationship with the driver.

If the educator says that he or she will do some follow-up, then it is critical that the follow-up be done. There may be a problem with the student that is beyond the authority of the teacher. The teacher can go with the bus driver to the administrator to report the problem.

Bus drivers have every right to become upset when there is valuable information about a student and no one provides that information to the driver. A bus driver reported that a student had a seizure on the bus and no one had told the driver that the student had a known seizure disorder.

At times, teachers may be afraid to provide information to the driver because of the confidential nature of the information. It is true that there is certain information that the bus driver has no need to have in order to transport the student. However, there is other information that the driver does need to have.

As part of bus driver training, all bus drivers should be trained on issues related to confidentiality; therefore, the teacher should provide the necessary facts to the driver.

As another example, if the student has diabetes, the bus driver needs to know that and also be provided with an emergency plan in the event that the student goes into insulin shock. All schools should have policies on how that information is provided to the staff, but it should be clearly provided.

The School Secretary

It is critical that teachers remember that the school secretary has a multitude of tasks to complete within a busy and distracting environment. Everyone is coming into the office wanting the secretary to answer his or her questions or to copy a test for him or her.

The secretary, to be successful, must be a juggler of sorts—answering the phone, dealing with an angry parent, managing the behavior of students who are waiting to see the principal, copying reports, and fixing the copy machine when it breaks. In short, the secretary frequently works in a crisis situation. The teacher needs to recognize this and understand the crisis element of the secretary's job and the fact that the secretary has to work for the principal, who may need work done quickly. The secretary also works for many other teachers in the building other than just one.

When the educator requests that a secretary complete an assignment for him, the educator must ask himself whether it is an assignment that he could do for himself or whether it is necessary for the secretary to do it for him.

A word of thanks for everything that the secretary does for the educator goes a long way in recognizing the effort that the job took. Sometimes educators take what the secretary does for granted—perhaps saying that it is the secretary's job and she should just do the work. However, a kind word of thanks or a special little treat for the secretary when the secretary is under stress and is working very hard goes a long way in building rapport. When the educator comes into the office and states that she needs something done right away, it should truly be an emergency situation.

Granted, those emergency situations may occur, but the less often they do occur, the better; and if the teacher has gone out of his or her way to recognize the secretary for his or her assistance, the secretary will be more likely to do work quickly.

Picture this scenario: a secretary was pressured by the superintendent's office about the number of copies that were being made in the school. This is a "big thing" in a number of schools—too much paper is being used, or the copy machine has to have too many repairs. The secretary may be the one who feels the brunt of this pressure.

The teacher may be making more copies than are needed or may jam the machine, thus causing the loss of paper. If this is a source of sensitivity to the secretary or other school personnel, teachers should be cognizant and cautious when using the machine. If the teacher has problems with paper jams—a problem that everyone can really relate to—he or she may want to ask for assistance at a time when the secretary is less busy. The teacher should also seek advice from the secretary about preventive techniques for paper jams.

Custodians

Custodians are sensitive about the looks of the school building—the looks of the building are a reflection on them. Although it is their responsibility to keep the building clean and sanitary, they need all staff and students' help. It is everyone's responsibility to beautify the school and to keep it clean.

Children need to be taught at an early age to respect and take care of property. When educators allow students to throw paper on the floor and not pick it up or to put their feet on the walls or on their desk, they are not teaching them care and respect for property. This is also an insult to the custodian, given that educators are sending a message to the students that it is not their responsibility to take care of property. The educator's attitude might be, "That's the custodian's job." However, that attitude does not reflect a true team effort in taking pride in the building.

The custodian may walk into a classroom after students have gone home and find a mess all over the room—the teacher has made no effort to require the students to clean up before they go home. The teacher may have even said to the students that the custodian will take care of cleaning up.

Remember that the custodian is responsible for the cleaning of the entire building, not just one classroom, and the easier the educator makes the job for the custodian, the more the educator will be appreciated by that individual.

The custodian needs to be considered an integral part of the school team and should be treated as such. The custodian knows whether the educator values him or her and respects his or her important job in the school.

A custodian relayed this story: One day, the school superintendent was walking down the hall and noticed a dirty window that the custodian had not cleaned yet. Rather than say something to the custodian quietly, the superintendent spoke loudly in front of staff and students, saying that the custodian had better get that window cleaned right away and that he was very displeased that she hadn't gotten it cleaned already.

The superintendent chose to evaluate the custodian's work performance in front of others—the custodian was embarrassed and angry.

On another occasion, a custodian had been asked by the boss to meet with a salesman for a company that specialized in bathroom deodorizers—a big item, particularly for the boys' restroom. The superintendent came in and contradicted what the custodian had said.

A teacher may finish her lunch and fail to clean up after herself; after all, she figures that it is the custodian's job to clean it up. Custodians in most buildings are overwhelmed with the amount of work that there is to do—they should not have to clean up something that would take the person who made the mess only a few minutes to clean up.

Educators must also teach their students to clean up after themselves, thus teaching them a life skill, given that most of them are not going to have a maid to clean up after them.

Fellow Teachers

In the beginning example in this chapter, the reader quickly learned that Ms. Brown did not like the fact that the "new kid on the block" invaded her space. The new teacher sat in the seat usually reserved informally for Ms. Brown. Educators understand the importance of respecting the space of students; it is equally important to observe that law when working with fellow teachers.

The classroom of the teacher and the materials of the teacher are his or her domain and should be respected as such. Going into the teacher's classroom and sitting in the teacher's desk is not respectful of space, unless the teacher has specifically invited you to sit there. A group of teachers may go into a teacher's classroom for a short meeting; one should pick up cues from the teacher who works in that room. It bugs some people when others come in and move around the furniture, especially if they do not put the furniture back when they leave.

Respect the privacy of the teacher's space. One teacher will look for something that a fellow teacher has. The "snooping" teacher will actually go through the desk of the other teacher. This is really a violation of space. Unless a fellow teacher has given permission to the person to do that, it should not be done.

Space includes the property of other teachers. A common and certainly worthy occurrence in some schools is sharing materials among teachers. This does not mean going into a teacher's classroom and taking a book without telling the teacher. In the real world of the schools, teachers pay for many of their own materials, so they are even more protective of those materials because they will have to replace them, again with their own money.

Educators should never openly or privately criticize the work of another, especially if they have not offered assistance to the individual. Even if the criticism is warranted, a teacher who criticizes a fellow teacher is not appreciated by the person being criticized.

It is so easy to criticize others without having all of the facts involved in the action. Before forming a judgment, the teacher who may have witnessed an action by a fellow teacher with which he or she did not agree can go to the teacher and ask questions worded in a supportive manner about the event. That may open the door to the teacher being questioned to ask for some assistance.

A colleague should be an empathetic listener or idea sharer, not one who critiques—that is the role of an assigned evaluator.

Fellow teachers are often asked to work together on a project, teamwork or collaboration, as it is called in the workplace. It is wonderful and highly successful when it works, but at times it is easier said than done. Members of the team can foster true collaboration only when each does his or her share of the work.

One can walk into most schools and hear the common frustration, "Ms. Johns isn't carrying her share of the load" or "Mr. Stemm was supposed to get us a copy of that lesson plan and didn't—I was counting on it." Although there may be those times when an individual can't get something done because of extenuating circumstances, not getting assignments done that one said he would get done should be an exception to the rule and not the rule.

If people lose faith in the individual's ability to do his fair share of the load, they lose respect for that person. If someone has an excuse, it should be a valid one. In schools this statement can be heard: "I am so sick of hearing how she had to go to her son's ball game and couldn't get her job done."

While discussing the topic of collaboration, it is important to realize that collaboration is working together for a common purpose. It is not defined as one person taking over and doing all the work. Some individuals find that it is just easier for them to go ahead and do all the work themselves. Some individuals are take-charge kind of people. Although some tasks need a take-charge kind of person, some do not, and it is important to recognize the contributions that everyone can bring to the task.

To survive in a school building, teachers must be able to share credit for a completed project or for recognition that is given. No one is recognized alone; everyone had assistance in their professional advancement and should recognize those individuals who have been of assistance.

If the group has worked on a project and one teacher tries to grab all the credit for the completed work, other teachers will be much less likely to be part of a work group with the credit grabber again. Teachers may recall instances where they worked very hard on a project and the administrator took the credit for the work.

When a teacher recognizes others for their assistance, it is critical that he or she recognize all who provided assistance. At so many of the awards ceremonies, award recipients thank those who got them where they are.

The audience members who have worked with that individual are sitting there waiting with bated breath and listening closely to whether their names are mentioned. If their names are mentioned, they are proud. If their names are not mentioned and they believe that they were critical contributors to the award recipient, they will be upset and hurt, and there may be resulting friction with the award recipient.

Although it may appear that it is a small thing, it can become a big thing and result in hard feelings and even the severing of what was a positive relationship. The important point to remember is to thank and recognize anyone who has contributed to the work.

The Administrator

In the words of one administrator, "Nothing irritates me more than a teacher taking an action and not telling me about it." Granted, the teacher cannot tell the administrator everything that he or she does, but if there is any suspicion that the action may affect the administrator, the teacher needs to tell the administrator.

Nothing is worse than a community member or parent or school board member appearing at the door of the administrator with the news about something that a teacher has said or done and the administrator does not know anything about it.

Sometimes in the teacher's zeal for obtaining funding or materials for the school and classroom, he may seek out donations within the community and not let the administrator know that he is engaging in such activities. The administrator finds out about it later. Many school districts have policies and procedures about the handling of donations. The administrator should always know if funds are being solicited on behalf of the school.

Ideally, teachers are active in their professional organizations to keep abreast of the most current state of the art in the field. Some teachers may become involved on the board of one of those organizations. Some administrators may be threatened by that involvement in outside activities—they may suffer from professional jealousy—a topic that is discussed in detail in Chapter 5.

A teacher may want to seek some time off to attend a board meeting or to go to a conference. It is critical that the teacher ask for that release time well in advance. She will decrease the likelihood of professional jealousy if she informs the administrator about her activities and thanks him or her frequently for the cooperation and support.

It is also critical that the educator not overstep his or her bounds. Any administrator is protective of his or her role and gets upset when the teacher does something that is the job of the administrator. The teacher may think that it is just easier to do it himself or herself and will go ahead and take an action that is the job of the administrator. The teacher should keep the administrator informed at all levels.

Communication is a key to any educator's success in establishing a positive relationship with the administrator—the administrator should be kept informed of actions taken by the teacher that will affect the administrator. When dealing with an angry parent, the teacher may request that the parent talk with the administrator—the teacher then has an obligation to warn the administrator that the parent may be visiting him or her.

Teachers should always be cautious of bad-mouthing the administrator—even though that is a common practice in many schools. The administrator may not have acted as quickly as the teachers think he or she should have acted. A teacher may not like the way that the administrator handled a situation. The teacher does not believe that the building principal supported her with a parent.

Whatever the situation, the teacher must be cautious. If the statements get back to the principal, the teacher has ruined his or her working relationship with the administrator.

Here is an example of a negative teacher who thought that she could do anyone's job better than the person could do it. This teacher was taking classes for administrator's certification. She would go to class and bad-mouth the school superintendent and whatever recent action he had taken that week.

As it turned out, the instructor of the class, as well as a few other teachers in the classes who were tired of her critiques, told the school superintendent what she had to say. Needless to say, the teacher who aspired to be an administrator killed any chance of getting an administrative position in her home district.

Teacher Aide

The teacher is so pleased this year that she has been assigned a teacher aide because of her large class size. She has not worked with someone else in her classroom before. Her classroom is her domain—she is protective of that domain. Consequently, the teacher aide may pick this feeling up and not feel like he or she is welcome in the room. The teacher may not be sure what the role of the teacher aide should be, and so the teacher has the aide do what she or he may perceive as a menial task—collecting papers, sharpening pencils, keeping the classroom neat.

The teacher aide wants to be treated as a valued member of the classroom—she or he would like to assist in instruction or help correct papers, but the teacher is reluctant to let her or him do so.

A common complaint heard from teacher aides is that the students won't listen to the aide because they know that he or she is not in charge of the classroom. The teacher may have inadvertently conveyed the message that the students need to listen to only the teacher and not do what the aide says to do. It is critical that the teacher communicate to the students that they must listen to both the teacher and the aide.

Sitting down with the teacher aide at the beginning of the school year to outline the individual's roles and responsibilities is a must. Ongoing communication throughout the year is also a must. If the teacher senses friction with the aide, he or she should sit down with that person as quickly as possible to figure out how they can work together to resolve the issue.

Pupil Personnel Workers—School Nurse, Counselor, School Psychologist, School Social Worker

"I feel like I have been left out of the loop, even though Jamie is on my caseload." This is a common concern voiced by school support or pupil personnel workers. Something happens with a child with whom they have been working, and it happens on a day that the social worker or psychologist is not in the building. The teacher fails to notify the absent personnel worker. The parent calls the social worker to ask about the event, yet the social worker doesn't even know what happened.

In another instance, the student tells the teacher some information that the counselor needs to know—the teacher fails to give the information to the counselor. The student is in crisis, and the teacher doesn't want to bother anyone, so he or she deals with the situation himself or herself. The student gets sick in the classroom, and the teacher fails to let the student see the nurse; the student then throws up in the classroom, and the nurse is called and learns then that the student has been sick all morning.

Pupil personnel workers are employed to support teachers and students, and they take pride in doing their jobs. They can easily be offended when they are not consulted when something happens with a student. Although they may not want to be bothered with minor occurrences, it is critical that they be kept in the information loop and be sought when the child is in an emotional or medical crisis.

School Volunteers

There is never enough help in a school building. Teachers always feel like they need about ten extra sets of hands. Volunteers fulfill a critical need in schools. At times, educators may get upset because they did not do exactly what they wanted them to do, or they thought they were going to do more than they did.

Before volunteers come into any school or any classroom or go on any field trip, they should be provided with an orientation training on what they can and cannot do and what is expected of them. It is critical that volunteers feel welcome, needed, and appreciated.

Some volunteers come into schools and try hard to figure out what they need to do. They think that they were helpful, only to learn that they did not meet the expectations of the staff. These problems can be curtailed with clear expectations of their responsibilities.

One of the authors remembers walking into the bank one day; this bank was the business partner for a local school. The bank provided volunteers for the school, and the employees would report to the school to read to the students. An employee of the bank was upset and vowed that he would never go back to the school.

When asked why, he reported that he had taken the time that had been arranged and had gone to the school. When he got there, there was nothing for him to do. The staff were busy and didn't want to take the time to find a student to whom the volunteer could read. The message to the bank employee was that the school personnel were just too busy to deal with the volunteer; they devalued the time of the bank employee.

How Do We Figure Out What the Small Stuff Is to Our Colleagues?

Throughout this chapter there have been lots of true-life examples of how the small stuff bugs people within school buildings. It is critical to realize that many times other school personnel with whom educators work do sweat the small stuff. It is critical to learn what the small stuff is to the colleagues and make a concerted effort to not engage in those behaviors that may upset others.

How can educators assess what those small things are that really bug other people? Educators may know fellow teachers or administrators who can't stand a picture hung crooked or a colleague who wants no one to use her room for any purpose other than her classroom instruction. How about the teacher who refuses to eat in the lounge at the same time as a colleague because he can't stand the way that the colleague slurps his coffee?

All individuals have actions or behaviors that bug them. The key for the educator's survival in the school building is to learn what those actions or behaviors are and to avoid engaging in those behaviors, especially when he or she knows that those behaviors bug a colleague.

Educators should get to know their colleagues by talking with them on an informal basis, not prying into their personal business, but just listening to what they are saying and showing an interest in their activities. They may learn that their child is on a local soccer team, and then the educator can show an interest in how the child did at the soccer game the night before.

Educators can learn about any common interests that they have with their peers. Perhaps they collect the same items that someone else does, or they have the same interest in a sport that another faculty member does. Educators can be good listeners and hear what their colleagues are saying to them while refraining from interrupting or passing judgment.

Educators need to listen to what their colleagues say about others without passing judgment on anyone. In future chapters there will be discussion about staff who make some negative statements about other staff and how educators must be very careful not to form an opinion based on those words.

Educators do best when they form their own opinion and do not pass judgment. One of the problems that occurs when one person makes a negative statement about a colleague is that another person may join in with the negative comment. The comment then gets back to the colleague, and relationships are severed.

Others may also poke fun at particular staff members' quirks. "Isn't it funny how he straightens every picture as he goes down the hall?" "I can't stand to watch her eat." "It makes me so mad when she uses the copy machine and always leaves it empty of paper." Educators should never allow themselves to get into those cruel behaviors where someone makes fun of someone else's behavior.

The bottom line is that each person has little things that bug him or her; some may have more than others, but everyone has them. Individuals need to respect each person and recognize his or her strengths. The key is to focus on strengths, not weaknesses.

Educators can learn a lot about their colleagues through observation. They can observe how others communicate with the students within their classrooms, how they communicate with fellow teachers and the administrators. Educators can also learn about what expectations they have for their students. They can look at how their colleagues have their rooms arranged. If they are neat, they have a strong indication that they do not like items out of order, and if their colleagues are messy, it may be a sore spot for them.

If our colleagues' students are out in the hall and being noisy and the teacher comes out and shuts his or her door, there is a good indication that the teacher is sensitive about noise, especially when it disrupts the class.

The key to establishing a positive rapport and not causing stress for colleagues is to respect each person for who he or she is, recognize the importance of each individual's role in the school, learn as much as possible about the person, and show sensitivity and concern to all individuals within the school environment.

ACTION PLAN

1. Educators should observe and listen to learn as much as possible about their colleagues.
2. Educators should talk with colleagues to clearly understand their roles.
3. Educators should learn about the strengths of their colleagues.
4. Educators should observe what bugs their colleagues.
5. Educators should always thank those individuals who do a task for them.
6. Educators should refrain from passing judgment without the facts.

Chapter Three

Surviving the Teachers' Lounge

I worked hard all morning
Did I need a break!
I went to the staff lounge
What a mistake!
Dumping and griping
I wanted some space
Negativity and complaining
I wanted to bolt from the place!
Could we just talk about positive things?
Tell us about some successes for a change?
Couldn't we include everyone in
Conversations that cover an interesting range?
Maybe tomorrow
I will find it better at noon
Back now to my classroom
Hoping for support and enthusiasm soon.

Whew! It'd been a really rough morning. Andrea, an elementary special education teacher, had begun her day early with an individualized education program conference that included a contentious parent, an emotionally absent administrator, and support staff colleagues that were anything but! They had all slipped out after making their individual contributions, leaving her holding the bag until the end of the meeting. She white-knuckled it to her lunch period, awaiting a pause in the intensity, eager for some downtime when she could regroup.

Jack, a secondary English teacher at a school not far away, had a morning that he would never want to relive. Not only did he have a face-to-face altercation with his department head, but he also heard that one of his more fragile students had been placed on suicide watch in a local hospital. To sit in the staff lounge and have a baloney sandwich in peace seemed like paradise at this point.

Both Andrea and Jack needed time away from the difficulties and frustrations of their challenging jobs. With lunch schedules in place, their next stop during the day was their respective faculty lounges. Instead of finding quiet, diversion, and solace, both Andrea and Jack experienced more of the same—a continuation of their difficult day.

When Andrea arrived in the lounge, she walked into a lively discussion of how challenging one of her students had been in mainstream math class. To top it off, a school volunteer who lived near the student being discussed sat drinking coffee within earshot of the entire diatribe. After a half hour of this discomfort, Andrea figured that she would have to continue blanching her knuckles until her after-school walk along the river.

Jack, on the other hand, swung into the lounge to encounter a cool atmosphere of indifference and disinterest. Colleagues sat in separate corners, their noses buried in student papers or the sports page. In his large school, he ached for time with like-minded colleagues to discuss his concerns in a supportive and trusting atmosphere. He would have to wait until he got home and unload the day's difficulties onto his cat.

Clearly, Andrea and Jack had certain needs and expectations to fulfill during lunchtime and were met either with a barrage of negativity and lack of professionalism or with isolation and unwelcome solitude. How can Andrea and Jack, who were created to illustrate educators in similar situations, find a time of much-needed and well-deserved refreshment and noontime renewal? The following are some suggestions to improve midday stress.

FINDING A WAY TO ADDRESS BREACH OF PROTOCOL AND CONFIDENTIALITY

Some staff use time in the teachers' lounge to blow off steam. Often, they find other teachers with whom they can commiserate and who will reinforce their perceptions of the students and situations. When things get going, such a group poisons the atmosphere for everyone else. In addition, staff discussions become unprofessional.

As a first step, it may be helpful for a concerned staff person to talk to the principal or a special education supervisor about the circumstances and also about issues of confidentiality. They can help take proper steps to ensure that students' dignity, reputations, and privacy are respected. Administrators will also help find a way to educate everyone on the faculty about data privacy and how it applies to school situations.

The Family Educational Rights and Privacy Act has strict requirements about who has the need and right to know information about a particular student; it is important that all school staff, regardless of their roles, are educated on the provisions of the law. It is even more difficult in small communities where school personnel may be related to students; if information is shared inappropriately within the teachers' lounge, that same information may get back to other family members.

PROMOTING AN INCLUSIVE LOUNGE ENVIRONMENT TO AVOID CLIQUES AND CRUELTY TO OTHERS

The reality in today's schools or other work environments is that cliques exist and cause hurt feelings, which can result in lowered self-esteem for those who are excluded from the cliques. Teachers' lounges can be dens for staff cliques. People who are part of the in-group congregate at specific times, and if someone who is not part of the group tries to invade the space of the clique, he or she will be ignored or ostracized by the group. (More information on ostracism can be found in Chapter 13.)

Such cliques cannot exist in schools where educators work together as a team and recognize the value of every individual. It is critical that each educator learn to recognize the warning signs of exclusionary behavior and vow to do his or her part to make all staff feel welcome and to recognize the value of each individual.

As an example, if a certain group is congregating in the lounge and talking about an event that they are planning that deliberately excludes certain people, an individual should vow not to be involved in such an event and should change the subject when someone who is not being invited comes into the room. Conversations should include everyone who wants to be part of the daily dialogue and chatter.

Members of cliques may also talk negatively about a person who is not part of their group. A person who hears such a conversation needs to be strong enough to not enter such a derogatory conversation but also to change the subject. This takes focus and deliberation of thought and speech to time the content and tone of conversational redirection.

Perhaps someone who chooses to insert a transitional topic into the conversation can come into the lounge somewhat rehearsed as to what to bring up because she or he knows from experience that the opportunity for such redirection will surely present itself. For example, if the topic is criticism about a teacher who just left the room to return to class, those in the lounge know that this teacher will not be coming back. They may have a sense of false freedom about what to say about this person.

They may mention something to the effect that this teacher repeatedly borrows materials because he or she tends to misplace things so frequently. Instead of continuing the topic using this teacher as the primary target of criticism, the individual who is changing the conversation to protect this person may still maintain the topic of misplacing things but could instead, with some mild humor and lightness of spirit, put the attention on himself or herself.

The contribution to the conversation, following the recent criticism, could be a funny comment about misplacing car keys or lipstick. The subject changer could then skillfully lead the topic forward to makes and models of automobiles or preferences in brands of cosmetics.

Besides building on the theme at hand and doing some creative redirection, a person could also pull from a bag of conversational tricks as adeptly as a substitute teacher pulls out a filler activity or draws from a repertoire of downtime activities. Having the newspaper at hand, a person could revert to sports scores, a cartoon, or a letter to the editor that is sure to create a stir.

Distractions and diversions of stronger impact will change the topic with no connection to the theme, clearly leading the group far from the petty criticism of a colleague. Both strategies can be used to redirect conversations that are critical of students, parents, or administration. The teachers' lounge is not the venue for verbally attacking anyone who is not present to come to his or her own defense.

CONTENT OF LOUNGE CONVERSATION

Sometimes teachers who eat together every day fall into a pattern of conversational topics. This may include student behavior, school-related griping, or small talk of various kinds. There may be teachers who are subject to these patterns due to designated lunchtimes who find the "same old, same old" frustrating and frankly quite boring.

They want to bring a new dimension into the lunchtime lounge talk but are unsure how to go about changing the pattern. Perhaps no one is under attack as mentioned, yet someone would like to add new dimensions to the conversation or find some refreshment from common and mundane conversation. What should such a teacher do to bring more to the table when it comes to lounge talk?

Perhaps it is a matter of ingrained habit, and those who are together so often are simply creatures of repetitious behavior, needing modeling and the introduction of additional topics. Bringing new topics to the lunch table may be as easy as ABC. The following are some suggestions for conversational content and starter questions.

a. Architecture in education—How would a teacher redesign a classroom if he could do anything he wanted to do?

b. Business—If this school were run more like a business, how would classrooms be affected on a daily basis?

c. Character—What can teachers do to make students more aware of developing the qualities of respect, courtesy, and tolerance?

d. Diet—What type of diet makes people most energetic and healthy?

e. Exercise—What are good exercise ideas and ways to make time to exercise?

f. Friday night—Do most teachers prefer to unwind from the school week by going out to eat or to a movie or crashing at home on a Friday night?

g. Gangs—What can the community offer youth that would give them a sense of belonging and would be a stronger draw than that from a gang that leads to negative behavior?

h. History—What events or people from local history would be of interest to students today, and where can teachers find out more about them?

i. Island—What island would be a good spring break destination?

j. Jury duty—How do teachers manage when they are called up for jury duty?

k. Karate—In what ways have students who are involved in karate or the martial arts transferred a sense of personal discipline into their classroom performances and social relationships?

l. Lunch alternative—What are some new options for lunch today?

m. Money—If a teacher won a million dollars in the lottery and had to give it to the school system or to this community, for what would they want it used?

n. Name—What is the latest name parents are naming baby girls?

o. Out-of-the-box thinking—What is a good way to present this topic?

p. Pie—What kind of pie do most teachers here like?

q. Quiet—Where do most teachers find quiet time at this school?

r. Reward—What have been some of the most rewarding events here at school this year?

s. Sleep—How much sleep do most of the teachers need each night to feel on top of things here?

t. Teaching overseas—If given the opportunity to trade jobs with a teacher in another country, where would most teachers here want to go?

u. Unglued—What are some stress management strategies to use to keep from coming unglued by Wednesday?

v. Verdict—Wonder what the verdict will be in the (current well-publicized national) trial?

w. Weekend—How can teachers avoid bringing much work home on the weekend?

x. What are most teachers here doing for exercise these days and how does it help with job stress?

y. Yard—What is a good idea for a landscaping project this summer?

z. Zero tolerance—Is the zero-tolerance policy as it relates to guns hitting the mark in this district?

One person has the opportunity to change the culture in the school lunchroom by making daily small steps to introduce different directions and topics into typical conversations, whether they be inappropriate and out of professional bounds or simply stuck in the mundane. Working together, teachers who want to improve the atmosphere of their staff lounge can introduce better topics than those involving backbiting a buddy or betraying the boss.

Two people or more who make a pact to elevate lounge talk can continue to keep things going in the positive direction and help one another with a glance or signal if they notice a colleague getting caught up in conversational styles and topics that they are working to avoid. When considering topics for lounge conversation, further alphabetical acrostic guidelines for the word *lounge* may be of help in setting lounge boundaries.

L: Listen before speaking. When entering the staff lounge, it is helpful to take a few seconds to assess the situation to determine the tone of conversations there. Making a seating decision may be determined by instinct upon arrival. Once seated, it is wise to take time to get the drift of the conversational patterns before jumping in.

O: Open the group to a variety of topics of general interest. Refraining from sharing things about oneself or students and families is respectful and professional.

U: Use time in the lounge to laugh and unwind from the intensity and stresses of teaching. Diverting energy from work-related topics that carry certain emotional and physical stress reactions, and pausing to rest body, mind, and spirit with light and refreshing subject matter enables one to truly find refreshment during this break time.

N: No discussion relative to a student's private or family-related information should occur among people who are not involved with a student. Educators should consider themselves as having the integrity of a doctor or therapist when it comes to confidentiality.

G: Give yourself a break. A true break should offer true relaxation. Selecting the company of staff who offer relaxation instead of more stress is important.

E: Enjoying a healthy meal enhances this time set aside to replenish the body, mind, and spirit.

GIVING EXPRESSION TO SCHOOL-RELATED FEELINGS AND FRUSTRATIONS

When frustration, anger, and concerns build up in the school environment, there is the natural need to give them expression. Yet if the lounge is not the best professional avenue to do this, where would teachers best give vent to these emotions? Besides a journal, family member, or friend outside of school, how might one manage to express these feelings in the school environment, especially when one has an immediate need to do so, and still maintain professional confidentiality?

Educational speaker Wayne Urbaniak (personal communication, July 1, 2005) "suggests venting. The purpose of efficient and effective venting is to verbalize a pent-up emotional reaction in a quick and safe manner—to prevent the symptoms of that reaction from emerging later in damaging ways.

The components of efficient and effective venting are:

- To a carefully selected person—a mature person, approximately lateral in the organization, who is prepared (understands the process of venting);
- In a carefully selected place—somewhere private (step outside for a few minutes if no empty classroom or office is available);
- With a clear purpose—'I need to vent,' (which signals to the other person that he/she should listen rather than problem-solve or counsel);
- In a blitzing, uncensored manner—to allow the anger and frustration to be expressed confidentially and safely;
- Ending with an assurance—'I'm alright . . . thanks for letting me vent.'

The benefits of efficient and effective venting are: it prevents embarrassing outbursts expressed randomly that would be confusing or harmful to others; it helps form supportive, constructive, collegial relationships; and it prevents 'contamination' between school and home" (personal communication, July 1, 2005).

EATING IN A DIFFERENT LOCATION

On certain days, when a teacher needs a time-out from school issues, personnel, and concerns, it may be time to eat alone. This may be contrary to school custom, which dictates that everyone on the staff eats with one another in the lounge, but there is no law to that effect.

Finding a quiet space such as a conference room, low-traffic alcove, or functional space that is unoccupied at the time may bring peace. One's own desk is an option, but being there signals work and offers the reminder of what is left on the to-do list. One can be creative and come up with a spot that best fits personal needs.

If one chooses to be alone to read a novel, write in a journal, listen to a soothing CD, or do some deep breathing, it is best to find an isolated location. When weather permits, ducking outside and walking around the grounds to get a breath of fresh air and clear the head either before or after eating a brown-bag lunch would offer a healthy change of pace.

Audrey Baumgartner, Lifetime Fitness personal trainer and Minnesota School District 192 paraprofessional, uses her lunch time for personal rejuvenation. She shares the following: "I love to run on my lunch break! There are a lot of benefits to it. I feel refreshed, am able to work better with the kids. If a project didn't go so smooth in the A.M. I think about it while I am running and sometimes come up with something that may work better, and I can share it with the teacher! Plus it really breaks up the day!" (personal communication, August 4, 2012).

Those who enjoy the company of others but like space from their school may take this break time to contact someone in another setting. This may be the time for an arranged conversation with a colleague in another building. With use of cell phones, one could even call a son in San Diego or a daughter in Detroit. Private lunchtime offers the opportunity to catch up with a trusted friend in order to use the time to discuss personal or professional concerns confidentially without using the school phone system.

One could find like-minded company in the school setting by putting together a smaller lunch gathering in the office of a colleague, such as a psychologist, department head, speech clinician, resource center director, or social worker. In such a setting, individuals can mix work and social chatter in a spot where only appropriate team members will hear it. Working lunches provide not only opportunities to catch up on school business but also the opportunity to speak safely and professionally about important issues in balance with social conversation.

SCHEDULING LUNCH AT AN OPPORTUNE TIME

Those who have a flexible role in the school and have control over their own schedule may choose to eat in the lounge, but plan their lunch during a time when a department or grade area known to be upbeat and positive eats lunch. Positive people will easily hear requests for conversation about topics other than school. They may even welcome an on-the-spot request that the subject be changed or that discussion of students be delayed to another time and place, for reasons of confidentiality as well as a teacher's own need for a break.

When small groups with positive mind-sets gather, they set the tone for a location. They become the barometers of the building by modeling ways to relax and converse respectfully and enjoyably. As they leave the lounge at scattered times, they influence those who trickle in one by one.

As new staff members enter the conversation, they follow the lead set by the tone and tenor of the discussion at hand. Even when the original positive conversational trendsetters have left the lounge, their influence can potentially set up a completely different group of people to have light, energizing, and renewing conversations.

Another option would be to eat during a different available time and use the midday lunch break for completing school-related work. Suppose that a teacher has prep time or a study hall late in the morning or in the middle of the afternoon. This individual could use the equivalent of the lunch period for eating a meal and finding diversion from the typical activities of the school day. When the official lunchtime comes, a staff member could use it for professional purposes, arranging work and personal time according to job commitment and need for balance and peace.

If one is alone or shares the break time with others, the individual could plan the time for optimal personal benefit. With as much conscientiousness as is used to plan daily lessons, one could also put the same seriousness into determining ways to refresh and renew in the middle of the school day.

Deciding where to spend this time, prioritizing it as a situation that includes people who bring enjoyment, or using the time for activities of personal choice are all options. One could go out for a walk on school grounds, make a phone call to schedule a massage, return to a best-seller on tape, or write a letter to a college friend who has chosen the same career. The opportunities are endless.

USE STRATEGIES TO IMPROVE LOUNGE ATMOSPHERE

Creative staff members can come up with endless ideas to bring fun and diversion into the teachers' lounge. They do this by encouraging special occasions and celebrations in the lounge on a regular basis. For example, staff members can post a menu from a local restaurant and order out regularly. Perhaps each month someone can sign up to select the restaurant and be the person to pick up the food.

People employed in certain roles in the staff have more flexibility about leaving the building premises during a school day as determined by school district policy. If it is not workable for someone to get the food, a restaurant that delivers is the natural choice. If a carryout is preferred, a volunteer on the staff could pick up the food the evening before or in the morning.

Birthdays and holidays lend themselves to decorating the lounge space to cheer up the atmosphere of a familiar and ordinary room. These occasions are great for inviting staff to sign up for potluck meals. To save time and work, staff may choose to bring something "as the spirit moves," given that such gatherings have ways of working themselves out and including diverse offerings.

Another way to enhance lunchtime is to choose a theme such as seafood or a coming holiday, having participants bring in a food dish fitting for the particular theme. When the climate of the lounge changes with new and different food being available for sampling, it is hard to introduce complaints and inappropriate comments into the conversation.

Those assigned to clean the staff lounge for the week may decide to bring in centerpieces, fresh flowers, table coverings, and pleasant music to support the message that this is a place of relaxation and to subtly state that this space is for switching gears and coming off the intensity of teaching.

New dimensions come into lunchtime and break conversation when people bring reading material to help lead others to discussions about the news, personal interests, or lighter topics. Magazines that feature sports, travel, hobbies, decoration of living spaces, fashion, and news analysis offer ready alternatives to the repetitive topics of classroom drama, parents, princi-pals, and playground pandemonium. It is a quick way to bring diversion in anyone's day.

ADJUST EXPECTATIONS

"Rome wasn't built in a day." It is important to keep in mind that all staff have had difficulties and challenges during their morning. They may need to let go of stress and, feeling overwhelmed, may not be quite sure how to go about it. In some instances, modeling stress management and using appropriate boundaries in the public atmosphere of the lounge may be actions that speak louder than words. It is critical that staff act as role models for students and also for other staff members.

Everyone can have a bad day and feel the need to "let it rip" or "blow one's top." There are times when a small cluster of trusted colleagues are the only ones in the lounge. During that time, a teacher may have latitude about what to say and how to say it. On the other hand, when a visitor, a parent, or a staff member who has no right to hear the details of a disaster important to discuss is in the lounge, it is best to refrain from the details and save the sharing for a time and place where this can safely and confidentially be addressed.

When beginning teachers come to a school, they may be unsure of what to say in the lounge. They are likely to slip and say something inappropriate. On the other hand, they may have been trained on "when and where to say what." Perhaps instead of being the ones to slip into breach of boundaries and confidentiality in the lounge, they may overhear conversations that are true-to-life samples of exactly what they have been told not to say by their college and university instructors.

New teachers burn out of this field, so it is critical that veteran educators model appropriate ways to deal with school challenges; likewise, new educators can model enthusiasm and interests in a variety of topics for their colleagues. Being open and respectful of others regardless of their levels of experience is the key to creating appropriate exchanges in the lounge and throughout the school.

DEALING WITH THE TEACHERS' LOUNGE IN A NEW SCHOOL ENVIRONMENT

Whether a teacher is just starting out in education or moving to a new workplace, the means to find this midday balance and discover the people and places in the building that lend support may take some strategizing. It is difficult to walk into a new school environment where the atmosphere is negative and divisive among the staff. The new teacher may wonder how the school climate became so negative. Perhaps there was an administrator who encouraged divisiveness to keep people from attacking himself or herself.

One of the authors is reminded of an administrator who would go into the teachers' lounge and make negative comments about other staff members to an individual to see what kind of response would be elicited. If the individual said anything negative, the administrator would then go to the original individual and tell that person what the other one said. The result was that staff members were continually angry at other staff members.

This kind of administrative behavior may sound familiar to some. Also familiar may be an individual who thought that he or she was the best teacher in the building and would make it clear that there was nothing to learn from someone else. That person might also have talked negatively about other staff members.

These situations can be frustrating when one is entering such a negative environment and balancing the need to be accepted with the importance of maintaining integrity and being kind and caring to colleagues. These suggestions may help make a smoother transition into a new setting.

Listening without being judgmental. When entering a new school environment where there is a lot of contention and negativity, staff members will be quick to share what is wrong in the environment and what is wrong with certain staff members. Listening to what they are saying but not sharing personal thoughts about what is wrong within the school is wise. It is likely that comments will be shared with others and some will perceive the new teacher as acting like an expert on the school situation when in fact this teacher is the "new kid on the block."

Forming one's own opinions of other people; not allowing negative comments from others to cloud personal opinions. It may happen that a new teacher will be told some negative comments about a colleague in the new school; unfortunately, the new educator will then avoid that person. That individual may be an excellent teacher who could have been an excellent colleague with whom to work. Instead, the new staffer will have allowed one person to cause him or her to block a positive working relationship with someone. The person who was the source of the information manipulated the new person into excluding someone.

Finding positive strengths among colleagues and recognizing individuals personally for those strengths. Schools can become negative when people are jealous of the accomplishments of others; there is no need to be jealous of the skills of others. Everyone is different and has strengths and weaknesses, just as students do.

And just as teachers and paraprofessionals recognize the strengths of students, so must they recognize fellow staff members who may be technologically savvy, who are assessment experts, or who are artistic and create beautiful bulletin boards. It is wise to ask for assistance from those people; doing so will be giving them the best form of flattery—recognizing their talent and letting them know they can help another in a positive manner.

Celebrating the successes of others. When someone in the new building is successful in an endeavor, sending a congratulatory note to him or her is a way to make a connection. Going out of the way to personally congratulate a teacher goes a long way in establishing positive rapport. Instead, if a new teacher becomes jealous of that person's accomplishments and resents this recognition, the teacher will begin a career by becoming bitter, self-centered, and negative.

How unfortunate when a person is so jealous when a positive event such as a special award is given to a colleague that he or she makes negative statements about the individual. That person was so threatened by the other individual that the focus was on being negative rather than celebrating the individual's success—such behavior makes a person look petty and non-caring.

Such jealousy can be destructive in a school environment, but an individual has the power to change that negative attitude by being positive and celebratory. Modeling the celebratory spirit in the teachers' lounge sets an excellent example for others—being happy for colleagues.

Avoiding making negative comments about a colleague. Although it is critical to form individual opinions of fellow staff members when getting to know them, it is also important if a new teacher has a negative experience with someone to keep that information private. If a new teacher starts talking about one individual to another, the teacher is then buying in to and contributing to the negative school environment.

Oftentimes, in a teachers' lounge, someone will start gossiping about a colleague, and the behavior snowballs. Everyone wants to chime in on the conversation. Then the comments will find themselves outside the teachers' lounge door and at times back to the individual who was being talked about.

If a new teacher truly needs to process the occurrence, it is important to find a trusted individual who is not part of the school system. Letting that person offer feedback on what happened or simply hear and validate the experience keeps the discussion contained and out of the school. After having been heard and having had reality and perspectives validated, the new teacher may then better be able to let go of a disturbing event.

Involvement in a variety of groups to become better acquainted with all colleagues. When someone is new in a building, it is important to avoid becoming ingrained with only one group of staff members. One may find a starting group that is either beneficial or negative. It may appear that the new teacher is excluding other staff members. It is a good idea to get to know as many people as possible within the school building. Offering to help with a project enables the new teacher to meet a variety of staff members.

Avoiding engaging in cliquish behavior, inviting certain people to join an activity to the deliberate exclusion of others. Although everyone forms friendships and engages in special activities with friends, it is far different when people are planning an activity in the teachers' lounge and another person hears the conversation and knows that he or she is being excluded from the event. Many can relate to being excluded from a party and how hurtful this felt. Sensitivity to the needs of others is critical in establishing a positive school climate.

Another consideration is for persons who come to the school as volunteers or as reserve teachers. They are there on occasion yet not often enough to know the latest events in the school. It is good to make them feel welcome. Words of greeting and inclusion help them know that they are valued for their contributions. Perhaps it would be helpful to them to ask them questions about their interests or whether they need assistance in finding something in the building.

People who pass through schools and the community at large have the potential to pass on their impressions. It may be because one teacher makes a positive impression that a whole school is represented positively in the community, and the lounge is certainly one place where impressions can be formed.

Vowing to work to make the teachers' lounge in the school a positive place for all staff is a fine way to contribute to a school. Vowing to make everyone feel welcome in the environment is a way to improve the school atmosphere. It is critical to remember that the break in the teachers' lounge can set the tone for the rest of the school day.

If it is a negative experience, the visit to the teachers' lounge that was supposed to be a relaxing break for rejuvenation may in fact be just the opposite—it may upset someone so much that the teacher will be angry for the rest of the afternoon, and the experience carries over into the classroom. If it is positive, a teacher can return to the classroom with a renewed spirit and do the best job possible with students.

Much happens in the course of a single school day. Some of those events occur within the teachers' lounge. Taking the time to pace oneself and, especially, to create space in the middle of the day makes a difference for the better.

As a teacher progresses through the lulls and intense moments of the morning, the anticipation of a time to relax and meet personal needs helps to sustain a teacher. Likewise, contribution to the needs of others is ongoing and important. Maintaining balance ensures the ability to continue to provide for the students and families served so successfully.

ACTION PLAN

1. Educators should consider healthy options for how to spend lunchtime.
2. Educators should all take responsibility for the lounge atmosphere in their school.
3. Educators should be sensitive about keeping conversations on topics that are inclusive of all those present.
4. Educators should have a repertoire of topics to talk about in the lounge when the conversation becomes inappropriate.
5. Educators should partner to employ strategies to improve the lounge climate in their school.
6. Educators should work hard to make reserve teachers and volunteers welcome in the staff lounge.

REFERENCES

Baumgartner, A. (2012). E-mail sent to Mary McGrath from Audrey Baumgartner, August 4, 2012.
Urbaniak, W. (2005). E-mail sent to Mary McGrath from Wayne Urbaniak, June 30, 2005.

Chapter Four

Dealing with Faculty Meetings

Meetings, meetings, more meetings
After one I feel like I've been through a beating
Oh what a bore
Sitting in meetings is a chore
Agendas there are none
The administrator is always on the run
The same folks seem to dominate
The rest of us, they alienate
Every week we have to meet
Complaining about students who lie and cheat
Covered is a lot of info
That could just be sent in a memo
Curriculum, instruction, I wish we could stress
I must work with others to clean up this mess
Productive comments I will make
The negative cycle I will work to break
I will vow to do my part
Next time, I will be positive from the start.

Jane has worked in the same school for ten years and has spent countless hours in faculty meetings—at the beginning of the year, every Thursday, during school improvement days, and at the end of the year. How many hours has she wasted in endless nonproductive meetings?

She wishes she could just spend the time in her classroom. The principal, Mr. Ford, started at the school during the same year that Jane did. He seems always in a rush, running from crisis to crisis. He holds faculty meetings because he knows it is the thing for an administrator to do. He is never on time—invariably, there is some crisis right before the meeting starts.

The regular Thursday meetings are quite a joke. They start at least fifteen minutes late, so everyone knows it's alright to be late. Everyone brings papers to grade so that the time is not a complete waste. Mr. Ford reads off a list of housekeeping items—students are using too many paper towels in the bathroom; a fire drill will be held next Wednesday; the secretary is upset because teachers are expecting her to do too much copying; the budget for paper is almost totally spent, and it is only November. The list goes on and on.

This is followed by a variety of directives from the district office. Mr. Ford then asks if anyone has questions. Invariably, Ron or Betsy has a complaint—teachers are not keeping their students quiet in the halls when they pass one of their classrooms; each staff member should have an assigned parking space; why can't fruit juice be included in the faculty vending machine? Mr. Ford then thanks everyone for coming, and the meeting is concluded. Such has been the pattern for many years.

After Jane's first year in the school when she felt comfortable in her role, she decided that she would bring up a curriculum issue at several of the meetings—she wanted to spend time in the meetings talking about ideas that would help her in the classroom. Each time that she brought up a discussion item dealing with curriculum, Mr. Ford would suggest that they put the item on the agenda for the next meeting—but there was never enough time to discuss it the next time.

Once there was time, and Jane brought it up again, only to receive no response or ideas from her colleagues. Jane finally gave up and accepted the fact that faculty meetings were always going to be a waste of her time. She wonders whether every school's faculty meetings are such a joke.

Bill worked for many years in the same school as Jane. This year, he has transferred to a school across town. Like Jane, he considers faculty meetings a waste of time. His principal is new to the school and to the district. Mr. Grant, having served as a principal for five years, has a much different practice. He sends e-mail bulletins to faculty about housekeeping items and informational items from the district office.

There are weekly meetings and the other traditional meetings—all have an agenda that is sent to the faculty before the meeting. Staff are asked to submit agenda items ahead of time. Meetings begin on time and end on time—staff are expected to refrain from negative comments about one another and to look at problems as a system issue that everyone must work on to resolve. Such issues are given a specific amount of time during the agenda, and every effort is made to come to closure on those issues.

The bulk of the agenda is devoted to curriculum and instructional issues—staff have multiple opportunities to talk about methods that will improve their classroom instruction. Bill is really in awe of the change in leadership. He actually looks forward to attending meetings and finds himself submitting ideas about curriculum and instruction for the agenda.

Most teachers wish that they could work in a situation where the administrator is a true instructional leader and where faculty meetings are devoted to improvement of instruction rather than gripe or housekeeping sessions. However, many teachers find themselves in frustrating situations like the one in which Jane has found herself. How can teachers deal with the challenges faced in faculty meetings and fulfill their part in benefiting from those faculty meetings?

Let's look at some of the real-world challenges faced in faculty meetings.

ADMINISTRATIVE ISSUES

Lack of Administrative Leadership

In an article in the *Kappan*, Jentz and Murphy (2005) stressed that new administrators often start off on the wrong foot and fail quickly. Administrators may operate in a time of confusion. They are bombarded by conflicting demands and heightened expectations, and they are not sure what they should do.

The administrator is a key in the process of ensuring successful faculty meetings, but some are torn about how to do that. Some of their leadership training may not have prepared them for the real world of the schools, where they must be multi-taskers and an instructional leader; they may complain that they do not know how to juggle the multiple facets of the job.

They may not understand that it is a matter of respect for staff to start and end faculty meetings on time. They may not know how to facilitate a meaningful discussion with the staff. Lack of administrative leadership is frustrating for staff.

Some administrators may be working to survive and are afraid to have meaningful discussions with staff for fear of learning information or receiving feedback that may be a negative reflection on them.

When teachers observe this lack of leadership, they must actively participate in meaningful discussions in staff meetings that are not threatening to the administrator. As an example, the teacher might meet with the principal and ask for some ideas on a curriculum issue; the teacher may ask advice from the administrator directly; and he or she may also ask if there is time on the agenda to solicit ideas from colleagues.

This is much less threatening for the administrator, who does not want to hear a teacher tell him or her how to run the meeting but who may be open to a request for help.

Lack of an Agenda

Some administrators are not as organized as we would like them to be, and this may be bothersome to us. There should be an agenda to keep everyone on track, with specific items to be discussed. A timed agenda is preferred.

If the administrator is resistant to an agenda, the teacher might want to request that an item be placed on the agenda—this may assist the administrator in seeing the need for time to be spent on specific items. Other teachers can then submit items to be discussed, thus increasing the likelihood that the principal will then prepare an agenda as a way for him or her to remember what items have been promised for discussion.

Failure to Stay within the Time Limits Designated for the Meetings

Everyone who works in a school is busy and has many demands during the day. If the teacher makes a real effort to get to the meeting on time and has to sit and wait until the principal gets there, the teacher is frustrated because the administrator has devalued the time of the teacher. The habit that then begins to develop is that all staff start coming to the faculty meetings later and later because they figure that there is no use in getting there on time.

The problem with this pattern is that such behavior is a vicious cycle and is disrespectful to all staff. To prevent the administrator from continuing this practice, the teacher can suggest that the meetings start later because there are conflicts in schedule—this may help the principal see what he or she is doing. Some administrators get so involved in the day-to-day pressures of the job that they may not realize that keeping teachers waiting is not respectful to all individuals.

Time Spent in Unnecessary Discussions in Meetings

It is certainly unfortunate when meetings are spent on discussions that are not necessary or on items that could be dealt with in a memo. Ideally, faculty meetings should be spent on school improvement and instructional topics that will result in meaningful positive changes within the classroom.

At times, administrators become so wrapped up with trivia that they cannot see the big picture. At other times, administrators may feel threatened by some faculty who dominate and want to spend the entire agenda as a gripe session about everything that is wrong with the school. The administrator genuinely does not know how to cope with dominating faculty and believes that it is just easier to let them dominate and talk about items that are not designed to improve the environment.

Effective administrators are prepared with an agenda, and they stick to the agenda while at the same time building time into that agenda for items that are submitted by the staff for discussion.

The effective administrator establishes rules or expectations for staff meetings that include the need for respect for all staff. That respect translates into refraining from put-downs; instead, rules encourage productive comments designed to build the school program rather than tear it down.

Bullying Behavior

Educators may feel bullied by the administrator in staff meetings. In the case of Melanie, a longtime teacher within the district who had received awards for her teaching, the administrator proceeded to make some negative statements about her in a staff meeting—such statements are inappropriate within a public meeting and violate a teacher's right to be respected and to not have a public evaluation of work performance.

Colleagues were afraid to speak up for the teacher for fear of being reprimanded themselves. However, the teacher spoke up for herself—she remained calm and simply stated that an evaluation of her work performance should be conducted privately.

Normore and Floyd (2005) have pointed out that even though administrators may be overwhelmed by daily social, economic, and political pressure, there is no justification for mistreating any teacher. Dignity and respect among teachers and administrators should be expected.

Unfortunately, the power gained by some administrators by virtue of having secured their role can result in corruption in their role. It is critical that the teacher not resort to such negative behavior in response. The administrator may be baiting the individual to show that the teacher is unreasonable—the teacher must monitor his or her own behavior. This is difficult because the administrator does have power over the teachers, and such inappropriate use of power might result in the teacher's leaving the field or in an emotional upheaval for the teacher.

Melanie then met with the administrator privately and discussed her feelings about how the administrator embarrassed her in front of her colleagues. Melanie wanted to give her administrator the benefit of the doubt, namely, that he did not realize what he had done.

If such behavior becomes a pattern on the part of the administrator, the behavior should be reported by the teachers to the school superintendent. Such bullying behavior cannot be tolerated for any period because of the damage that it can do to the morale of the entire faculty and, ultimately, to the instructional environment.

Examining the Functions of the Administrator's Behavior

Teachers may feel frustrated by the failure of the administrator to run an effective faculty meeting. They just can't seem to understand why the administrator is so dysfunctional in his or her leadership ability.

It is important to try to understand the behavior of the individual; only through doing that will educators be able to grasp the reason for the dysfunction. Readers learned earlier in this chapter that some administrators act the way they do to access something—attention or power and control. Others act the way that they do as an avoidance or escape tactic.

Some administrators engage in behaviors that affect faculty meetings and are attempts to gain access to attention or power or control. Some administrators may feel insecure in their role, and because of that insecurity, they feel the need to exert their power and control over their faculty and staff.

When administrators are late for a meeting, they could be wielding their power or control of when the meeting will start—after all, in their eyes, the faculty work under them and will wait until the administrator gets there and not leave until he or she says that they can leave.

Administrators could also be engaging in escape or avoidance behavior—they really do not want to deal with a faculty meeting because they are afraid that they may be confronted with a difficult situation and will look bad in front of the staff.

The administrators may also not prepare an agenda because they want to be in control of the situation and keep staff on their toes—staff never know what will be discussed in the meeting and therefore have to always be vigilant. There is a fear of the unknown, and the administrator is keeping control by not providing necessary information to the staff.

When the administrator spends the bulk of the meeting on housekeeping items, this may actually be escape or avoidance behavior. Not really feeling comfortable in discussions about curriculum and instruction, the administrator devotes the time to items that require little thought. The administrator may have been a high school teacher who is now the principal of an elementary school building and may be without expertise in elementary school curriculum.

This principal may also want to avoid any controversial discussions that would show his or her vulnerabilities, so instead focuses on trivial issues as a way to avoid the major issues facing the school.

When the administrator engages in bullying behavior, such as in the example of Melanie's negative experience with her administrator, she or he is engaging in access to power and control. Generally, bullies are into power and control. They may feel inadequate and try to make themselves feel better by wielding power and control over those they perceive as being less important than they are.

Such bullying and the wielding of power in such a manner may be the kiss of death for many administrators because such bullying and negative treatment of faculty within a building harbors resentment, lack of satisfaction, and lack of willingness to work as part of a team when the team leader is such an easy-to-dislike individual. Power struggles will abound in such schools when administrators behave in such a fashion.

The administrator is a role model for the entire staff, so when that individual engages in bullying behavior or lacks respect for other people's time or issues, that administrator sets a poor example, and soon faculty may find themselves copying this behavior. This results in a poisonous environment that is detrimental to all employees and can result in low staff morale, poor attendance, and, finally, resignations.

COLLEAGUE BEHAVIOR

Although the administrator is the instructional leader in the school building, there are also fellow faculty members who engage in behaviors that are detrimental to the positive school environment. Those faculty members may even go as far as setting the administrator up for failure from the beginning.

Picture this real story. A faculty member was upset over the hiring of an administrator—the faculty member had applied for the administrative job and had not been hired. She has been out to get the administrator from the very beginning. She has designated a notebook in which she keeps a log of everything that she observes that the administrator does wrong. She makes negative comments about the administrator in the faculty meetings. She is determined that she will get rid of the administrator no matter what she has to do.

Many faculty members know that what she is doing is wrong, but they do not know what to do about it. This is just one example where a colleague's behavior can make faculty meetings almost unbearable for fellow educators. Here are some of the problems that may be faced within the framework of faculty meetings.

People Who Dominate Discussions

It is very frustrating when educators feel that they cannot say anything because other people are taking up all of the time. It may be even more frustrating when these excessive talkers are dominating discussions with items that are not important to others.

Colleagues believe that the meetings are a waste of everyone's time; the dominating ones are using the time to listen to themselves talk. They may believe that they are the experts in the important matters in the school, and they do not want to listen to anyone's ideas. This situation can be even more frustrating if the administrator does not make any effort to stop their domination or tries to do so but is unsuccessful. The administrator and other staff members may be afraid of these dominating people—afraid that if they say anything or interrupt them, they may incur the dominators' wrath.

There is not a great deal that one can do if the administrator continues to allow it—colleagues may want to talk with the administrator and share their frustration but only if they are sure that the administrator will not quote them to the dominator. At some time in educators' careers they may have to complain to the administrator, and the administrator may go to that dominator and say, "Ms. Johns has come to me and complained that you take up too much time in our faculty meetings with your discussions."

An individual who does make a complaint is then likely to incur that teacher's wrath. One of the educator's options when someone is dominating discussions is to listen carefully to what the person is saying and write down any good ideas that can be gleaned from the dominator's comments.

If there is little option of changing this individual's behavior and the ideas are not relevant to the situation, then make the best of a bad situation by taking paperwork to do or by sitting and brainstorming ideas about what to do the next day.

Staff Using Sessions as Griping Opportunities

Anyone who works in school buildings knows some people who seem to do nothing but complain; they bring others down with their negative attitude.

Some of the educators may be feeling positive about something that has occurred in the school building only to find the negative teacher who is bad-mouthing the occurrence. These people look for something negative and thrive on looking at what is wrong rather than focusing on what is right.

It may be easier to change these people's behaviors than it is to change the behavior of the person who dominates the meeting. How? Educators should look for anything they say that is positive and reinforce them by strongly agreeing with them. When they make a negative statement, colleagues may want to try one of several effective techniques.

1. Educators should not respond to the negativity by agreeing with the statement. When they do that, they are allowing themselves to be brought down and to be part of the negative cycle that becomes harder and harder to break.
2. Educators should change the subject, reframe the comment into a positive one, or make a positive statement about what they do like about the particular situation about which their colleague is being negative. What does this mean?
3. Picture this scenario. Ms. Johns is complaining about the fact that the building is not clean, and she is tired of it looking like a "scum pit." Ms. Mathur comments, "I have noticed that the hallway looks so much better this week than it did last week." Ms. Richards says, "What one thing could each of us do to make the building look better?"
4. Educators should practice empathetic listening. They should recognize their colleague's feelings but then reframe the statement in to a proactive action. As an example: Ms. Johns says, "This building is just filthy, and it drives me up a wall." Ms. Mathur replies, "I hear you and know that the condition of the building really bothers you. What can we do to fix the problem?"

Bullying by Staff Members

Earlier there were discussions about bullying behaviors of administrators, but educators also know fellow staff members who bully others. There is an entire chapter devoted to bullying by ostracism, but what about individuals who bully through put-downs or intimidation? They have the need to have power and control by tearing other people down. They want to control the meetings and will do whatever they need to do to control.

The administrator may actually be afraid of these people. He or she knows that they can make his or her life miserable.

Recently, a principal reported that she was released from her job because the superintendent wanted to get rid of her. The superintendent went to a teacher in the building and had her document everything wrong that the principal did.

This type of situation may certainly occur in the building, although it was certainly not professional of the superintendent to request that a teacher do his dirty work. A new administrator might be more intimidated by teachers who are experienced and have been in the building a long time. If they do not like the administrator, they can certainly make his or her life miserable.

These seasoned teachers may believe that they are in charge of the building and want to assert their power. Consequently, they try to intimidate anyone who is new or anyone who may attempt to bring up a new idea that they do not want to try.

One of the most successful strategies for a teacher who is being intimidated or put down in the faculty meetings is to recognize that bully's need for power and control and give power to the individual when you agree with that person's statement.

As an example, let's say that Ms. Deppert is a bully in meetings and that Ms. Johns makes a statement about a new idea that she has found to work in her classroom. Ms. Deppert comments, "Well, that isn't a good idea." Ms. Johns might reply, "Can you tell me why the idea hasn't worked for you—I really appreciate your experience in this area." This does not condone a negative statement but gives Ms. Deppert some power by asking her advice.

It is also critical that this dominator be positively reinforced when he or she engages in an act of kindness with fellow staff. If at the faculty meeting the bully does engage in a positive statement or attempts to include someone in a discussion, that person's behavior should be reinforced. A simple statement could be made, such as "Thank you for including me in this discussion" or "I really appreciate your openness in discussing this issue."

When the Real Meetings Occur

Some educators have found that they have gone to a faculty meeting and felt like they had missed a chapter. Maybe they did miss a chapter. A group of people may have gotten together in someone's classroom earlier that morning and decided what they were going to do in the faculty meeting, and the other educators believe they have been left out of the loop. Decisions have already been made.

Even worse is when the administrator gets together with a small group of people in the hall or in the parking lot and the group decides what will happen and announces decisions in the faculty meeting.

Other educators were indeed left out of the loop. Such occurrences happen frequently in the real world of the schools. What can educators do about it? An effective lobbyist used to say that the best way to find out what was going on was to lurk. What did he mean by this? He simply meant that you have to hang around and listen to what people are saying.

Educators need to be in the right place at the right time. If the administrator seems to be listening to a core group of people, other educators need to examine who those people are and how they have gained access to the administrator. They need to try to gain that access. If specific people seem to be making decisions, they should observe where those people frequent. Do they hang out in certain classrooms before school or after school? Do they eat together in the teachers' lounge? Do they congregate in the parking lot at a certain time after school?

The key is to keep ears and eyes open—other educators may not be comfortable breaking into their group, but by careful observations and listening, they can prevent any surprises. Educators will know what is going to happen ahead of time.

Exploring the Functions of Others' Behavior

Everyone engages in behaviors for a purpose. In this chapter there has been discussion about some of the functions of the administrators' behavior—this section looks at similar functions of fellow staff's behavior. It is important to recognize those functions so that educators have a better understanding what drives their behavior and what can be done to fulfill their needs.

Faculty may feel a need to gain access to attention or power and control, and they may see the faculty meeting as the golden opportunity to gain center stage. They may dominate the discussions because they need attention, and what better way to gain attention than to call attention to themselves through domination. They may also want to gain access to power and control—they want to run the meeting. They want to show everyone that they are the ones who are in charge in the school.

Fellow faculty who use intimidation tactics in the faculty meeting are engaging in bullying behavior and are gaining access to power and control within the buildings. They have a significant need to control others—perhaps they do not feel good about themselves and compensate for those feelings by trying to dominate others.

Faculty may spend their time in escape/avoidance behavior, as evidenced in griping at the faculty meetings. At times people will gripe about minutiae to avoid discussions of the real problems within the schools. They want to escape the hard-core problems—they may be part of the problem, and they want to avoid attention drawn to the fact that they might not be doing a satisfactory job.

Picture Ms. Kelly—she runs around before faculty meetings complaining about what another teacher did; she then goes to another teacher and complains about a different teacher. By the time that everyone arrives at the faculty meeting, many are mad at each other and are so self-absorbed by what Ms. Kelly said to them that they don't care if Ms. Kelly gripes. Ms. Kelly has manipulated a situation quite well to escape any conflict for herself.

TAKING OWNERSHIP OF THE INDIVIDUAL'S BEHAVIOR

It is critical that all educators within a building each accept some responsibility when a system is broken. Just as this chapter has reviewed the functions of other people's behavior, educators need to explore their own behavior and whether they have contributed to the breakdown of the system.

Making Other People Look Good

It has been said that the number-one thought that is always on a person's mind is, "How will I look?" "Will I look good?" This does not refer to physical looks alone but the fact that what is always on a person's mind is whether one will look good.

No one wants to be embarrassed or to look bad. People are driven by how they believe they will look in front of others.

Students are always worried about what their peers think. Adults are no different—they want to be accepted and liked. It is important for them to remember this as they sit in faculty meetings. They need to make their colleagues look good. Sometimes this is difficult—particularly if the administrator is disorganized or if a fellow faculty member talks too much about trivia. However, they need to treat those people with respect and look for comments they make that are positive or something that they do that is positive.

An administrator loves to be thanked publicly in front of his or her faculty for something that he or she did that was helpful to someone.

People also do not want to be put down in front of peers. It is often easy for individuals to get into a contest about who can have the last cutting word.

If someone cuts another person down, that person wants to cut them down even more. However, then both parties are buying in to a demoralizing practice. Educators should certainly not let someone cut them down without a response, but what is more effective is to give a productive positive response.

Here is an example with Connie and Barb. In the faculty meeting, Connie is making some negative statements about how no one is helping her with the faculty fund-raiser and that she is doing all the work. Barb speaks up and says, "I will be happy to help you." Connie retorts, "Well, you certainly weren't much help last year. You didn't sell much of anything."

It would have been so easy for Barb, who was upset by Connie's put-down, to say something nasty. Instead, Barb replies with "Connie, I'm sorry that you didn't think I was much help last year—I believe I worked hard; perhaps you can explain to us what needs to be done this year."

Barb could have reminded Connie that she would not allow anybody to help last year, but she instead chose to have Connie explain what she needed this year. She also let it be known in a nonthreatening manner that she believed she did work hard.

This is a common scenario that happens in schools—some people play the martyr role. (See Chapter 10, Martha the Martyr.) Woe is me—they have so much to do and no one will help them. However, when someone tries to help them, they say it's okay—they will do it themselves. They really do not want help—they just want to complain and have everyone feel sorry for them.

These martyr-type issues invariably come up in faculty meetings and are best dealt with by asking the person what you can do to help and by having the person provide specific ways that other faculty can help. Many times these people need to be needed—doesn't everyone? Colleagues need to frequently stroke their egos and recognize them for all they do.

Think Carefully before Speaking

In everyday lives, how many times have people said something when they were angry or feeling frustrated? They just blurt a statement out and then regret it later.

In faculty meetings this happens frequently—educators get caught up in the moment and blurt out what is on their mind, often regretting it later. They just get tired of a colleague's bringing up the toilet paper in the bathroom or the noise level in the hall, and they say, "I am sick of hearing you talk about this again. Can we move on to something important?"

The person to whom we made the comment is offended, and then many of the other staff jump on the bandwagon for that person, even if they were also sick of hearing about the same gripes. The educator who spoke alienated more than one person with that comment.

Lustbader (2001) compiled a book about wisdom from the elderly—those who have lived over seventy years. She interviewed these people about the most important piece of knowledge that they have learned in life. An eighty-six-year-old man, Herb Johnson, said it well: "Before you blurt out your feelings, consider where you're heading" (p. 176).

He went on to comment that we let ourselves be driven by emotion; we speak before we give ourselves a chance to think about what we want to say, and then we regret what comes out of our mouth. His advice centers on the importance of focusing on what individuals really want to achieve: they need to keep their eyes on the target.

Looking at the Function of Your Own Behavior

Throughout this chapter, there has been discussion about the function of others' behaviors during faculty meetings—the behavior of the administrator and faculty members. Readers have learned that they may engage in specific behaviors to get access to something—attention, power, and control. They have also learned that they may engage in avoidance behaviors—they do not really want to deal with a specific problem.

At the same time as educators look at the function of others' behaviors, they need to take a look at the function of their own behavior. Educators do not like to be left out of the loop—they may also need access to power and control.

Some educators are the type of people who always want to know what is going on and want to have the most current information. They may also want to be at the center of attention, so they are offended when someone is dominating the group discussion at the faculty meeting because they want the attention and do not appreciate the fact that the attention is taken away from them.

Many educators just want everyone to get along and be one big happy family; so, when faculty meetings turn into negative confrontations, they just withdraw and remove themselves mentally from the meeting. They are engaging in escape behavior.

Many educators do not like conflict, and they will do just about anything to avoid it. They therefore may allow a person to dominate discussions or bully them because it is easier to do so than to confront the problem. Their behavior becomes part of the problem. Instead of engaging in assertive and productive behavior, they withdraw. They take the path of least resistance. It takes courage to stand up for what they believe in, and courage may be very difficult for them to practice.

Let's look at the example of Judy. Judy likes everyone to get along—she has never liked any conflict. She often caves in to others' demands just to keep peace. Mary has learned that Judy will do most things just to avoid conflict. Mary has taken advantage of Judy's kindness—borrowing materials from Judy's classroom and not returning them, asking Judy for favors frequently.

Judy attends the faculty meeting one day and shares an idea concerning the upcoming school fund-raiser. Mary comments, "That is a really bad idea, and it certainly won't work." Judy immediately backs down. She does not defend her idea by giving reasons why it would work. She chooses to avoid a conflict with Mary. Mary gets her way—she has engaged in power and control tactics. Judy has engaged in escape behavior. Neither is engaging in healthy behavior that improves the climate of the school.

FIXING THE PROBLEM

One of the most difficult issues for educators to face is that they may not be able to fix the problem; they can certainly do their part to not contribute to the problem so that it is not perpetuated, but some things may indeed be out of their control.

Educators have to figure out what they can and cannot change and focus on what they are able to do. When something is going wrong in faculty meetings, they need to ask themselves, "Am I contributing to this problem?"

If the answer is yes, then they need to work to change their behavior—they need to identify the problems that they are causing and make a conscious effort to be part of the solution.

If the answer is no, then they should focus their efforts on ways that they can learn to cope with the situation and support the individuals who are working to make necessary changes.

Faculty meetings can be a waste of time or a productive means of sharing information that will improve performance in the classroom. All educators need to do their part to be positive and productive by recognizing the strengths of those meetings and working together to contribute to their success.

ACTION PLAN

1. The educator should provide constructive items for the agenda.
2. The educator should always be respectful of others by being on time for faculty meetings and by listening to the suggestions of others.
3. The educator should adopt a positive attitude when going to faculty meetings.
4. The educator should commit himself or herself to giving undivided attention at the meeting.

5. The educator should work to communicate frequently with the administrator to understand the challenges the administrator faces.
6. The educator should reflect continually about his or her own behavior in a difficult
   situation to determine whether there is a different way he or she can handle the situation.

REFERENCES

Jentz, B., & Murphy, J. (2005). Starting confused: How leaders start when they don't know where to start. *Phi Delta Kappan*, 86(10), 736–744.

Lustbader, W. (2001). *What's worth knowing*. New York: Penguin Putnam.

Normore, A., & Floyd, A. (2005). A roller coaster ride: The twists and turns of a novice teacher's relationship with her principal. *Phi Delta Kappan*, 86(10), 767–771.

Chapter Five

Coping with Professional Jealousy

Enthusiasm
Then came a chasm
Between who you are
And their desire to block your star
With envy and lack of esteem
They seek to undercut your dream
It's not about who is inferior
Or who is superior
So affirm those at school
Detach when they are cruel
Invest in your learning
Validate each yearning
Keep your heart burning
Stay focused on what is new
Value everything that is in you
In spite of what "they" say or do.

Sara just completed her master's degree in special education and got a job in a nice urban middle school. This was her dream job; she always wanted to teach in a middle school. At the end of the year, the principal informed Sara that her students had done pretty well on the state tests. Parents were happy with Sara. Her participation in different school activities was appreciated. In about two years, she had created a positive relationship with her students, peers, administrators, and parents.

During her third year of teaching, the principal, Mr. Robson, asked her to serve on a five-person professional development team to mentor beginning teachers. She felt honored to be part of this team. She enjoyed the professionalism of her colleagues because she was part of such a brilliantly talented and professional faculty. She gained self-confidence and truly enjoyed working with other teachers who needed help. Collaborating with the four other members of the team inspired her energy, esteem, and self-confidence. She could not ask for more and was satisfied with her career goals.

She thought that she was part of this professional community where she was learning leadership skills and offering her mentoring support in various ways. The following year, the principal asked her to run for a seat on the advisory panel to the school board. The principal welcomed her input and discussed every major initiative or policy that affected the school. He listened to what she had to say and acted accordingly.

His perception was that Sara really knew the teachers and their needs, and he trusted and valued her opinion. During this time, Sara developed an innovative plan of student-led individualized education programs (IEPs). The committee appreciated her ideas and assisted her in carrying out her plan. The results were positive.

After a year of implementing this plan, the school received an excellence award in special education by the State Department of Education. The demonstration teacher in her school building always bragged about Sara for her implementation of student-led IEPs. The principal and parents were sending accolades. Sara felt successful, but she also noticed that the eyes of some of her colleagues were green. She heard her peers make comments like "She's always trying to show everyone that she is better than others" or "Anyone can come up with these ideas. What is so special about such IEPs? In fact, I think it's a lot more work than the regular IEPs."

Sara struggled with accepting the recognition she received for her success and unfortunately did not feel any pride and honor about her accomplishments. She knew that she was doing the right thing; however, the environment around her was making her feel frustrated with her own success. Fortunately, she had a mentor, Bryan, who was a seasoned science teacher in the same building. He figured out that Sara was struggling with accepting her success.

He decided to talk with her, and he shared his professional insights with her. In his conversations with her, he brought the term "professional jealousy" to her attention—(and explained to her) what it is; how it is related to a feeling of incompleteness, insecurity, and envy; and how it may serve as a breeding ground for more jealousy to erupt. He also shared some strategies for dealing with unhealthy professional jealousy. With his support and mentorship, Sara was able to deal with some of these barriers, and she began to enjoy her work again.

Teachers must know that as they enter the profession of teaching, not everyone around them is going to celebrate their desire for innovation and creativity. It is the same as when they were taking courses in college; some teacher candidates committed themselves to working more than others. Teacher candidates who wanted to get the best out of each college experience invested themselves in the learning process more than others did.

This chapter reminds the beginning teachers of examples of professional jealousy that they may experience as they begin to enhance their likelihood of professional recognition and success. They may encounter collegial jealousy, and it can become a barrier to innovative teaching. It is important that they understand this concept and learn to elevate themselves from professional jealousy. There are some ways of dealing with these types of situations without compromising teachers' desire for success.

CAUSES OF PROFESSIONAL JEALOUSY

Several causes exist that may give rise to the development of professional jealousy. Colleagues may feel jealous because of their own problems and limitations. When they are suffering from a lack of self-worth and a feeling of inferiority, they tend to think that if they do not support the person who actually demonstrates strengths, they may be able to restore their self-worth.

Another reason is a fear of vulnerability in colleagues; they show their inability to let themselves down by accepting others' success. Inside they feel that others may reject them. Before others actually do that, they reject others and their successes. This way, they do not have to face rejection. Teachers' attitudes toward these vulnerable colleagues should be professional and businesslike. Teachers should give their colleagues a feeling that they are open for communication; however, they should not allow colleagues to demean them.

Closeness with administrators may become a cause for jealousy among peers. Some peers may not give the beginning teacher full acceptance for his or her successes or may even consider damaging his or her relationship with others. Beginning teachers need to develop healthy and positive relationships with their colleagues.

The more they develop awareness and understanding with peers who have similar interests, who are interested in growth and learning as they are, and who are invested in producing positive outcomes, the more likely they are to develop positive relationships and connections with peers. Learning about why people become professionally jealous in the profession of teaching may give awareness about how teachers should be maintaining relationships with their colleagues.

REMEMBER: SOME WILL ENVY PROFESSIONAL SUCCESS

In Sara's case, some of her colleagues had a difficult time in sharing the same philosophy for student-led IEPs. They were not fully convinced that it was indeed a process that might work for many middle school students. Other peers just had no time to learn a new method. Many of these peers were resentful that they had to learn it, especially since the principal mandated its implementation without seeking input of Sara's colleagues.

If Sara would have explored the idea with her peers, they would have felt more comfortable with the process, and she might have felt less alienated by her peers. Buying peers' input may be one way of gaining their support. The root of professional jealousy lies in a limited definition of self. If teachers build their self-confidence and comfort with others, they are likely to be more successful in celebrating successes.

Here is another example. Cindy is a collaborative teacher, and she likes to adopt teaching approaches that are based on collective vision and teamwork. Because she values teamwork, she may overindulge in creating team environments, and she may push for sharing ideas about new instructional techniques and the effective use of new technologies because she sees benefits for peers and students.

She needs to learn that some people do not value teamwork. When she asks them to engage in collaborative problem solving, they come up with excuses of lack of time, resources, and administrative support. She heard some of them say, "I just cannot attend any more meetings. My job is to teach, and I am sick of these new projects that have no relevance. I only work from 7:30 a.m. to 3:00 p.m. per my contract."

Cindy's choice is to show them benefits and leave them at that. She cannot push them to agree with her philosophy of collaboration. She may find that some of her colleagues are so entrenched in old traditional ways of instruction that they do not even want to know the new and emerging approaches to teaching that are based on integration of technology or best practices. What she can do is share the positive results of teamwork. She can show them the products and deliverables that she has collected through the teamwork process. It is only by providing them information on tangible outcomes related to teamwork that she can attract her peers to see the value of teamwork. Data will speak as the success of her efforts.

DO NOT PUSH IDEAS: SHOW THE BIGGER PICTURE

It is especially difficult for Elsa to deal with Cindy as she is receiving recognition for teamwork. Elsa becomes so envious that she begins to manipulate situations, such as faculty meetings, presentations, or conferences. For example, she changes Cindy's space in the program or the order of her name in the presentation, and she tries to take "the whole pie" instead of the "slice" offered.

First, Cindy notices it and thinks that it is just a random occurrence. Then it becomes obvious because Elsa has also started to receive awards for teamwork. She has started to make her name, and now the principal thinks that Elsa is equally capable of the job that Cindy used to do. She never invites Cindy to the discussions, and Cindy has recently noticed that Elsa does not attend the meetings that Cindy coordinates. Elsa has clearly separated from Cindy. Cindy resents the process that Elsa undertook to sabotage her success; however, Cindy has no problems with Elsa's success.

On several occasions, Elsa did not show up for the ceremonies until she had to get some award or incentive. In fact, she stopped masking her lack of consideration with a friendly smile. Some other colleagues have also noticed this change in her. The principal has now started to hold Elsa in regard and is bragging about her accomplishments.

These situations are not so common, but when they happen they are pretty consuming and need to be addressed. One suggestion for the teacher who is going through such a situation may be to let the colleague who is manipulating the situation know how his or her actions are affecting the situation. The teacher may decide to provide clarification to the principal, who once supported her accomplishments. The most important action for the teacher will be to become smarter in his or her own actions.

Teamwork is always a great way for dealing with such situations. The teacher can start with giving the team of colleagues a broad picture of what needs to be done to accomplish the goal, and tell them in a supportive and encouraging manner how it is crucial to be fair to all members. The teacher can show the team that he or she is involved in teamwork only because it produces greater results for students and peers. She can make it clear to them that she is not doing these things to get notoriety or recognition. By sharing the results with team members, she raises expectations and encourages others to do the same. All the team members are encouraged to share information on success stories that they have created.

Once this climate of sharing is created, teachers like Elsa have a choice to either meet those expectations or manipulate at a higher level. In such environments colleagues develop a pretty good sense of which teachers are credible, and they begin to support them. Teachers gain respect by their interest in teaching and their desire to contribute to the growth of their students. These teachers thrive on their students' success. Teachers should not expend their positive energy on colleagues like Elsa and get involved in their tactics of putting others down. These tactics promote unhappiness and negativity.

BELIEVE IN GOALS WITHOUT MAKING OTHERS HOSTILE

Sally just completed a master's degree and has a desire to go for a doctorate. She has started to notice that every time she begins to talk about pursuing further education, her colleagues/peers begin to challenge her goal by making remarks such as "I don't think a PhD does any good to anybody" or "You really need to be a good teacher, and for that you really do not need the letters after your name." Sally gets disheartened and asks her department head about his opinion. He encourages her to get admission to a doctoral program. Sally has also indicated that next year she wants to go to another district if she doesn't get to enroll in the program.

It is clear that peers who are close to Sally have decided not to enhance their own professional lives or have decided that they do not need to go for further studies. These peers tend to undermine Sally's career goals and perceive her as having a self-centered approach toward her career. Teachers like Sally enjoy accumulating their professional experiences; these growth experiences enable them to do a better job of teaching in a classroom.

Oftentimes, peers whose educational experiences were not so relevant and did not contribute to the actual teaching in the classroom may have caused these peers to have negative opinions about obtaining a PhD degree; they perceive a doctorate as separate from enabling them to do a better job of teaching.

Teachers who would like to grow in their careers and consider that they would benefit from a doctoral degree do not worry about what their peers would say. They utilize the opportunity, they evaluate their own strengths, and they seek out tuition support to finish their doctorate. They are not worried about disclosing that they are enrolling at the state university to get their doctorate. They are not worried about peers' reactions.

Teachers need to engage in soul-searching from time to time to figure out what they are trying to achieve professionally. They also need to informally clarify common interests, shared values, and professional goals with their colleagues. In this process, they may find that most fellow teachers have been doing the same thing for a long time. Many of them dreamed to be in a safe position of teaching, and that's it for them.

There are always a couple of teachers who may get more excited about new learning and may be eager in increasing their personal growth. They believe in innovative ideas and are willing to take a risk to achieve them. They gravitate toward those who show similar interests; they take the time to become acquainted with one another's interests, values, and goals. This seems to help professional relationships, and it provides a common understanding without creating a threat.

These teachers keep discussing their professional expectations and share some positive examples with other colleagues like Sally. They mutually desire to accomplish their professional goals as successful educators. It is possible that these educators may get frustrated and dubious about their goals when their peers make negative comments. Gradually, they learn to alleviate those concerns and feel ready for the professional growth and challenges.

Effective teachers redefine their relationship with a colleague, peer, friend, or someone who cares about professional achievement. They make it clear to their colleagues and peers that they will support them in acquiring new knowledge, skills, and standards of professional competence; that they believe in ongoing professional growth; and that, as their colleagues' performance will evolve to new levels of competence, they will still be supportive of them.

REDEFINE SUCCESS

Success goes beyond achieving or reaching a landmark; it is constant engagement with the process of growth. A doctorate may symbolize an achievement in this ongoing process of growth, but it is just a landmark. Teachers' confirmation that they are on the right track comes from students who are learning and engaging in academic tasks and who are demonstrating a high level of concern and commitment to learning.

Teachers should not fall into the trap of evolving from a high-performing teacher to one who now has a doctorate but never uses the new knowledge. These teachers may begin to put pressure on others because of their new degree and also may become apathetic and negative. They need to remind themselves that when they first started five years ago, they were ushered away from many teachers who lacked interest in innovation and professional growth. At that time, they felt that they were surrounded by many talented seasoned teachers who were seemingly burned out.

As teachers continue their professional journey, they see many teachers join the profession. Seasoned teachers should not be negative around the beginning teachers nor should they squelch their enthusiasm. By working in this environment for a while, they have figured it out that in a resource-scarce environment people rely on discussions of tenure or seniority to empower themselves.

Effective teachers make a commitment to themselves that they will not be a senior member who has adopted the path of discouraging young teachers from expressing themselves or even trying new ideas. They know they have to begin the path of providing mentorship to these new teachers.

CELEBRATE GROWTH OF OTHERS

It is important to learn valuable lessons of leadership and professional growth from people who have gone through many different circumstances. Teachers should find motive for themselves to continue to learn new lessons. They should invite, encourage, and enable others to begin their own professional journeys. As they reflect on their own learning and reflect on the learning of others, they must encourage the educational growth of others.

Everyone needs to feel acknowledged and respected, even the least productive or least powerful. Valuing all fellow staff members and their thoughts and feelings and listening to their perspectives, even when in disagreement, will augment a healthy professional environment. Open communication will enhance the feeling of belonging to a community in the school. The more the colleagues feel that they are part of the school community, the more likely they are to become connected to the ultimate goal of achieving teachers' success.

At the same time, it is critical to recognize that peers and colleagues are individuals who have their own perspectives and opinions. Teachers should take time to acknowledge and celebrate the accomplishment of their peers. Things that may help in building these relationships include ideas such as bringing light refreshments or snacks to faculty meetings, sending simple greeting cards or thank-you notes to colleagues, posting written notes, and sharing information related to common interests.

One of the reasons that people become less interested in celebration is that too much emphasis is placed on achieving the results. Once the desired outcomes are produced, a new list of goals emerges. Educators should achieve the goals and take a moment to cherish the accomplishments.

ASSIST IN CREATING AN INTEGRATED PROFESSIONAL CULTURE

The environment that is characterized by a mix of veteran and beginning teachers provides a breeding ground for the best practice and innovation. The school in which the new teachers are supported by seasoned teachers is characterized as having "integrated professional cultures." In this environment, one can expect frequent meaningful interactions among faculty members across all experience levels and an appropriate novice status that accounts for the need for mentorship and support, while not underestimating one's potential contributions.

In addition, responsibility for the school and its students is shared among all colleagues, seasoned or new, within the school. In contrast is the environment where many new teachers find themselves subtly excluded from professional contact with veterans, feel a lack of support and collegiality, and leave the profession without giving it a fair try.

Teachers who want to make a difference have decided that they are not going to loiter around the edges in front of seasoned colleagues or sit in a corner chair in faculty meetings so that they will not be noticed. They have decided to participate in the discussions and have made themselves more visible. At the same time, they have decided to listen to the good pieces of advice from seasoned colleagues. They do not take it personally when seasoned colleagues challenge their new ideas.

Effective veteran teachers keep doing the right things; they keep track of past initiatives; and they demonstrate social competence when they are dealing with colleagues. They always try to bring their strengths and talents to work and continue to search for values that align with those of the school.

GET PAST DISTRACTIONS: KEEP FOCUS

Several opportunities emerge in schools where teachers are nominated for recognition and rewards. The principal may nominate a teacher for election to a state board for the school's best teacher award, for distinguished community service, or for other recognitions. Usually teachers support each other for these opportunities. Once in a while, one or two teachers may try to sabotage these opportunities by bad-mouthing or misrepresenting the teacher who is receiving the nomination for election, recognition, or an award.

Let us take an example of a teacher who is nominated for election to a state board. The principal nominates her because she is a well-deserving candidate. She is collaborative and maintains excellent relationships with all stakeholders. A couple of colleagues who are showing professional jealousy have started to defame her on no solid grounds.

The deserving teacher may have to become assertive about this situation. She may have to state her observations in a factual manner. She may have to say, "It has come to my attention that there has been misrepresentation of my position." The deserving teacher may like to add how she feels about it and the tangible outcomes and effects of this misrepresentation. She may have to create an opportunity for other colleagues to discuss this situation. She must reach out for others and have them talk with each other about her situation. Her forthrightness will help in having colleagues understand her position.

True colleagues do not want to second-guess, and as a result, they may reward her with affirmation. She may have a better chance of getting elected now than she did before. The key is not to blame the one who is bad-mouthing but to redirect colleagues' attention to the real focus. She should display her focus to her colleagues with ease and should not let them drift off. She should not let them think that she is not in this election process anymore.

She can change the system only by being part of it. She must keep building enough trust in herself to impel her to participate in this process, even in the face of twists, tentative action, or doubts. She must make sure to give her all to the process and not let a couple of nonsupportive peers get in between her and her desire to succeed. The more she manages to deal with them in a neutral way, the more confident she will become about her focus and purpose of participating in this election process.

KEEP FOCUS ON INNOVATION

Sometimes when teachers are confronted with people who show professional jealousy, these teachers tend to punish their own attributes of innovativeness. They may start thinking that maybe they are making it harder for themselves and others; maybe they are difficult and do not get along with others; maybe they need to change. They may indulge in unhealthy self-criticism.

Teachers need to reflect on who they are and remind themselves that they are innovators and agents of change. They must assist in dislodging the old thinking and not give up on creativity because it is their strength. They should keep engaged in the process of inquiry, discovery, and reflection; they should keep introducing new ideas and spreading new models through teaching and maintaining relationships with other professionals.

Oftentimes a veteran teacher with a strong paradigm may ignore or deny the validity of new experience, as it may appear contradictory to her or his experience. The new teacher who lets other teachers see the results of his or her thinking can create an appetite for them to learn a new way of teaching.

For some people, implementation processes are necessary, such as providing details about how to do it—that is, how to plan, design, and execute. If seasoned teachers begin to question the new teacher's ideas, the new teacher can provide them with tools such as details and share success stories of teachers who have applied new ideas. The new teacher can help the seasoned teachers by connecting them to a group that has applied new ideas and to websites where they can find more information.

Innovation and brainstorming are two different processes. Brainstorming refers to generation of multiple ideas, solutions, and outcomes, whereas innovation must be sharply focused on the areas of highest impact on student learning outcomes. For example, the principal of Farmer Junior High School is experiencing an increase in bullies on the playground. His afternoons are spent conducting in-school suspensions for at least eight to ten students during the week.

Heather is a behavioral specialist and has been charged by the principal to come up with an innovative solution to this problem. Heather decides to involve all her colleagues in a brainstorming session and seeks their input on various aspects of behavior management in their school. She discusses with them whether bullying has become an issue for them and gets their agreement on the importance of doing something about it.

In the second phase of discussions, she asks her colleagues to generate solutions to this problem and asks them to evaluate the effectiveness of each solution. She has used the collective brainpower of her colleagues to identify the extent of the problem, generate solutions, and evaluate solutions to the problem. Brainstorming sessions have provided a forum for open communication of ideas and generation of innovative solutions. These sessions help tap in to the brainpower of every teacher in the school so that each feels that she or he has had input in discussions. Heather also knows that she needs to effectively manage the collective brainpower without making these sessions chaotic. If not managed appropriately, these sessions can easily turn into gripe sessions.

The third phase is to implement the solution that was generated. This is the phase when creation of ideas turns into innovation. Brainstorming processes are geared toward getting a creative idea or solution; innovation, however, refers to creativity implemented. During this phase, Heather found that many of her colleagues became hesitant and showed a lack of commitment to the process. Heather knew that if she could get the group of her colleagues through this phase, they could really experience success in reducing the number of bullies in their school.

During this time, she began to show the results of positive-behavior supports from other schools and shared their success stories. She invited people from sites that had implemented a systemic approach to behavior management specifically designed to address bullying behaviors. This sparked her colleagues' interest, and they refocused and recommitted themselves to engage in similar approaches. Heather knew that for coming up with an innovative solution to bullying, she needed to have her colleagues engage in a conscious, collaborative, coherent approach that ensures dependability and best outcomes.

If the school values innovation, it needs more than just new ideas, multidisciplinary teams, and keynote speakers. It needs to establish the kind of school culture that is conducive to sustainable innovation, which takes all the teachers to a higher level of excellence.

ENEMIES MAY TURN INTO FRIENDS LATER

Reacting in a hostile manner toward those who decide to think and act differently rarely helps anyone. At the same time, new teachers do not want to be intimidated by those who become scornful and angry with them because of their success in the field. Teachers need to use these conflicts as learning experiences that raise awareness about differences of opinions, and not take them as personal attacks on them or their work.

Hostility begets hostility, so teachers need to be watchful that they do not treat others who are maintaining differences with a little charge of their own hostility into the equation. They want to have clear thinking about the vision they have for themselves and their students. They do not want to compromise their ability to communicate clearly about the vision and, hence, their freedom to choose skillfully between the options that contribute to student learning.

CONCLUSION

This chapter summarizes various types of professional jealousy that teachers may experience, and it provides reality-based solutions to some of these experiences. The key is to elevate oneself and disengage from acceleration of hostility. By deliberately detaching from an escalated hostile interaction, teachers do not lose a battle; instead, they make a conscious choice of staying as a professional in their field.

ACTION PLAN

1. Educators should understand the causes of professional jealousy.
2. Teachers should not deplete their positive energy on colleagues who spend their time in being negative.
3. Educators should believe in their goals and assist others in accomplishing their goals.
4. Educators need to assist new teachers in getting settled in the profession of teaching and should encourage innovation.
5. Educators should disengage from hostility and keep in mind the real purpose of joining the teaching force.
6. Teachers should work toward building their self-confidence and comfort with others; they are more likely to be more successful in celebrating successes.

Chapter Six

Avoiding Stagnation:
Dealing with the Pressure to
Stay with the Group and Not Excel

To grow into all education has for me
doesn't fit with what "they" want me to be
inside me a vision is forming
outside me, seems there's a warning
you'll be ignored and even rejected
pushed back, instead of being selected
resisting, onward I continue to move
honoring my priority to improve.

Natalie had worked for twenty-six years in a large corporation. She eventually reached the point where she sought more meaning in her life. Instead of seeking it through after-hours volunteering, she opted to return to school and obtain a degree in elementary education. After her first six months in the classroom, Natalie had become acquainted with the school staff and procedures. She found her niche in the teachers' lounge and enjoyed talking with her team members there during lunch.

All of them had children that were about the same age and in similar after-school activities. The lunch group also covered topics such as local bargains, movies, books, and television shows. This small talk at noon gave Natalie a welcome relief from the pressures of her classroom. Having a corporate background, she missed the big picture. While working for her company, Natalie had several opportunities to travel for professional purposes. Not only did she do business in other cities, but she also enjoyed the benefit of flying to other locations to attend training sessions.

One day Natalie noticed a brightly colored teachers' union flyer in her mailbox, and it caught her attention. It stated that funds had just become available for some interested teachers to attend national professional conventions. Applicants were given guidelines as to types of conferences, monetary limits, and connection to district goals. Just a few days before finding the flyer, Natalie noticed a conference being held in another part of the country that fit in perfectly with her curricular interests.

After reading the union flyer, she could see how the theme and content of this convention would match well with district goals and objectives. That evening, after she had completed her plans for the next day and had settled her children in bed, Natalie gathered her thoughts and prepared her application for the convention. The next day she sent it to the union contact person through the district mail. Natalie hoped that she would be selected to attend this upcoming four-day spring convention.

After two weeks had passed, Natalie had still not received a response to her application. Her hopes began to dim. She decided not to tell anyone on her staff that she had even applied. Because she was new to the district, she thought that her chances might not be that good. After one month, she received a letter through the district mail stating that she had been accepted to attend this convention. Due to the funds available, her airfare, hotel, and conference registration fee would be paid.

According to district policy, Natalie was to find a substitute and make the travel arrangements herself. She would be reimbursed once she offered proof of her expenses. Natalie was ecstatic! The bell rang, signaling that it was time for her to be at her classroom door to greet her students, so she had no time to share her excitement with anyone. She looked forward to surprising her team with the good news over lunch. When noon came, she burst into the staff lounge and announced her opportunity to her team members.

Their reaction stunned her. When she showed them her letter and the conference brochure, they passed it one to another. Each in turn glanced at the material, but instead of commenting, they continued their discussion of fund-raising for an upcoming soccer tournament that involved all of their own children. Instead of sharing in her excitement, they talked about the current cost of sports uniforms, carpooling detail, and balancing that with their quarterly report card deadlines.

Natalie left the staff lounge feeling unacknowledged and mystified. This was the same group that she had felt part of for six months, and today she felt like a misfit and a perfect stranger. What was going on? Why was everyone so indifferent to her opportunity? In her corporate job, conferences were an everyday event for someone in the office. What was different about this seemingly amiable group of teachers? What Natalie had just done was break one of the group's cardinal rules: stay with the group personally, socially, and professionally.

Natalie had joined the group as a personal and social match. Her application to the convention was a violation of the group's level of professional involvement. None of the group members had the time or the interest in traveling out of town alone to attend a convention with a group of strangers. They also had no desire to spend four days away from their classrooms listening to university professors and educational consultants present updated instructional information.

They had been to school once and had no intention of putting themselves in the position of having to return and apply what they had learned. They believed that things were going well, and they were comfortable with the status quo. When Natalie presented them with her acceptance papers, she signaled to them that she was interested in moving forward and further developing herself as a professional.

Unbeknownst to her, Natalie presented herself as a threat to the modus operandi of the team. By revealing to the group members her desire to grow in this manner and ultimately upset the familiar dynamics of the team, Natalie had placed herself in the position of having to make a choice between pursuing her own professional vision or staying with the pack. Until this time, she had no idea that she would have to make such a choice while working with people that she perceived to be mature professionals.

THE PURPOSE OF THE PACK

In nature, animals gather in packs for group preservation and survival. They help one another detect danger and come to one another's rescue. It is to the advantage of the whole group that each member of the pack is strong, able, and healthy. Birds in the northern hemisphere, for example, begin to flock in the fall in preparation for their long journey ahead. Some even migrate as far as South America. When doing so, they depend on one another in various ways to make this long journey. In effect, they support each other as they advance to their destination.

Ideally, in education, teachers have the opportunity to provide one another with similar support. As with animals seeking to grow strong for the good of the group, teachers have the option to see a peer's advancement in academic and professional growth as a benefit to the whole. For example, even though a teacher cannot take the time to attend a graduate class with the teacher across the hall, one can still benefit by taking time to learn about the class's highlights from this close resource.

Observing the results of a peer's attendance in any class, whether formally or informally, strengthens two professionals' ability to teach. When teachers decide to enroll together in a graduate program, taking turns driving, sharing ways that they are applying new learning in their classrooms, and working cooperatively on a project, they are moving forward in somewhat the same spirit as migrating birds.

Because they are traveling together through new territory, they are there every step of the way to offer encouragement, support, and confidence as they face the unknown challenges of academia together. Unfortunately, in some schools teachers have fallen into social patterns that subtly define growth parameters that they determine as being acceptable to the group. They place limits on the advancement of others by discouraging departure from group norms of professional development.

When a teacher steps forward and charts her or his own course of growth, the pack, as in the fictitious story of Natalie, chooses to ignore mention of it. Instead of asking questions, showing interest, and giving encouragement, the pack responds to talk of continued learning with indifference. Pack members do not understand the importance of continued mental stimulation. When a peer completes a class or earns an advanced degree, pack members find themselves unable to affirm these efforts, offer congratulations, or show enthusiasm.

Not only that, but they may even go so far as to begrudge a colleague this chosen opportunity. If a teacher, despite these unwritten but strong rules about limited professional growth, decides to proceed ahead anyway, he or she may be lonely when with the group. Perhaps he or she will be part of the conversation when the topic of interest is considered permissible. Peers may be cordial and friendly. But the teacher may risk being relegated to the fringe of the pack if he or she goes beyond the parallel paths of peers.

In high school, students who choose honor roll status instead of staying out late with the gang end up with a certain stigma. The gang will rule that honor students will be on the periphery of the action. Similarly, the teacher who chooses a more distinctive path may have to pay the price of some isolation. To grow, the teachers who know who they are, what they want, and what unique path they plan to travel to get there may have to travel alone.

Unlike the animals that reach their potential in a pack or the birds assisting one another on the journey, such teachers may have to fly solo. To make it to their selected destinations, they will have to somehow mentally transcend some subtle rejection. They may have to do without certain social components of the school day that they would otherwise have experienced had they chosen 100 percent compliance to the code of the teacher pack.

DIVISION VERSUS UNITY

Ideally, one would think that teachers who are united and moving together are doing the best for one another and their students. That is true when staff can lay down their personal preferences and serve the greater good through cooperation in a group effort. Unity serves students and families when it involves a group decision to speak positively about students, families, staff, and school programs in public.

Division does not serve the best interests of others when teachers continually challenge the efforts of the majority to accomplish curricular and building programs and board mandates. Energy that fights the common good is energy misspent. Such efforts are wastes of the time and talent of all involved. However, there are certain circumstances when the reverse is true and growth demands abandonment of unity in favor of division.

Those circumstances call for the choice of division from forces on the staff that thwart forward and individual movement of those seeking to grow professionally and personally. If a team, hall, or faculty behaves in a way that shuns, ignores, or dismisses the efforts of a teacher who is sincerely working to improve teaching methods and students' lives and learning levels, then this teacher has a choice to make.

Cliques, factions, and groups who directly or indirectly work to keep a teacher from growing beyond the pack's established horizons are using unity improperly. Teachers who face the loss of unity with the group and the potential for division from the pack face an important professional choice.

IDENTIFYING THE CHOICE

Teachers in such circumstances are put into an unfair position due to the nature of the social patterns established in their immediate school environment or department. The message comes across that they have a choice. Acceptance comes with relinquishing dreams of a doctorate or plans to become an administrator, speaker, educational journalist, or after-school class instructor for staff. The list of possibilities is as unique as the teachers who dream.

Teachers who come into environments where the pack rules arrive with ideas of where they want to take their professional careers. They also come with openness to growth that is responsive to student needs. They have no expectation that their ideas will create issues with peers, and they come with the expectation that the system in which they work will foster their efforts to improve and grow professionally.

They have no awareness that the "who do you think you are?" message will be sent directly or indirectly in an attempt to curtail their advancement to their full professional potentials. Then it happens, as it did to Natalie. Their plans and dreams are challenged through indifference, a sharp remark, or a clear attitude of disapproval.

With the challenge comes the choice to submit to building standards for professional growth or to go forward in an honest response to the heart, the needs of students, and the dream to become a fully developed and mature professional. Teachers who are alert to the challenge will know they have to decide, and decide they will, either to give in and find satisfaction and acceptance with the status quo or to risk going forward into the unknown of further professional pursuits.

BREAKING AWAY FROM THE PACK

No one knows the true price of breaking from the pack until one actually does it. The break can be done slowly and gradually or dramatically, publicly, and consistently. For example, if a teacher chooses to take a graduate class to improve behavior management skills, no one need know about it. Time spent after hours and on weekends is personal. The new skills acquired can be applied in the confines of a classroom.

Those who launch out onto their own paths of professional growth may do so with little fanfare, reserving their enthusiasm for coffee times with professionals in other settings. Supporters met at a convention or on a state or national board may be the people with whom to best share candidly the journey of growth. Moving in this manner is a break with the pack that is protective of the teacher who has to work with a potential naysayer.

Perhaps a teacher in this position is testing the waters of graduate school, feeling fragile about one's ability to actually achieve an advanced degree. Protecting the dream from someone who would readily snuff out confidence and interest in such an endeavor is wise indeed. Others who break from the pack see clearly that to be their true selves, they must come out with it and make it clear that they have a plan in mind to go a certain direction.

An example of a teacher in this position is one who has made a decision to teach for five years and then pursue a certification enabling him or her to work as a principal. This kind of teacher plans to move to another district once certified and is clear to everyone on the staff about these plans. An invitation to a home party or a saved chair with the gang at lunch is of little importance to this individual. This professional sees the big picture and is rock solid in his or her decision.

Eventually, such teachers as in the previous example find acceptance for who they are. If this were not to occur, they are not concerned because they have a mission for the moment, learning everything they can about their own students and how schools are run. They objectify the behavior of the pack and add the awareness of such dynamics to other information that they are gathering that will be helpful in their future job.

In some instances teachers do not pay a large price for their actions. Are there circumstances where teachers will pay a heavier price? Teachers who choose to be who they are can share their goals and desires with peers and test the waters. If they tell one of the pack members about having an article published in a professional journal or of their success in securing a spot as a presenter at a state convention, the teacher may start the group moving against them.

They may experience a distancing or, even worse, a retaliatory action, such as misrepresentation in a gossip mill or overt cruelty in another circumstance that does not appear connected to their breach of the pack code. On the other hand, this staff person may be overloaded and not care one way or the other and not recall much of the conversation about the teacher's desired growth experience.

Sharing success could work out well in the long run. Perhaps the teacher who seeks to achieve a dream also has social abilities that affirm and entertain peers. In spite of any jealousy or pack loyalty issues, certain teachers may find avenues of connection with the coworker who chooses to grow. They may come to realize that they admire this person for going ahead with his or her ambitions, noting that he or she is sincere and is doing it for the purpose of helping others as opposed to personal glorification.

In seeing that genuineness, they may give the person a pass and continue relating in an amiable manner. Rejection may or may not occur when one is true to one's dreams and desires. If it does, however, it is important for the teachers choosing their own growth path to realize that such staff sanctions come from unhealthy individuals and are not about them.

DEALING WITH REJECTION

Suppose that staff members succumb to their jealousy or feelings of discomfort or inferiority that are stirred up when they see peers take off in the direction of their dreams. Maybe the pack will rule strongly and, when a leader pulls the switch, will lead the way in ignoring, shunning, and rejecting—what happens then? Although it will be unpleasant to be excluded from the center of the flow of a staff or department social system, the teachers who take the risk and are treated unfavorably can choose to see the situation as a test of their own truth.

Do they want to pursue their endeavor? Can they pay the price of peer pettiness for a potential payoff down the line? Can they see the big picture and fuel their dreams with hope and optimism in spite of coworkers who do not reinforce this dream? Those professionals firm in their identity and direction find ways to verify individual professional goals and dreams not shared by coworkers.

They find clarity in their personal decision to move ahead with their professional goals in spite of any rejection that is experienced in the work environment. For these individuals, determining, clarifying, and continually renewing commitment to professional goals helps maintain a steady direction toward meeting them.

DETERMINING PROFESSIONAL PRIORITIES

Each day teachers are flooded with ideas, duties, and unplanned events that need to be addressed. Staff members become saturated in the crisis of the day or the emergency of the moment. Keeping a clear sense of a professional dream challenges the most determined of teachers. It would be so easy to abandon ship and let the priorities of the immediate wash one ashore.

It is hard to continue to persist in the pursuit of dreams when such desires get fogged in, appearing vague and distant when so much in the work environment can pull one off course and drown out deep desires for further development. When the culture of the building overtly and subtly attempts to define one's destiny, how does one remain true to professional priorities?

Apart from the demands of the job, a personal discipline rises from within to steer teachers in the direction that is their "true north." With an internal compass that aims to lead such teachers onward, they continue to make small choices in thought, professional behavior, and selection of association supportive of their ultimate destination.

Teachers on track, following their own priorities, pull back from conversations and connections where there is criticism of the kinds of behaviors needed to become all they can be. They break from bonds that keep them back instead of reinforcing their true natures. They read materials that support their growth as educators and find other professionals who believe in advancing their cause. Teachers who know their priorities can easily detect people who are unwilling to get onboard with their best interests.

Those who desire a doctorate, plan to develop a curriculum that will benefit the broader educational community, or hope to advance their students in the state debate competition remain steadfast in their dream. They work daily toward developing the character qualities, knowledge base, and mind-set to get them where they want to go. Through pursuing their own vision, they value reaching out to others to share their expertise. They take interest in others, knowing that their professional lives are about helping others achieve their best as well.

All professionals who are sincere about doing their best daily make efforts to function in an organized and efficient manner. They develop a system to ensure that their classrooms and offices run smoothly. It means a great deal when they can end the day satisfied that they have managed their time for the optimal benefit of students and team members. Goal-oriented teachers choose to arrange their workspaces to avoid wasting time shuffling around looking for the essentials. They remain determined to use each moment in the workplace wisely.

Though they realize that building themselves from the inside matters most, teachers en route to fulfilling their professional potentials are attuned to externals that enhance their progress as well. They work to create a positive and productive atmosphere when working with students and serving on committees. They forge bonds with parents based on respect and courtesy. Consistent professionalism builds their outer environment and reflects their inner attitudes and desires. One manifestation of professionalism is how a teacher chooses to dress while at school.

THE MESSAGE OF DRESS

Jean earned her undergraduate degree as a young woman. When her children had grown, she followed her previous course of study with a master's program that enabled her to specialize as a teacher of children with learning disabilities. During her university years, she wore casual clothing to class and enjoyed the comfort of blue jeans and a sweatshirt when she studied late into the night.

When Jean prepared for her first job, she purchased clothing that she believed appeared comfortable yet professional. Though she planned to wear slacks often, she thought that wearing a jacket with slacks or a scarf with a blouse or sweater distinguished her from the students and gave her the look of professionalism that she chose to present.

When Jean arrived at her first job, she was surprised to see the attire that most teachers chose. Though some dressed tastefully and fashionably, many opted for current youth fashion or what she considered to be Saturday-morning clothing. Jean wondered how students felt about their teachers wearing trendy tops, denims, and sneakers. She faced the decision of using the clothing that she had bought for school or going with the clothing code that seemed to be already set in her school.

Max prepared to work in the same school. His ideal was to dress comfortably yet to support his image as a professional through his clothing. Max's college roommate, John, had earned a degree in business. He planned to go to work for a software firm in the fall. Both young men shopped together for their work-world clothing, buying sport shirts and white shirts along with comfortable khakis and dress pants.

They parted ways on selection of their ties, with Max choosing some bright and figured ones that he thought students would enjoy and with John selecting more conservative tones. When Max intentionally wore a short-sleeved white shirt with a tie on the first day of school, he planned to send the message to his students that, though young and new, he was an adult and he intended to be taken seriously.

On that first day, when an older parent en route to work at a corporate setting stopped in to introduce herself, Max felt confident in his ability to meet her as a professional and to stand toe-to-toe with her as an expert in his respective field. These imagined individuals decided to dress in a way that they believed to be appropriate, comfortable, and professional while on the job in their classrooms and offices. They realized that there would be field trips, outdoor events, and designated theme days where they would depart from standard dress.

They also respected teachers in roles such as physical education and special programs that called for different attire, and they noticed that, though clothed appropriately for their unique roles, through posture, presence, and demeanor, they presented themselves as adult professionals. At times Jean and Max wondered if their peers thought that they considered themselves above the other staff members.

On the contrary, Jean and Max chose their dress from the point of view of self-respect and a professional identity that they intended to maintain, not only with students, but with parents as well. Jean and Max chose to break the general code of teacher wear in their school and set their own tone and direction through dress.

Collectively, teachers speak of wanting to be treated as professionals. So often, less desirable pay and public perception distress and disturb teachers. They may feel helpless, uncertain of their identities and how to present themselves. Choosing to dress the part of a professional, in accordance with specialists in fields outside education, gives them part of the edge that they deserve. When teachers present themselves to students, administrators, parents, and peers, their professional attire sends a strong message that they are, in effect, exactly that—professional.

BREAKING AWAY YET STAYING CONNECTED WITH THE PACK

Is it possible to break away and still remain in a daily relationship with those at school who, whether overtly or subtly, intend to deny a goal-directed teacher his or her dream? Why would one want to? Those who are goal driven and have made the internal decision to move in the direction of their dreams still remain in their school situation on a daily basis. Their goals may be years in the future, though they have selected to begin them now. Consequently, they come to school daily, harboring the ideals and ideas that they intend to follow to reach a particular professional goal.

By daily physical proximity with these negative people, positive teachers already have an established identification and connection. They ask themselves what they can do to make each day as pleasant and as productive as possible. To do so, they seek to build social relationships and contacts that are constructive, clear, and workable to their situation. They put their best foot forward in minor exchanges, such as borrowing a pen, or major ones, such as working for consensus at a staff meeting relative to the organization of school conferences.

In doing so, they are psychologically bolstered and find betterment in knowing that they are making a contribution to their current school situation. In this mode, they are suited to enter into exchanges with students and parents. They have made their contribution to the balance and function of the school as a whole. They find satisfaction in reaping the rewards of investing their talents and time into their school community.

With this satisfaction, such teachers find emotional growth and further personal maturity and professional development. As they proceed in social conversation, psychological certainty, and emotional awareness, they distinguish themselves in terms of their own boundaries and goals. As they approach each day and each person in their school sphere, they realize clearly what their purpose is in the moment and where they intend to direct their career goals and projects in the future.

They remain in tune and in touch with the pack on their pathway to their chosen professional fulfillment. They alone know the nuances of their vision. They are inner directed, but they relate responsively, assertively, and confidently with their outer world as well.

FINDING A NEW FLOCK

As noted previously, teachers will flock and function according to rules and codes determined by their group. Sometimes flocks can be supportive and protective. At other times, they prevent personal growth and self-development from flourishing and meeting their full potential. When that is the case, teachers find new flocks with which to associate.

During the evening, on weekends, and in the summer, they build relationships with like-minded individuals who share similar goals and dreams. Perhaps they meet with a writers group over coffee on a Saturday morning. Maybe they attend a national convention in the summer, even at their own expense if need be. They know that the price of a plane ticket and a conference registration fee is invaluable because they are validated in the presence of others who share their professional passions.

Whatever groupings they find, whether in a graduate class study group or in a support group formed with teachers in similar roles from other school districts, the power of the group propels teachers who are determined to achieve their goals forward toward these dreams. In making the decision to opt for personal plans over the vision adopted by a group who has set parameters for growth, teachers choosing to move forward empower themselves to become all that they are capable of becoming.

They work among people who have professional limits, yet they refuse to take on these limitations as their own. As they continue to reach out for like-minded professionals, they become stronger in their resolve. Eventually, they look back at the pack and wonder why they were concerned about the pressure to stay with the group and not excel beyond their defined limits of growth. Achieving their dreams was well worth the choice to see their vision clearly and pursue it in spite of messages to remain with the flock.

ACTION PLAN

1. Educators should list people supportive of their professional growth and note how and when these individuals can offer work-related support. These support teams or groupings may choose to communicate on a regular basis to sustain excitement and incentive.
2. Educators should read educational magazines, journals, newspapers, websites, and blogs as well as participate in chat rooms that discuss relevant educational subjects.
3. Educators should determine the behaviors and situations in their school culture that may be a detriment to achievement of a professional goal and then strategize actions and attitudes to offset these outer conditions.
4. Educators should list motivational statements to strengthen their resolve to stay the course.
5. Educators should join a committee or organization in tune with their professional interests and goals.
6. Educators should identify through journaling or art the qualities they need to maintain professional growth.

Chapter Seven

Working Effectively and Professionally with the Building Administrator

Administrators come and go
It's the good ones we hope to know
They come in all manner and style
Some remain calm; some easily rile
Some truly know how to lead
While others would rather mislead
Some are eager to do
Others worry too much that someone will sue
Some like to interact and talk
When others see a problem, away they walk
Attention to detail, some have lacked
Educators want to know they will be backed
Some thrive on power and have a "pet"
The true leader assures that collaborative goals are met.

Today is Susan's first day as a real teacher. She is excited, apprehensive, and ready to assume the challenge. She is relieved that there is no more university supervision and nobody is coming to observe her while she is teaching. No one is going to mention her strengths and weaknesses on a daily basis. She will have her own class with her own students. She is eager to assume the responsibilities of a real teacher.

As she enters the new school building, she gathers a sense of the school environment, how students are taught in each class, how the teachers are collaborating, how the office staff is functioning, and so forth. She goes into the office, the receptionist greets her with a warm smile perking her up for the day ahead of her and making her feel welcomed to the new surroundings. The receptionist shows Susan the lounge and she moves forward to make herself comfortable on her first day of being a real teacher.

Looking back, she begins to think how hard she had worked. She reminisces about her rigorous coursework that she endured while maintaining a high grade point average as well as the field experience that she completed with flying colors. Susan would also think back to the student teaching with a hard-nosed mentor teacher that enabled her for the real challenge.

After she takes a few steps, she finds her second-grade classroom nicely arranged and organized.

As Susan begins to create a blueprint of the location of where the children will keep their backpacks, hang their coats, and place their lunch boxes, she notices Ken, the principal of the school, coming toward her with a roster in his hand. He seems to have an amicable personality. He calls her by her last name and says, "Ms. Mitchell, welcome aboard. We are so glad to have you in our school. Here is your roster for your class. Please feel free to let us know if we can be of any assistance."

It is obvious that he is a caring administrator and wants Susan to feel comfortable on her first day of teaching. He shows her the office of the vice principal, Ms. Larsen, and says that she helps him with day-to-day operations of the school. Susan notices that he delegates authority and develops the leadership skills of others. Then he asks her to join him for a little visit of the school, and he shows her the media room, library, cafeteria, music room, auditorium, counseling center, and the nurse's office.

Susan is a bit overwhelmed but feels that she is in a school where the school leader is providing direction. Ken cares about the cleanliness of the school, ensures that students follow the rules, and makes certain that the school building looks orderly. She feels inundated but also relieved that she is going to work in a great school where learning is important.

The positive effect of his leadership is reflected in all day-to-day operations. The day begins with announcements and reminders, as expected. Students are well dressed and eager to learn. Susan begins to count her blessings and starts to get ready to instruct her students. As she starts to get to know her students, she becomes more comfortable in her teaching.

Next door is the classroom of Ms. Roberts, a fourth-grade teacher. She notices that Ms. Roberts is sitting with a group of students laughing and talking. Two other students are trying to do their math and are showing problems of concentration and inattention. Susan hears her say, "Alright, Jimmy take your book out and look at the examples on page thirty-four and figure out how to multiply. I taught you last year how to do multiplication of two digits."

Susan begins to wonder about Ms. Roberts's instructional style for these two students who are struggling with such unclear instructions. Again, she hears her speaking, this time to the other student, "Kate, it is time to start working." Both the students still maintain the looks of apprehension and show themselves to be busy. Ms. Roberts keeps talking to other students, keeping the noise level up for the two strugglers. Ms. Roberts sees Susan taking notice of her class surroundings, and she begins to move toward her. She introduces herself to Susan, "I am Kelly Roberts."

Without giving Susan the option of introducing herself to her, she goes on, "I hope you like this place. I have been here in this school for five years, and nothing has changed. If you are thinking about changing things around here, forget it. Our principal is a micromanager and doesn't let people think on their own. I kind of stay away from him, and he knows that I do not agree with his management style. He wants me to work with the special education teacher to help these students learn. How is she going to help me? I know that I have control over my class, and he has a tendency to continually intervene. Well, I got to see what these two strugglers are doing in math." Without waiting for Susan's reaction or response, she leaves.

Quickly, Susan realizes that she is hearing about a conflict in the leadership style from a teacher who has a less-than-effective instructional style. She warns herself, "Don't alienate yourself from this colleague; but at the same time you can't let her bad-mouth the principal and blame him for the problems that she is experiencing in the school." Susan notices that Ms. Roberts is not really interested in helping the students who truly need help. In the case of these two students who are struggling in math, she needs to think about the learning context that seems to be productive for them.

Susan also wonders why Ms. Roberts was so quick to give her a negative tip on her principal. Susan does not want to ruin her relationship with her on the chance that she may have to work together on a team project. She is being cautious, and she knows that she cannot trust her. It is much easier to destroy the possibility of collaboration, and who knows, she may need some assistance from her down the road. Her personal encounter with the principal has not been too bad. In fact, she actually likes him and finds him professional and supportive of her. She perceives him as having strong interpersonal and organizational skills, and his management style is respectful.

Toward the end of the day, Susan receives a note from the principal asking her to check with him before she leaves. Susan goes to his office, and he asks about her day and reassures her that he would offer her any assistance that she may need down the road. This is one of the many experiences that beginning teachers have shared with one of the authors of this book.

To deal effectively with the building administrator, the first thing beginning teachers need to do is to know themselves. Instead of judging people around them, like colleagues, staff, students, or parents, they may need to find time to get to know themselves, their own habits of mind, their strengths, their needs, and what type of leadership style will help them thrive. Then, it is necessary to find a school that fits their needs.

It is great that Susan has found a right fit for herself. This school has the same value system and teaching philosophy that Susan encompasses. The school cares about each student's education, and teachers and administrators want to involve parents in their decision making. Ms. Roberts's style is the only issue that she may have to deal with. She has figured out that she is not going to reinforce her bad-mouthing behavior. At the same time, she will maintain a professional relationship with her colleague.

Fortunately, she spends a good year at this school, and the building principal decides to move on to another school the next year. Susan ends up having a principal who is not so involved with students and parents and is too keen on creating his own image. Nothing Susan does is noticed. Some of her other colleagues are also experiencing this change and are contributing to a low morale.

This transitory nature of educational leadership has endangered her professional enhancement, and her career goals may get compromised. She and her other colleagues do not feel like committing themselves to long-term changes because they find themselves uncertain about their future. Her superintendent is unwilling to make or follow through on commitments that she needs for her professional success.

It is important for the teacher to understand leadership style and dispositions and develop a repertoire of coping skills for when the teacher experiences dramatic changes in the leadership style. The teacher clearly needs to know the difference between an effective versus an ineffective leadership style. Also, if a veteran colleague like Ms. Roberts has had issues with effective leadership, the teacher needs to discern for herself whether the veteran teacher has issues of her own or whether there are genuine concerns that relate to the leadership.

This chapter presents some practical issues concerning the effectiveness of leadership that many teachers have experienced in their professional careers. Issues are presented with case studies, and suggestions for future teachers are offered.

WORKING WITH A PESSIMISTIC LEADER

Michelle, a beginning teacher who is enthusiastic, ends up being with a principal who has forgotten the real purpose of his existence in school. He refuses to examine his own expectations and leads a life of boredom and disinterest in students and their learning. Michelle finds herself trapped in a cycle of losing desire for her job. Oftentimes, she asks herself if she is experiencing burnout, has lost her touch, or needs to go back to college for a few more courses. She is unable to distinguish that the problem is actually not with her but with the school climate that has been created with inactive leadership.

Sara had a similar experience. She was an energetic, task-oriented, and competent first-year teacher who was trapped in a school where the leadership never thought of building morale, providing guidance, or offering opportunities for professional development. The principal always worried about the budget cuts that were guided by the realities of time; however, he was never able to see what good staff and faculty he had.

Everyday experience at that school became an aversive situation for Sara, and she decided to move to a different school. She did not want to bad-mouth the administration and figured out that she needed to change the location and climate for her to be successful, which was not a bad choice for her.

These scenarios clearly indicate that a principal is the central figure who affects the quality of teacher instruction, student achievement, and the degree of efficiency in school functioning. The responsibilities of a school administrator are enormous. Effective leadership creates a positive and healthy climate for staff, faculty, and students where gossip, ostracism, and upsetting events do not cause interference with one's teaching.

Educators should expect optimism in a leader, which is characterized by progressive outcomes, strength-based instruction, and a positive change in the environment. It is important that educators are able to figure out where the issues are. If they find out that the leadership has a negative tone, they should not question their own strengths. They should assist in raising the awareness in other colleagues about the issues of the leadership in a positive way. Once educators figure out that they are working under a pessimistic leadership, they may decide to adopt a collective approach to change the leadership.

DEALING WITH AN UNAPPROACHABLE LEADER

Maria had great difficulty approaching her principal, who never had enough time to listen to her concerns and never foilowed up on her requests. She needed to seek advice on a student issue, but he was always busy with meetings, fund-raisers, and other events around the school.

She had left several messages with his secretary to no avail. She kept making decisions in collaboration with some seasoned teachers who were experiencing similar issues.

Once she ran into him in the morning when he was heading out for another meeting with his board members, and she asked him if he could give her some time to discuss a student concern. He assured her that he was going to be back in his office after a couple of hours, and they could discuss the issue then. As she expected, he came back the next day, and she had already resolved the situation. She wanted to share a proposal that she had put together on peer-assisted learning for students with disabilities and had not heard from him for about three months.

Although this had enabled her to be a better decision maker on day-to-day issues, she always feared that if something went wrong, she may not have support from her principal. One Friday, Maria was called to the principal's office. Lo and behold, she was asked to provide an explanation about why she had taken her students on a field trip without his permission. They had gone to see an art museum, and she had sought his approval in writing two months before. But he did not pay attention to what he was signing off on.

What had triggered this event was that one of the students' parents had met with the principal on the weekend and complained about their son's dislike for the trip. The boy was not interested in seeing various exhibits in the museum. He went home and complained about the trip to his parents. But other kids had a lot of fun. The principal told Maria that she needed to tell him a day before going on the trip where she was going, how many students were going, and why she thought it would be a great experience for her students. He added that he did not want parents complaining about the field trip in the neighborhood.

Maria felt like she had informed the principal, took all the precautions necessary for the field trip, and had received parent permission before taking her students on the field trip. The principal was never interested in listening to her when she was informing him during the planning phases and had the nerve to become overagitated on account of the dissatisfaction of one parent. She felt unsupported by her principal. She was frustrated with his selective memory loss.

In circumstances like this, it is important that the teacher develops sound relationships with peers and has allies. He or she may ask for their support if things get unclear with the administrator. It is also important for teachers to keep documentation of requests.

DEALING WITH AN INEFFECTIVE INSTRUCTIONAL LEADER

Successful principals are effective instructional leaders; usually, they possess instructional qualities and respect those who have them. They are strong educators who anchor their work on central issues of learning and teaching and continual school improvement. They envision connections between instructional effectiveness and positive student outcomes and promote professional development and capacity building for instructional effectiveness in their faculty members. They ensure that they create a positive climate by promoting the significance of learning.

They model goal-setting behaviors and demonstrate the capacity to translate their vision into action. They enable the teachers to work as a team, and they emphasize the school-wide goals and expectations and provide a supportive environment for them to succeed. They do not take refuge from instructional issues and problems. Rather, they find opportunities for their staff and faculty to access the most updated information on instructional effectiveness.

Teachers who work in supportive environments tend to report satisfaction with their own functions of teaching and evaluating, dealing with parents, and developing a curriculum. On the other hand, when teachers meet with a disorderly school climate charged with low morale, they tend to burn out soon.

Where the principal is always hiding behind the desk in his or her office and is acting as the busiest administrator, teachers, students, and parents feel that they have no idea what is going on in the school. The effective principal, on the other hand, continues to find time to interact with teachers and parents and is willing to respond to their concerns.

In the times of shortages of effective teachers, it is essential that administrators begin to expand their responsibilities as instructional leaders and understand the pulse and the climate of their surroundings. They must show interest in the professional well-being of their staff and faculty and provide access to opportunities that may enhance their career growth. If the principal forgets his or her priorities of producing positive outcomes for students, educators have two choices: the first is to keep reminding the principal of student needs, and the second is to assist him or her in developing a vision that includes positive student learning and outcomes.

WORKING WITH A TALKER, NOT A DOER

Educators may encounter a principal who does not get back to people who were promised answers, does not respond positively to people who have differing points of view, and proposes great ideas at faculty meetings but does not follow up on them. Dr. Nelson was that kind of a principal: very articulate, very charismatic, and a people charmer. But that image did not last for too long because parents and teachers realized that he was offering only lip service and that no actions ever resulted from his proposals and speeches.

Effective principals devote significant attention to being cheerleaders and create a positive climate for students and faculty. They make tough decisions. They listen to faculty and student concerns.

Ineffective principals, on the other hand, try to procrastinate decisions by stating, "When everyone is on board, I will consider that." They want to maintain their image but do not want to take tough steps. They want to get along with everyone and adopt the path of inaction. They cannot deal with conflicts, which are actually a healthy part of an organization. They do not make time to communicate about sound ideas and best practices, and they demonstrate failure to provide competent oversight.

What should educators do if they get stuck with the principal who fails to take actions and make decisions? They have two choices. The first is to stop being inactive just because the principal fails to model activity for them. They need to work with their intrinsic motivation and do the right thing. They may wish to create a small group of teachers within their school who believe in doing the right thing and who support one another for doing the right thing.

The second choice is to let the district-level leadership know about the issues that educators are experiencing with their principal.

WORKING WITH A LEADER WITHOUT A VISION

Almost every action that a principal takes conveys a message about his or her vision for the school. If the principal does not believe in seeking parental input, parents will not be involved in the decision-making process, and teachers will not make sincere efforts in communicating with parents. If the principal allows time to be wasted or squandered on unproductive activities, the value of instructional time and the importance of student engagement will be diminished. If the principal celebrates only one form of student achievement, such as standardized scores, other forms of achievement that reflect improvement or progress will languish.

If the principal ignores inappropriate, undesirable student behavior, so will everyone else. If the principal avoids technology, it will never get integrated into his or her school. If the principal does not value special education, special educators in that school will be treated as the second-class citizens of the school. If the principal does not support fine arts, there will be no promotion of art, music, theater, or extracurricular activities.

As a result, the effects of every decision resonate throughout the school, communicating to everyone exactly what is important and meaningful and what is not. It is one thing to disagree with the components of the vision, and it is another to have no vision in the leadership. Without a vision, educators may find the school climate to be chaotic, with teachers working in disarray and with students not producing positive outcomes for themselves.

If educators end up being in such a situation, they may want to have a mentor outside of school and may want to seek advice in how they need to be handling day-to-day issues without being caught in confusion. They may like to keep a log of requests and responses that they have made over a time of chaos.

Some other suggestions for educators in such situations include the following: educate and raise awareness of staff members about the importance of vision and how it affects the school climate; make a collaborative request for developing a clear vision for the school; and ask about being involved in the development and revision of the vision and the mission statement of the school.

WORKING FOR A LEADER WHO DOES NOT CARE ABOUT DETAILS

Effective principals have oversight on details of the school day. They ensure that their teachers and staff have materials and supplies that they need, that the classrooms are supplied when school opens, and that everyone has procedures for making appropriate requisitions. They attend to the minor details and provide careful oversight of books and materials ordered by secretaries. They are not so busy as to think that this is something they do not need to manage. They may delegate these responsibilities, but they have the knowledge of how the day-to-day operation is being handled.

A principal who has no interest in details and no patience to find out about failures of operations does not provide adequate resources to his or her staff and faculty. Such principals are not effective managers, and they fail to create an effective management system that takes care of daily needs. Although teachers may not expect them to be taking care of each detail, they do expect them to create a system in which details are taken care of. They should show interest in knowing whether things are working out for the teachers and their students.

Don is sensitive to staff needs and has a great heart but shows a lack of patience for details. When a teacher tells him what she needs, he shows the signs of boredom: he begins to yawn and directs her to talk to his secretary. He has given too much power to his secretary, and his secretary has started to consider herself to be the boss and actually treats the teacher in a condescending way.

Once a teacher asks about pencils for her class because her students are going to take the state tests this week. The secretary reminds her that she had given her a half-dozen pencils three weeks ago and questions her, "What happened to those?" The teacher feels like the secretary is not just controlling supplies but also controlling her. The teacher is so tired of asking for things that she ends up spending her own money for her class needs.

When a teacher is faced with such challenges, he or she may like to find out if there is someone else experiencing similar issues. If there are peers who are experiencing similar issues, they all may consider developing an advisory committee to provide suggestions about how to maintain supplies for the whole academic year and present a report to the principal.

PRINCIPAL'S PET

There are some other issues that may interfere with the teacher's relationship with the administrator. One of them is being labeled as the principal's pet. In the beginning, the teacher may enjoy all the attention that he or she may receive in being considered as the principal's favorite person, but later he or she may dislike the attention. How should teachers follow their administrator's directions, support their administrator, and not be perceived as a principal's pet?

The teacher, Ms. Gonzales, knows she is liked by her principal because she always contributes to the principal's goal-setting process in which student achievement data is analyzed; she assists in identifying areas and actions for change when the principal asks for her feedback; and she works collaboratively with staff and the school community and helps the principal identify discrepancies between current and desired outcomes. Instead of defending, she sets and prioritizes goals to help close the gap and assists in developing improvement and monitoring strategies aimed at accomplishing the goals.

Ms. Gonzales finds that as she has shown some of these strengths, some veteran teachers have developed hostility against her and have started to spread a rumor that Ms. Gonzales is a snob. They dislike the fact that the principal has taken note of Ms. Gonzales's work and appreciated her work in faculty meetings. Ms. Gonzales finished one of the projects that were assigned to her way before the expected time. The principal went around and bragged about her work, and now she finds herself isolated from her colleagues because they have stopped having conversations with her. How can she deal with this situation?

One way to solve this problem is to have an open conversation with the principal. The principal has full faith and trust in Ms. Gonzales and depends on her advice and guidance. It is therefore her responsibility to be objective in giving him advice. It is not easy, but it can be done with diplomacy. Another suggestion is to find out who else is a good worker among her colleagues and collaborate with them. Next time when the principal assigns Ms. Gonzales to work on a project, she may want to ask to work with someone else.

Given that she has the ear of the principal, she may also highlight some of the collaborative work done with other colleagues and build their status in the eyes of the principal. She should make sure that she is still communicating with her peers and has their trust. Ms. Gonzales may have to initiate some of these conversations herself, but she is perceptive if she does that. For more information, see Brown Nose Rose in Chapter 10.

TRAITOR OR "TATTLETALE"

Nancy is a general educator who works hard but neglects to provide accommodations to Jason, a third grader. Jason goes to Nancy's class for math and receives resource services for reading from Sam, the resource teacher. Nobody ever says anything against Nancy. She is well respected, and the principal likes her, but she is not serving this student with learning disabilities.

Sam did try to talk to the special education director, and she suggested that he talk to Nancy directly. Well, the best thing for Sam is to think about what he really wants to accomplish. Does he want to tattletale, or does he want to have a positive outcome for Jason?

One thing that a teacher must remember is that he or she can change the system only by becoming part of the system. If he or she gets tired, he or she will not be able to develop the influence that is needed for a significant change. Change does not arise in short periods of time. Sam cannot be against Nancy, and he needs to have Nancy understand his concerns. He needs to increase Nancy's awareness about what needs to be done with regard to Jason's educational outcomes.

Instead of working through the principal, Sam should directly work with Nancy. In a neutral way, Sam should attempt to raise her awareness about accommodations that can benefit Jason by giving her information about various types of accommodations that have produced desirable outcomes for students with learning disabilities.

Teachers must be cautious about alienating their colleagues. They can maintain a great professional relationship with their principal and colleagues at the same time. If a teacher has specific concerns about his or her colleague, he or she must communicate those with the principal, but to entertain the principal with daily news about his or her colleagues is not a healthy communication. It really does not create a positive climate for work. People tend to develop feelings of apprehension, suspicion, and mistrust when they have to work with "tattletales" around them.

Randy was a secondary education teacher and taught social studies to tenth graders. His students really liked him. He had a colleague, Patty, a science teacher who happened to have the ear of Mr. Parry, the principal of the school. Whatever she said to Mr. Parry, he listened and believed it to be true. For some reason, Randy and Patty were not great friends, but Randy thought that he could always work with her on a professional basis.

They had a curriculum night in their school, and the principal wanted to announce a fundraiser. Patty offered to help the principal, and Randy was busy grading papers because the report cards were due the following day. Patty saw that Randy was busy with his work, and she went to Mr. Parry and said, "I really don't know what's up with Randy; he never helps when we need his help." Mr. Parry, as usual, took notice of this comment, came back to Randy, and asked him about his lack of interest in the fund-raiser activity.

Although Randy explained his side of the story, he felt that Mr. Parry had this preconceived notion that he was not willing to help out. Randy developed an attitude of being by himself and not talking to anyone. The state tests were approaching, and he became busier in his schedule. He has decided to eat in his own classroom lately because he does not seem to get time to eat in a faculty lounge. The other faculty members have started to think that Randy perceives himself as being above eating with them.

The reality is that Randy has limited time and a few aversive experiences with people who thrive on being tattletales. How can a teacher avoid being a victim of such circumstances? It is wise for teachers to keep channels of communication open. For more information, see Inspector Hector in Chapter 10.

HOLDING THE PRINCIPAL ACCOUNTABLE

Educators should hold their administrators accountable for meaningful teamwork, clear and measurable goals, and the regular collection and analysis of performance data. Effective administrators lead their schools through a systematic goal-setting process in which student achievement data are analyzed, improvement areas are identified, and actions for change are initiated.

Some aspects of leadership are collaborative. Providing a high-quality public education is every individual's responsibility in the neighborhood. Educators can strengthen the leadership by working together in setting and prioritizing goals, in developing improvement plans and monitoring strategies aimed at accomplishing the goals, and in communicating goals and outcomes to the entire school community.

Oftentimes, teachers may need training in how to hold administrators accountable for their actions. Teachers need to do their job of teaching and administrators should take care of providing leadership.

Some other suggestions to promote accountability for leadership may include developing opportunities for teaming and collaboration; participating in advisory committees that engage in the examination of various leadership models; engaging in solution-oriented approaches rather than focusing on red tape; becoming nonjudgmental and taking time to evaluate biases; and leaving biases out when conversing with peers, parents, or the principal. Educators need to support the leadership that promotes positive action conducive to producing positive student outcomes.

If teachers work under a supervisor who is less professional and ethical than they are, they may have two choices: either to feel worse about their situation or to keep doing what they believe in. All teachers experience leadership changes at several points in their career. These changes may affect their ability to plan, manage, and follow through, and in some cases may disrupt career choices and professional and family lives. Teachers need to remember that they have options. Accepting this leadership is one choice. Offering suggestions for change is another.

DEVELOP RESILIENCE

As professionals, teachers must reflect on their own inadequacies and develop strategies for dealing with ineffective leadership. They should continually strive to develop a positive relationship with the principal and communicate effectively without harming their relationship. Every principal is not going to be great. Oftentimes in some schools disorganization becomes a way of life. If teachers are open to wisdom and enthusiastic advice from peers and other colleagues or can find a mentor, they may be able to develop resilience toward these risk factors.

All teachers are vulnerable to stressors. If they have to submit to chaotic leadership, they need to take good care of their mental health and personal needs. They should refrain from reacting personally to the mixed messages from the principal, take the time to sort them out, provide themselves with options, and talk to peers to clarify the intent of the message. They should not consider themselves to be victims but consider themselves to be agents of change.

They should think about strategies that may work in the environment they are in. They may seek advice from their mentors and invest in developing collegiality and trust with their colleagues. In today's results-oriented educational environment, they need to work on developing their support system for long-term survival in the field of teaching. Strong teachers continue to work on their knowledge, skills, strategic behaviors, and motivation to face the challenges of leadership. They don't allow themselves to become tired of teaching, even when they are faced with crisis moments of leadership.

ACTION PLAN

1. Educators should understand the difference between competent and incompetent leadership.
2. Educators should adopt a positive attitude toward the principal who clearly demonstrates a positive leadership style.
3. Educators should assist the principal in developing accountability for student outcomes by working together in setting and prioritizing goals and in developing improvement plans and monitoring strategies.
4. Educators need to develop healthy relationships with peers and allies.
5. Educators should know their strengths and develop resilience to withstand changes in leadership.
6. Educators should have a mentor outside of school to seek advice in how to handle day-to-day issues without being caught in confusion.

Chapter Eight

Maintaining Professional Behavior with Parents

Every year as I look over my class list
I see parents who will complain, those who will assist
Some parents I will want to clone
Some parents think they belong on a throne
Some parents think they carry a lot of weight
I hope many cooperative parents are my fate
I know I must take heed
For I will have to meet parents' needs.

It is August 1, and Ms. Davis is eager to go to school to see when she can get her class lists. The administrator, Mr. Pilger, has told the teachers that they can get their tentative class lists on August 10. Ms. Davis goes into school that day to get her list of fourth graders.

There are two fourth grades, so she is not sure what group she will get. Mr. Pilger gives her the list and comments that he knows that she will be able to handle Billy's mother because she has such a positive and calm manner. This statement makes Ms. Davis nervous. She asks what he means because she is not familiar with Billy; he is a transfer from one of the district's other schools.

Mr. Pilger shares with her that Billy was transferred at the request of his mother and that the superintendent agreed to the change. The superintendent had to listen to multiple complaints from Billy's mother last year—the classroom work was just too easy for Billy; the teacher did not give Billy enough attention; the teacher did not spend enough time on social studies; and the list went on.

Ms. Davis thinks, "Oh great, what a way to start the year." She goes to her classroom and ponders a plan. How can she win the confidence of Billy's mother? How can she meet Billy's needs? Ms. Davis has taught enough years to know that if Billy's mother isn't happy, then Billy won't be happy. Furthermore, Ms. Davis won't be happy.

She formulates her first steps. She always writes a letter home to all the parents, introducing herself and inviting the parents to meet with her before the start of school. She readies that letter and sends it. She does not stop there, however.

She decides that within a couple of days she will call Billy's parent to make sure that she has gotten the letter. In the meantime, she gathers more information and learns that Billy's mother is a single parent and that he is an only child. She also learns that Billy's parent is a teacher at the local community college and is active in the community. She learns that Billy is a good student.

When Ms. Davis calls Billy's parent, she lets her know how happy she is to have Billy in class and relays that she is looking forward to meeting both her and Billy. She shares with Billy's mother that she has learned that Billy is a good student. She asks Billy's parent if she would like to come in and meet with her before the start of school. Because she knows that Billy's parent works full-time, she offers to meet with her during her lunchtime or before or after work. Billy's mother is pleased to meet with her and says that she can meet over her lunch break the next day.

When Billy's mother arrives the next day, Ms. Davis has fruit on the table and offers her something to drink. Ms. Davis talks about the profession of Billy's parent. Ms. Davis asks for helpful hints about working with Billy—she asks about Billy's interests and his strengths. She tells Billy's mother that if she notices anything about Billy's work performance or homework assignments that Ms. Davis should know about, Billy's mother should call her right away. Ms. Davis offers to meet with her at any time. Billy's mother leaves the conference feeling pleased.

Ms. Davis got off on the right foot with Billy's parent. She followed her letter up with a phone call. She opened the call positively—complimenting Billy. She recognized that Billy's mother was a busy lady and gave her a choice of times to meet.

She provided snacks because Billy's mother was giving up her lunch. She established a positive rapport with Billy's parent by getting to know about her profession. She asked for input about what was successful for Billy. She requested feedback and made Billy's mother feel important. She opened the channels for positive communication.

Just as all of the students within each classroom have different needs, so do the parents. As teachers proceed through the school year, they will hopefully recognize the needs of the parents and strive to meet them. Without the parents' cooperation and support, the year will be a serious challenge.

Unfortunately, some educators have left education because they could not deal with the challenges that some parents presented. The field of education needs top-notch teachers. Educators should not have to expend a lot of negative energy dealing with problematic parents. Instead, they should be able to establish a positive rapport with the parents of their students.

This chapter is designed to acquaint readers with the various types of parents with whom they may work, then to offer some practical strategies to meet their needs.

THE COOPERATIVE PARENT

Cooperative parents are the parents educators would like to clone. Educators wish there were more of these parents who recognize their own role and the critical role of the educator. They help their child with homework; they volunteer in the classroom or for special projects when they are needed; they support and work with their child.

When the child has a behavioral problem in school, they reinforce the consequences that the educator has given. These are the parents who always show up for conferences about their child. They may be active in the PTA.

The real danger with these parents is that educators may take them for granted and not appreciate them enough for their efforts. Educators may be so focused on the squeaky wheels that they forget to stop and appreciate the cooperative parents.

A simple phone call, e-mail, or a nice note sent home to say how much their efforts are appreciated will mean a lot to the cooperative parents. Educators need to remember that they need all the friends they can get; so, the more parents who are on their side, the better.

THE PARENTS WHO THINK THAT THEIR CHILD DOES NO WRONG

Some readers remember the old days when, if they got into trouble at school, they also got in trouble at home. Parents were more likely to support the school; now, increasingly, when students get into trouble at school, they go home, tell their parents, then the parents come into the school and inquire, "What did you do to my child?"

Many students do not want to take responsibility for their own behavior, and some parents discourage students from taking responsibility for their own behavior. Teachers have probably all heard these words: "You must be mistaken—my child wouldn't do that." Some people have great difficulty accepting their responsibility in an event.

Educators need to teach children at an early age that they cannot always control what happens to them but that they can control their own response to the event. It is unfortunate that some adults also cannot accept that responsibility, and they transfer that inability to their children. It is much easier to place blame elsewhere than to examine their own role and accept blame.

Here is an example of a parent's refusal to accept that her son did anything wrong some years ago. The parent was asked to attend an IEP meeting for a student with behavioral problems. The student had slammed a girl into the wall and kept slamming her several times. The police were called and charges pressed.

A meeting was being held to see what different placement was warranted and whether a new evaluation of the student was needed. The parents came in angry—they felt that it was unfair that their son had criminal charges pressed against him and that the girl whom he slammed had caused the whole thing because she called him a name. Attempts were made to get the parents to focus on what their son had done and to move away from what the girl had done, but this was difficult for the parents to discuss at all.

When the parent comes in and tries to place the blame elsewhere, it is important to stick with the facts and explain specifically what the student did. It is critical that rules and consequences are delineated to parents so that they know up front what the consequence will be if a student engages in a particular behavior. Educators must be firm, fair, and consistent with students, and parents need to know from the beginning that the consequences will be applied fairly.

THE ARGUMENTATIVE PARENT

A parent may come into the classroom or to a meeting and want to argue about what seems to be every statement that the teacher makes. It would be easy to get into an argument back, but this will only agitate the parent even more and will become counterproductive. Here it is important to focus efforts in active listening and in trying to find common ground—where does the teacher agree with the parent? Often, the educator is quick to interrupt the parent to get his or her point across—especially if the parent is arguing.

Educators should not allow themselves to get into an argument—they should listen closely to what the parent is saying. If there is something they do agree with, they should comment on that.

THE HOSTILE PARENT

The parent seems to be angry at the world, or at least the educational system, and the teacher cannot figure out what they are angry about. Perhaps the parent had a bad experience with the first-grade teacher and has never forgotten that and is hostile to everyone within the school system. The parent may believe that the teacher is being unfair to his or her child or may not agree with a particular method that the teacher is using.

When dealing with this type of parent, the old motto "An ounce of prevention is worth a pound of cure" holds true. As an example, the teacher looks up and sees Ms. Smith coming down the hall. She has a scowl on her face, and she knows that she is not a happy camper. She greets her with a smile and says, "It's so good to see you. Thanks so much for coming by." Or the teacher might say, "I am so glad to see you—do I have some good news for you about what Trevor got done today."

When the teacher knows that the parent is exuding hostility, it is important to remember to smile and make a positive statement. This can diffuse a potential struggle. It is hard for the parent to continue to be hostile when the teacher is positive.

THE APATHETIC PARENT

It is frustrating for the teacher to have a parent who refuses to get involved with the class. This is the parent who will not come to conferences, attend open houses, or respond to teacher notes. This may be the parent who does not send her or his child to school on a regular basis.

It is important for the teacher to look at the reasons why the parent may appear apathetic. Perhaps the parent may have had a bad experience in school. The parent may have so many responsibilities at home that she or he is overwhelmed and just does not have the time to get involved in the school situation.

With the apathetic parents, it is critical that the teacher look at the function of the parent's behavior—the parent may be avoiding the school because he perceives school as an unpleasant situation.

For parents who will not come into the school, the teacher might offer to meet with the parents in a neutral setting—a local coffee shop might work. It is a good idea to send a welcoming letter to the parents before the start of school and to follow up with a phone call. If this does not work, the teacher may want to set up a home visit and take other school personnel with her, such as the social worker or the administrator. It is a good idea for two individuals to go together for safety reasons and so that there is a witness to what was said.

Many years ago, educators used to frequently conduct home visits to get to know the family much better; as the years have progressed, some school personnel have stayed away from home visits for safety reasons. Educators should not just drop in on parents because they may be self-conscious about their home situations; it is always a good idea to prearrange the visit.

Once educators arrive for a visit, they should take the lead from the parents on whether they will be allowed in the door of the house. Educators may find themselves standing outside meeting with the parent; the parent may be embarrassed by the condition of the home. The parent's embarrassment should be respected, and the home visit can be conducted outside. It may mean a great deal to the parent to have someone take the time to go to the home.

THE DUAL-ROLE PARENT

A tenuous situation is created when the parent happens to be someone who is affiliated with the school—teachers are on pins and needles that they are going to do something that the parent does not agree with and that their actions will have ramifications on their job. The parent, because of his or her role within the school system, may think that he or she has the answers.

This is not to say that all parents who serve a dual role as parent and educator will cause problems; some, in fact, may be even more understanding. However, in this context this discussion focuses on talking about the parents who have difficulty separating their roles.

School Board Member

Any teacher would be nervous if he or she has the child of a school board member in his or her class. After all, the school board ultimately determines the hiring and firing of the staff within the school. The school board member can also voice a negative opinion about the teacher to the building administrator, and that opinion may translate into a negative evaluation. It is important that the teacher not give preferential treatment to this student; the other students in the class will witness what is going on and will learn that the teacher is not firm, fair, and consistent.

The teacher should work to ensure that she or he is being fair to all of the students within her or his classroom. At the same time, the teacher should make sure that she or he keeps the parent informed of the child's progress and tries to involve the parent in classroom activities, just as he or she does with any other parent.

Fellow Teacher

There are a number of scenarios within this category—the parent may be a teacher within the same school building, even at the same grade level in a larger school that has multiple classes within the school; the parent may teach at a different grade level within the same school; or the parent may teach in a different building in the same district or in a neighboring district. In any case, these teacher parents can be helpful or a hindrance in working with their children in the classroom.

Teacher parents may see themselves as the experts and believe that they have all the answers concerning what the child needs. They may be critical of a colleague's work because there is a difference in teaching style.

It is important to engage in frequent communication and to establish common ground with the parent. Colleagues must find topics that both can agree on, and build on those topics.

Administrator

The teacher's worst nightmare—he has the superintendent's daughter in his classroom, and the child is a pain. The superintendent believes that his daughter does no wrong. Sound familiar? If it is not, the teacher should consider himself lucky.

It is critical here that the teacher not provide special favors to the child—otherwise, the other students and their parents will know that this is taking place. The grapevine works quickly within the school. Teachers must remain fair.

It is also a good idea to review with the administrator, before school starts (as teachers should do with all parents), what teacher expectations are for all of the students within the class. Just as teachers do this with students, they should also review expectations with parents so that there are no surprises. That way, teachers find out up front about any issues that might cause some disagreement with the administrator.

Good communication throughout the year will be critical to the teacher's success this year. The teacher needs and wants the support of the administrator yet does not want to compromise values and expectations for the student or for the rest of the students.

Teacher Training Parent

A teacher once shared that the teacher training parent had caused her a great deal of anxiety. The parent was an assistant professor at a university in the same community and was in the education field. This university trainer believed that her son was bright, and she became upset when the teacher called her in to share some concerns about the motor skills of her child. The teacher was also concerned about the social skills of the child.

The teacher trainer did not want to hear this—she often bragged in the courses she taught about how bright her child was. He was bright, but he had deficit areas. The teacher shared that, in retrospect, she had approached the situation incorrectly. She wished that she had talked first about how bright the child was in specific areas and then asked whether the teacher trainer noted any issues in motor or social skills.

The teacher could then have provided factual information about the areas of concern and asked the parent for advice on how they could work together to meet the needs of the child.

THE HOVERING PARENT

At some time, teachers will encounter the parent who hovers and calls so often that the teachers think they will lose their mind. What a frustrating situation! A true story comes to mind. A parent had a child with a significant disability, and the parent worried so much that she would call the teacher several times per day—the teacher had a phone in her class and the parent knew the teacher's extension.

The teacher got so that she just did not answer the phone during the day because she did not want to disturb her class. Feeling frustrated, the teacher decided that she needed to meet with the parent as soon as possible. The teacher explained to the parent that she was not able to be disturbed during class time for phone calls, and she assured the parent that she would call her if anything happened that the parent should know about.

Some schools have established procedures that teachers cannot be interrupted during class time unless it is an emergency. Of course, that does not prevent the parent from leaving several messages to call after school or from stopping by every day after school.

Educators must learn strategies for dealing with this type of hovering parent without offending him or her. Again, it is important to establish clear guidance on when phone calls are allowed and when visitors can be accepted.

Educators also need to keep phone calls and visits short and to the point—recognizing that the parent does have the right to the information that he or she is requesting but that educators have constraints on how much time they can spend. This is a parent who needs to establish confidence in the teacher, and it is important that the teacher provide reassurance when he does speak to the individual.

The parent may also have too much time on his or her hands or may just need a little extra attention; in this case, the teacher may want to get the parent involved in a school-wide project, or may want to solicit the parent's help in specific projects.

DIVORCED PARENTS

Educators certainly welcome parents who may be divorced and are on amicable terms, but what about the parents who parted ways negatively? They do not agree on how the children should be raised. They want to argue with each other, no matter the topic. They may play the children against each other. They may even go as far as to tell you that they do not want you talking to the other parent.

Educators may remember conducting a parent conference with them during which they proceeded to argue with each other throughout the conference.

It is important that educators respect the needs and rights of both parents. They will probably maintain more contact with the custodial parent, but, remember, unless the divorce decree says otherwise, educators have a responsibility to both parents. They will need to communicate with both, and it is important that they remain neutral in the process.

They will also need to be careful what they say to each parent; they do not want to be put in the position where the parents use their statements against each other—"Well, Ms. Johns said you should spend more time with our son." If the parents come to conferences together and begin to argue, it will be important to bring their focus back to their son or daughter and to establish common ground. At times, educators may feel like they are mediators, and, in a way, they are.

SOME HELPFUL STRATEGIES

Be Empathetic

Although educators cannot always put themselves in the parents' shoes, they need to attempt to understand what their background and experience bring to the interactions with them.

The parent may have two children with special needs and two other children. They are trying to cope with the many demands of all four children. Educators are talking to them about one of the children and are expecting them to assist that child with homework.

They need to understand that this may be difficult for them to do. When teachers are empathetic and attempt to see the whole picture of parents' lives, they will better understand why the parent may not appear to be cooperative. Arnold (1999) defined empathy as the ability to imagine, often intuitively and instinctively, how the other person feels.

Educators must be culturally competent (Muscott, 2002). They must recognize and understand the cultural differences and the different value and communication systems. There are a number of nonverbal cultural differences that can result in miscommunication—personal space, smiling, eye contact, touch, silence, and time concepts (Gonzales-Mena, 2001). Educators must also go beyond cultural knowledge and develop a specific understanding of how each parent expresses his or her own culture.

Educators also need to listen actively to what the parent is saying; that is, they must engage in active listening. As an example, the parent might be saying that "Keller has too much homework." The teacher should not deny the statement but recognize what the parent is saying and respond with "I hear your concern—can you give me an idea on when Keller is doing his homework and how long it is taking him?"

The educator may find out that Keller is waiting until 9:00 p.m. to bring out his homework, and by then he is tired and whines. A teacher can then certainly share the parent's concerns about the situation and work with the parent to look at alternatives for when the student does his homework. Educators might also hear the parent's frustration that the parent is unable to help the student with his homework because the parent does not understand what is expected.

Accentuate the Positive—Praise Often

A good idea to ensure that educators recognize parents for their positive efforts is to keep a set number of postcards on their desks and make it a point to send at least five postcards per week to parents who have done something positive for them. Another way that educators can assist in providing positive comments to parents is to include a nice note in students' assignment notebooks or home-school journals or in an e-mail.

It is critical that parents be recognized for everything positive that they do. This is the motto that should be used with children—never take good behavior for granted; reinforce it. This certainly holds true with parents. They need to be appreciated for their cooperation.

Martin and Hagan-Burke (2002) suggested a simple technique that works well when teachers are dealing with a student who is engaging in negative behavior. What happens in working with such students is that educators become negative about the student, and that negativity carries over to the parent.

To combat this, the teacher keeps an index card with him or her. The teacher records a list of accomplishments of the student that day. The teacher then sends that card home to the parent. The teacher gains better rapport when he or she focuses on the progress, and the parent is provided realistic hope about what the student is accomplishing in the classroom.

When meeting with a parent, teachers will find it important to start with positive statements—even a simple statement, "Thanks for coming in today—I know you are very busy," can set the stage for a positive meeting.

Do Not Withhold Necessary Information

A common mistake that educators make is to fail to provide the parent with pertinent information. This seems to happen a great deal with children with special needs. As an example, the child is having behavioral problems—the teacher does not tell the parent. The student is then suspended because of a series of events—the parent is angry because he or she did not know what was going on.

One of the authors remembers attending IEP meetings where students had been referred for special education in the area of behavioral disorders. The school district personnel did not want to provide the factual information about the specific issues that the child was having because they did not want to offend the parent—the parent was then upset because the team was recommending a special placement and the parent was not given enough information to believe that such a placement was warranted.

Another common occurrence is the parent who is told toward the end of the school year that his or her child is being recommended for retention. The parent is shocked because he or she had not been told about the child's lack of progress. Granted, there are times when the teacher has told the parent, but the parent has failed to listen or was in denial that there was a problem. But there are also times when the educator has not told the parent because the teacher wants to be nice and not provide the parent with realistic information.

There is a nice way to provide factual information, and it is much better to provide that information rather than to withhold it.

If the educator is going to try something new with the students or if there is going to be a significant change in the schedule, the parent needs to know that information.

When an educator withholds information that is important for the parents to know, they become suspicious. When they are suspicious, they lose trust in the educator and his work.

Seek Their Input and Assistance

A form of flattery is to sincerely ask the parents for their input or assistance on an issue or a project. The parents will be able to provide teachers with information about what the children's interests are, what the children do and do not like to do.

Teachers should always ask parents what their goals are for the child during the upcoming year—this provides the teacher with helpful information about the parents' expectations. Teachers should also ask parents about their concerns for their child.

The parent may have expertise in an area that the students are studying. Teachers can ask them to provide a program for the students on that topic. Parents have different levels of ability with which they can provide assistance. Because of time or fear, there may be certain things that they are willing to do and certain things that they are not willing to do.

Therefore, teachers should provide a list of choices for how the parent can assist within the classroom—from activities that are low commitments to those that may require a higher level of involvement.

Avoid Educational Jargon

Educators are notorious for using jargon in their work—they utilize acronyms and technical terms that parents may not understand. They assume that because those acronyms and terms are a part of their world, everyone knows what they are saying. Imagine how any educators would feel if they were around a doctor and did not understand all the medical terms being said. Therefore, all educators must work to keep their language exact and to the point.

Watch for facial cues that suggest that the parent does not understand what is being said. Too often, educators make statements like "Your child was given the WRAT and the WISC and DIBELS." The parent probably does not have a clue about what is being talked about, unless he or she is an educator, and even if the parent is an educator, high school jargon may be different from kindergarten jargon.

Focus on the Issues Rather Than the Personalities

This is so much easier said than done. It is difficult for the educator to ignore a personal statement against him or her. However, doing so is critical to success in dealing with the difficult parent. Picture this scenario. A father came into the school superintendent's office and was angry. He yelled at the superintendent, saying that he was "the worst superintendent the school district had ever had." The superintendent became angry and immediately responded loudly, "I don't have to take that kind of grief from you. Get out of my office." The parent had attacked the superintendent's value, and the superintendent got mad.

What could the superintendent have done? Rather than take the statement personally, he could have said calmly, "I know you are upset. Can you tell me what the problem is?" This would have been an effort to focus on the issue rather than the personality of the superintendent.

Teachers may have participated in a meeting on a student where the parent is upset because the student is not progressing at the rate that the parent desires. The parent attacks the teacher by saying, "You just aren't doing your job" or "I have talked with some other parents, and they aren't happy with you either."

This is hurtful, particularly to the educator who is working so hard and is going above and beyond to help the child. However, if the parent thinks that he or she can get to an educator and really bother him by these attacks, the parent will keep doing it. Through these events, it is critical that the educator remains calm and gets the parent back on the point.

Parents may be bringing a great deal of emotional baggage into their interaction with educators, and educators do not always have the information about the baggage—parents may have had a difficult time in school; they may have had a bad year the previous year. Educators don't always have all of the background and therefore may tend to take the statements personally.

It is difficult to ignore the parent's statement when the parent attacks an individual's value as a teacher—"you aren't as good as his teacher last year." However, it is critical that the educator separates the problem from the value attack.

Educators should not allow the parent to get them off the point. The parent might try to argue and get the educators away from the point. The child is not doing well at school—the parent comes in and says, "Gary never had any problems when he was in Ms. Jones's class last year."

Educators should not buy in to this—oftentimes, educators will then try to remind the parent that Gary did have problems the last year. The parent has actually, once again, attacked the educator's value as a person, just as the parent did with the superintendent.

Educators don't want anybody to think that they are not as good of a teacher as the teacher last year was; therefore, they become upset and react negatively rather than focus on the issue at hand—how can educators help Gary with the class work with which he is having problems?

Maintaining Confidentiality—Watching What Is Said in Various Venues

All educators must be cognizant of the importance of confidentiality—both with individuals within the school building and those outside the school building. The rule of thumb for discussing the specific needs of a student with someone within the school environment is to remember this adage: "Does the individual with whom I am sharing the information have the need to know?"

Certainly, the bus driver needs to know that a student has a seizure disorder and what should be done in the case of a medical emergency. However, there is no need for the bus driver who is not transporting the student to know about a student's condition.

One of the biggest mistakes that educators make is to make subjective statements or assumptions—instead, they should stick to the facts. When the educator says to a colleague, "I think that Mr. and Ms. Jones are having trouble at home," it is easy for the rumor to get started that the parents are not getting along and may get separated. Just as in the game of gossip, the word might get out that Mr. and Ms. Jones are getting a divorce.

Imagine being in a restaurant with fellow teachers. The reality is that educators all like to talk about students when they get together. However, if they talk about a student, someone else in the restaurant may hear the information and may spread it in the community. The waitress may be related to the child and hear the comment.

An educator may attend a staff development workshop and run into someone from the neighboring school—the educator asks if Jason moved to that school. When the educator learns that Jason did indeed move to that school, she proceeds to tell someone the information about Jason. Other people overhear what was said—the educator has violated that student's right to privacy.

If educators need to share information about a student, they must, first, ensure that the person has a right to know the information and, second, make sure that those who do not need to hear the information are not within earshot of the conversation.

Telephone Calls

As a word of caution, educators must be careful with whom they speak on the phone. If they do not know the voices of the parents in their class yet and someone calls and identifies himself as a parent and proceeds to ask questions about the child, educators should not give information. Instead, they should ask for a phone number at which they can call the person back, and then verify that the number is indeed the one listed for the parent.

Educators should not give information out unless they know that the person on the other end of the line is the legal guardian.

Here is another scenario. The aunt calls and asks for information about the student, and the teacher gives information to the aunt. However, if the aunt is not the guardian of the child, the teacher should not be discussing information with her; she is not someone who is the primary caregiver of the student. These can be touchy situations—when Grandma or a sister or brother calls to ask for information about a student.

But teachers must remain professional and not share information. They cannot jeopardize the privacy of the student, and they must comply with laws governing confidentiality.

There is a lot to think about as educators work with their students' parents. Parents can indeed be their allies within the school system if educators recognize their needs and their efforts, practice respect, and develop a collaborative partnership.

ACTION PLAN

1. Educators must strive to get off on the right foot with parents of the students with whom they work by adopting a positive attitude toward them.
2. Educators should solicit the assistance of the parents by gaining as much information as they can from the parents about what works and what doesn't work with their child.
3. Educators should provide as much positive recognition to the parents as possible.
4. Educators must remember to be firm, fair, and consistent with students regardless of who the parent of that student is.
5. Educators should learn about confidentiality laws so they know with whom they can share information.
6. Educators should avoid passing judgment on parents until they have worked with the parent(s) themselves.

REFERENCES

Arnold, R. (1999). *The role of empathy in teaching and learning.* New South Wales, Australia: Education Network, University of Sydney.

Gonzales-Mena, J. (2001). *Multicultural issues in child care* (3rd ed.). Mountain View, CA: Mayfield.

Martin, E., & Hagan-Burke, S. (2002). Establishing a home-school connection: Strengthening the partnership between families and schools. *Preventing School Failure*, 46(2), 62–65.

Muscott, H. (2002). Exceptional partnerships: Listening to the voices of families. Preventing School Failure, 46(2), 66–69.

Chapter Nine

Communicating in a Political Minefield

Below the ground
Hardly a sound
Lest a teacher disturbs a land mine
Part of the school that is not benign
Use of analysis, observation
Wisdom, insight, and determination
Intuition, to name just a few
Helps staff to act and know what to do
Should she speak or should she be silent?
How does he trust she said what she meant?

Once the teacher is more aware
He will know when to dare
To build bridges with those in other fields
Working together, not putting up shields.

Gina began her work at a public school with great hopes for a fulfilling career working alongside colleagues with whom she could find compatibility. She took seriously her mission to improve the education of young people. After working in the corporate world for twenty years, she decided to return to her local university, taking classes on evenings and weekends to attain an educational degree.

She found learning about teaching exciting and exhilarating and with each course looked forward to being part of a world in which she would make a difference in the lives of young people. She had traveled extensively before getting her degree and thought that her background would somehow help her in the teaching profession. Strangely enough, it proved to be helpful but not in a way that she would have ever imagined.

After beginning at her first school, Gina had a flashback to her early thirties, when she was touring the Middle East. She recalled sitting in a bus while the person next to her pointed out a field to the group. It looked like ordinary terrain, the same as any she had seen that day. However, according to this knowledgeable other traveler, the difference between this area and the rest of the land was not visible to the eye, yet it was dangerous.

The field contained land mines, left there from a military conflict. Lethal and dangerous below the surface, these mines waited for an unsuspecting person to walk on them. Once treading in the wrong spot, anyone would risk loss of limb and great trauma by proceeding totally unprepared for an unexpected explosion. The group unanimously decided to err on the side of caution and avoid going near this hazardous field.

Why did this stop on her tour come to mind for Gina after she had spent a few weeks at her new school assignment? Gina's school looked like any other school in the area. No danger was apparent to the eye. Yet, beneath the surface, as in the Middle Eastern field, communication traps, sensitive issues unbeknownst to her, and subtle professional dangers awaited an unsuspecting staffer.

Gina slowly learned that there were certain things that she should not mention, certain people that she could not trust, and certain personalities that required a particular approach. In addition, due to events in the school's history, still unknown to her, she realized that by bringing up a certain topic to some people, she could potentially set off an explosion of offense, mistrust, and even chaos.

Gina wished that she could sit safely in a bus out in the school parking lot and feel protected and secure, as she had on the tour some years back. She had a little distance then and a vantage point apart from the field. This time, she had to step inside the school, walk on the minefield, and risk stepping into a psychological or social spot that could cause her possible emotional and professional harm.

How would she discover where these mines were hidden? What did she need to do for her own safety in this environment? What would constitute the right "face mask, armor, and gear" to protect her from an "explosion" here at school? Would she survive in this building long enough to find out?

Like Gina, others may have encountered minefields in their educational work. Innocently, a teacher may have misspoken and caused feathers to ruffle or been the victim of unprofessional reactions to an innocent and sincere statement. Perhaps this individual had no warning, and all of a sudden felt wounded, suddenly and savagely, for no reason, by the comments of a coworker during a meeting.

Or maybe an educator was "hit" simply for being in the wrong place at the wrong time, doing and saying the wrong thing—at least according to a single human land mine or even a group of land mines encountered during a typical school day. Instantly, those people, clustered in a corner, may have reacted to a certain teacher's actions and collectively set off a colossal verbal explosion. Seeing the invisible is nearly impossible.

Yet after practice and with increased awareness, teachers become astute to the location and potential damage of land mines that exist in a school organization. With time, trial and error, and sharpened intuition, it is possible to not only detect such trouble spots, but also find the safe spots, build trust with peers, and reach across social and philosophical barriers that may have once been considered impossible. Time, maturity, and uncompromising professionalism hold the key not only to surviving, but also to effectively communicating in the political minefield of a school.

GATHERING INFORMATION ON LAND MINES

Identifying land mines in a school organization can be done in a systematic manner. The following is a format to utilize for data gathering. A teacher might want to spend several days collecting information by observation and through communication to build experience and awareness of locating the land mines in the immediate work environment. Keeping this information among private materials prevents discovery. This would only set off more reactions, causing the observer to be the victim.

Presented are categories of experience that might constitute a land mine. These include social exchanges inadvertently observed and heard in the lounge or in the hallway. Direct comments made among staff, by tone and innuendo may indicate minefield material right in the immediate vicinity. Political events, locally and nationally, might trigger comments and opinions among staff members.

Philosophy of education or philosophy of life differs among teachers and parents. Finding like-minded coworkers and determining topics for discussion with those having an opposite viewpoint helps sort out persons to list in these categories. Personality qualities of individuals cause them to respond and react in certain ways. Knowing the range of reactions of those people in the work arena helps determine an approach to them and appropriate dealings with them. An observer eventually learns how and when to best approach others.

Over time, observations help staff members to know what to say to colleagues and parents based on their predictable social behavior. Teachers also gain understanding of their opinions relative to political events and their philosophical viewpoints. Such gathering about their personalities offers a more complete picture of what could cause potential flare-ups among those in the school environment.

Relevant information, when compiled, can help to offset the explosion of a land mine and provide protection for the observer. The following format can be created in a personal journal. Within these categories, an observer may want to list circumstances that appear to be difficult and list persons (coworkers, parents, administrators, others) that operate as land mines in the school.

Land Mine Record
 Minefield Categories Circumstances Persons

   1. Social
   2. Political
   3. Philosophical
   4. Personality

Maintaining Professionalism amidst Backstabbing

Besides being alert to internal cues regarding one's response to the school situation, one must also defend against negative dynamics that ultimately become hurtful. Over time, when educators listen strategically in the lounge or observe conversational patterns with colleagues, the sources of this destructive habit become clearer.

For example, when teachers speak critically about another staffer, parent, or administrator, they are also sending up a red flag that anyone else could be their next topic of criticism. When someone confides directly to another colleague by sharing negative information about another coworker, it indicates that that person has the ability to take something they heard described or something that they saw and reinterpret it negatively to another.

For whatever reason, such persons have developed the unfortunate practice of taking the opportunity to speak poorly of another without that person's knowledge or consent. Backstabbers take the knife verbally and leave another wounded in some way without any willingness to administer the first aid of reparation. Backstabbers habitually leave a coworker in pain and move on to their next victim.

Defense against such individuals is difficult. There is no way for an educator to stay on top of everything that is said about him or her. Circumstances may sometimes eventually bring forth information about what is said and even who said it. In that case the person who is the topic of negative conversation may choose to confront the one who started the talk, explaining awareness of the source of such information.

If false or negative information was spoken and spread, and it turned into an exaggerated form of the telephone game, the victim should reinforce the reality of the actual truth and how it contrasts with what information went around. The subject of the talk may want to continue to say something to the effect that such words cause others to misunderstand him or her and that as a professional, misrepresentation is not appreciated under any circumstances. The subject of this talk might want to emphatically add that he or she trusts that this will never happen again.

Beyond that, an educator cannot trail backstabbers to monitor their conversations. If a staff member hears that he or she is the continued victim of backstabbing, this issue may ultimately have to be taken to the teachers' union, the district human resources director, or another administrator. It is important to choose the most beneficial action and consider all ramifications before sharing this with those who have the authority to be of assistance.

Before taking action, an individual may want to consider discussing this with trusted family, friends, a mental health professional, clergy, or a legal counsel.

Seeking collective wisdom is important in this instance because systems that tolerate such behavior and have done so for a long time are not easy to confront or change.

These dysfunctional and destructive systems contain deeply buried land mines, and extracting them cannot be done overnight and easily. It may be safer for an educational professional to know their location, learn to live with them, and step around them whenever possible.

DETERMINING HOW MUCH TO SAY AND SAYING IT WELL

Empowered by experience in a system and some data gathered in the field, teachers who decide to use discretion about what they say, where they say it, and to whom they say it will become savvy in their work-related communications. They will withhold comments that they might have spoken in a more casual manner. They will speak strategically to adults that have proven to be untrustworthy.

By keeping more private information in conversations where they will be honored, they begin to add the protective equipment necessary to more safely operate in their work environments. By withholding information that has potential for reactive gossip and backstabbing, they offer less and less fuel for those looking for tidbits to embellish and spread on their networks.

Networks in schools exist for good and for ill. In some departments, hallways, and schools, the dominant network traffics in negative information. In others, positive, valuable, and supportive conversations dominate the airwaves. One alert and astute individual in a building that has habitually fostered negative talk can gradually help transform such a school by modeling new ways to speak, positive conversational content, and the initiation of pertinent professional dialogue.

Repeating healthy words and modeling professional behavior has the power to offset and diminish the ingrained and unsavory habits of those who have controlled the dark and dreary communication networks in a system for so long. One dimension that may bring challenge to schools is the use of technology for interpersonal communication.

Teachers who have the means to text and communicate with phones can share without anyone in their surroundings overhearing what they are saying. This method of communicating can be used to affirm and encourage or to pass on the negative. Various schools may have individualized policies on the use of phones during the workday.

Nevertheless, whether communicating via phone or social media during the day or outside of school hours, a teacher is wise to remember to communicate with respect and integrity at all times. When there is need to express feelings and issues of concern in order to process them, a teacher who insures that the situation is confidential and beneficial is acting with professionalism and integrity.

Safety for oneself and for others should always be taken into consideration. If teachers have support, strength, and integrity, they and their developing network can become formidable and refreshing competition to that which exists for the sole purpose of entertaining others with the least common denominator of social exchange. Positive professionals maintain their own dignity and use their time at work for the intended purpose of teaching students effectively; relating to colleagues, parents, and administrators professionally; and growing personally.

KNOWING WHEN TO SAY IT

As a new teacher, Rod came to his first assignment bursting with energy and with ideas that he wanted to try. He also came "bursting at the mouth," openly speaking the free-flowing thoughts in his mind whenever he was moved to do so. Eventually, seasoned staffers became uneasy in his presence. They thought that because Rod said anything anywhere, they would be safest to say nothing to him about anything that mattered to them. They became cautious about sharing with him anything that they believed to be of a confidential nature about students and their own lives.

When Rod began to speak, his attempts at dialogue turned into monologues. He received little reaction or response from his coworkers. At his first evaluation, his principal took time to give him some pointers on communication skills. Rod took his principal's advice to heart and over time gained a good sense of knowing when to speak his thoughts and ideas. What might his principal have suggested to him?

This fictitious principal and teacher offer an illustration for consideration on how to address such a situation. Teachers are wise to refrain from sharing personal topics in the school setting. Wisdom dictates that professionals use discretion and bring up such topics only if they believe that it would help someone else or if they are in a trusted one-on-one or small group situation. Perhaps details about a family member's health or disability could give support and strength to someone in a similar situation.

They realize when the tone and content of a conversation or meeting goes out of bounds and pull out if the group has gone negative or has begun backbiting others. They may choose to refrain from joining, leave the situation, or do their best to bring the group into a more positive tone by using humor or changing the subject. Such wise staff members filter their thoughts and feelings through their sense of judgment before openly and freely expressing their true sentiments. Some situations benefit from a candid response.

Certain circumstances warrant that the prudent thing to do is to say nothing. Being spontaneous can be an asset in stand-up comedy, but in professional situations teachers may face unwanted consequences for saying too much, too soon. Sometimes it is wiser to process opinions in a journal instead of at a staff meeting. Wise teachers also spare the staff the details of their weekends.

When new to a school and especially if teachers are right out of the university world, they must remember that the faculty is composed of a variety of people from various generations, genders, and value systems. Young staff should not give anyone any material that could be used against them. Social adventures are best left behind while keeping a professional demeanor in the workplace.

It is also important for teachers to respect the confidentiality of students and families and to share only what is pertinent with those who work with the same students. Considering who can help the student by knowing a certain bit of information and determining if the others can work just as effectively with students without a certain fact will help decide who needs to know sensitive information.

DETECTING WHOM TO SAY IT TO: FINDING TRUSTWORTHY COWORKERS

Marla had enjoyed ten years in the same school, teaching students from the same neighborhood. In fact, the elementary school where she worked was also the setting of her pre-service experience. She felt comfortable at this school teaching third grade, but she also wondered what it would be like to transfer to another building in her district. A posting for a sixth-grade position at the middle school across town caught her attention. She decided to make the change, and she put in for a transfer.

When she completed her interview and received notice of her new position, she experienced a sense of adventure and renewed enthusiasm for teaching. That fall she settled in early and got her room ready. She spent long hours alone in her room preparing for her sixth-grade students to arrive. Marla kept so busy that she had little time to meet the other teachers in her building and even those on her team.

When the school year officially began, she and the other sixth-grade teachers met to plan the details of their curriculum and to determine when to team-teach and when to work separately. Together, they drew up plans for the days ahead. Marla found them to be a congenial group, but she missed her former third-grade team. They had worked with a sense of camaraderie and cohesiveness. Confidentiality and trust were typical of their meeting sessions. Marla suddenly realized that she had given up a great deal of earned trust and comfort by making this change.

Student teaching plus ten years counted for a lot. Now that she had made the switch, how would she know which staff she could speak to about certain things? She had to start over. How would she determine who was trustworthy? When Marla realized that she was on her own and had to figure out the social territory of her new school all by herself, she decided to come up with plans and guidelines to detect trustworthy people.

Because the school was already established, she thought that everyone there already figured out whom they considered to be trustworthy. Would they trust her, since she was also new? During Labor Day weekend, she took some quiet time by herself to develop a plan. Bit by bit, she drew up her strategy for the fall quarter. After assessing the situation, Marla made the following decisions:

1. *Listening and watching during interactive time.* Hearing what people say to one another in order to figure out the composition of the groupings and social clusters is beneficial. Noticing what topics these groups discuss helps to determine what bonds them.

2. *Getting acquainted with others who are new to the staff.* Finding out how they are experiencing the transition to this new setting and what they liked about their former jobs helps form a connection. It is also helpful to find some common experiences to share and build on for future conversations. As time passes, figuring out more about the new situation together can aid staff new to a school.

3. *Checking with trusted colleagues from the former school.* By doing this one can learn if they have any good connections in this current school. Mentioning their names and making links due to common relationships can be a means of introduction and building bridges.

4. *Leaning on others.* Colleagues from other settings, family, friends, and other resources can provide support and sharing. Communicating by phone or e-mail is a way to retain and build a wide outside supportive communication network.

5. *Giving the new staff time.* Remembering that it takes time and shared experiences to build new bonds while joining in and getting involved eases the transition. During the days ahead, through participation and familiarity, the bonds of connection in the new school will become more comfortable for all parties involved. Letting things evolve naturally, being friendly, sincere, and enthused are assets in the process. Trust will grow in its own way and in its own time.

By looking at school through the eyes of Marla, an imaginary character, one can realize ways to assimilate into a new teaching environment. It is important to grow, and new situations offer just that.

BRIDGING THE "MY FIELD/YOUR FIELD" DIVIDE

While observing the groupings and social clusters in the middle school, Marla noticed that a clear divide existed between classroom teachers and those working with children with special needs. This existed to some extent in her former elementary school, but the chasm at the middle school level seemed even more obvious. In fact, here the special educators rarely socialized with the classroom teachers, and vice versa.

Sometimes it appeared to her that conversations between these groups seemed strained when they discussed student placements, mainstream accommodations, assessments, and qualification for services. In the staff lounge, Marla picked up on classroom teachers' comments comparing working hours, student loads, and job responsibilities of regular and special educators. She also overheard two special educators talking in the hallway. In low tones, the resource room specialist spoke critically of a classroom teacher's methods of managing a student's behavior.

Marla noticed as well that Tamitha, one of the other staff persons new to her building, was recently hired by special education. Marla's and Tamitha's lunch breaks occurred at the same time. They began to share insights and observations about educational topics and their own jobs. Marla noticed that when she and Tamitha got involved in conversation, time went quickly and she lost the consciousness of any apprehensiveness and caution.

They eventually reached the point of trust where they acknowledged the reality of the divide that existed between regular education and special education in their school. Eventually, the lead special education teacher assigned Tamitha to the role of case manager for one of Marla's students with autism. Both teachers decided to meet weekly to discuss ways to best meet this student's needs. Marla valued learning about autism from Tamitha, given that Marla's training was more general in this area.

Tamitha knew the latest information about autism and willingly shared it. She also offered Marla concrete tips on how to help the student stay organized, and she even made recommendations on ways to arrange the classroom and the child's work space and personal schedule to enhance focus and concentration. Marla realized that this helped not only the child with autism but also other students with unique needs as well.

Tamitha often asked Marla about her other students, what they did after school and what their family lives were like. She found it refreshing to have a point of comparison between their lives and the lives of students with special needs. Tamitha valued the perspective that she gained when hearing about the daily experiences of typical students.

Tamitha often asked Marla about the content of the social studies and science curriculums. This exchange gave her a sense of what the class learned on a weekly basis. Marla's methods of presenting information to a large group, as well as her strategies for keeping the attention of thirty-plus students, earned her Tamitha's respect.

When Tamitha spent time with Marla, she learned about upcoming school-wide events, and together they pooled their skills and planned how the student whom they shared could successfully participate. They also discussed the latest research and trends in their particular fields and gave one another feedback on the methods' validity and potential application.

After Marla and Tamitha became better acquainted, they moved their informal discussions to other venues. They took after-school walks in a nearby nature center and talked about a range of topics, from fashion to fiction. Sometimes, they met for coffee at a small local spot, and besides talking about their favorite cappuccino or latte selections, their conversation covered their career desires and even the social and political dynamics in their school building.

Marla and Tamitha established valued professional rapport and trust. They did this gradually and respectfully. Not being bound by the unwritten rules of their new school, they broke through previously established barriers that seemed irrelevant and outdated. They forged their own path to trust and found mutual growth and benefit in the process.

Marla and Tamitha discovered the ways that their fields complemented one another. They found the means to enhance the lives of their students and families through mutual exchanges and ongoing dialogue. They realized that they could greatly benefit one another, and they grew in the awareness of their need for continuing their professional supportive exchanges.

The following are seven simple steps for establishing solid relationships with those in other educational fields.

1. It is helpful to identify in a notebook one to three faculty members who would be open to collaboration. These individuals will add motivation for seeking out this relationship.
2. It may be beneficial to list their fields and potential gain from a closer working relationship with each person.
3. After each name and field, listing one to three things to do to enhance each person's work with students adds focus to the vision.
4. Choosing one person and requesting an informal meeting with him or her brings about the opportunity to share the benefits. Social media affords the dimension of the visual as well as the immediate interactive component. A vigilant and tech-savvy teacher finds ways to easily stay connected with many people through this means.
5. During the meeting, asking if he or she would be interested in any one of the suggestions that a colleague has to offer brings about the possibility for more exchange.
6. Further stating interest in what that person can offer to another's teaching situation affirms and encourages the individual.
7. If he or she expresses interest, beginning small with a simple educational exchange may lead to broader exchange.

Ideally, taking one small step will lead to further exploration of opportunities for collaboration. If not, gathering courage and proceeding with approaching another person on the list will open a door. Over time, after taking small steps, the results of these small ventures in collaboration will become apparent. Others, seeing such modeling and realizing the benefit, may choose to get onboard to build alliances.

Willingness to reach out, take the risk, and affirm their skills while explaining the benefit to them is an offer that many educators could not refuse. Sincere approaches and intentional efforts bring to all teachers the opportunity to find full and meaningful professional exchanges as well. With confidence, educators can promote offerings and point out ways that their input and added dimension of the skills from others creates mutual benefit.

The following parable offers encouragement and suggestions to anyone interested in convincing a coworker that understanding of another field may actually enhance the effective functioning of one's own field.

A Tale of Cooperation

There once lived a weaver in a cave on a remote mountain. Each day she removed the wool that she had spun, and she worked at creating what she perceived to be well-crafted rugs. After completing five carpets, she placed them on the back of her burro and headed into the village to sell them. The villagers purchased all five of the rugs, and she returned, satisfied that she offered them a fine product.

The weaver then resumed creating more rugs for sale in the village. After several weeks, she had produced enough for her burro to carry down the road to the village. Again she sold her five rugs to five satisfied villagers. She continued in this same manner over several years. One day while she was selling her rugs in the village, a child riding on a horse passed by. He looked at her rugs and remarked to her that they were indeed made very well.

The young rider complimented her on her skill and stated that the rugs would certainly last a long time. He added that he would not tell his family in the valley about them because they lacked one thing. These rugs were all the same in that they remained the color of sheep. The child could not understand why any of the villagers would want to have rugs that looked alike and were the color of sheep. The weaver could not understand why the child would care that these rugs were the color of sheep because wool was wool and it came from sheep.

Anything made from wool, she believed, would naturally become the color of sheep. She thought of no other option to what she had always done. The boy looked at her in dismay and asked if she would like to hear about his neighbor. The weaver really had no interest in someone who lived in a faraway valley, but because the boy seemed to want to tell her about this person, she agreed to listen as he shared about his neighbor.

According to the boy, his neighbor was able to extract color from plants to use for dying cloth. All of the people in his village wore clothing the color of the sky, the trees, and bright mountain flowers. He thought that if the weaver and the dye maker could meet and learn from each other, they could produce carpets of many colors.

The weaver agreed with the boy and asked him to tell his neighbor about her rugs. The boy then bought one to show the neighbor. The dye maker gathered his best colors into parcels and rode up the mountain the next day. As a result of their meeting, the weaver found a new dimension to creating carpets, and the dye maker found a new way to bring color to the world.

ACTION PLAN

1. Educators should learn to gather information on the social, political, philosophical, and personality aspects of school dynamics.
2. Educators should develop a private approach to viewing school staff and situations.
3. Educators should determine a wise course of action ranging from confronting the source to accessing internal systemic help or outside advice when defending oneself against backstabbing.

4. Educators should protect themselves by using discretion in sharing some aspects of their personal lives at school.
5. Educators should work to build a relationship with a professional opposite (e.g., general educator with special educator and vice versa).

Chapter Ten

Dealing with the Dynamics Created by Emotionally Unhealthy Staff Members

I hate to complain after one week at school
when I say some are angry, immature, sad,
jealous, nosy, breaking each social rule
. . . this is just the start
There is mistrust and some "woe is me"
big ears, big eyes, and a brown nose or two
some try to be bossy,
others only do the minimum
My counselor leaned forward, any more to say?
some are quite disloyal
and when asked to do work they try to delay
does this make sense?
The counselor empathized in the usual way
sounds like you've got a very tough class
no . . . what I am trying to say
is how do I deal with this unhealthy staff?!

After studying to be a teacher, Bill remained idealistic and enthusiastic about entering the profession. When he advanced to the status of pre-service teacher, he worked long hours and put effort and energy into his lesson plans. It was not uncommon for this dedicated young man to stay up late at night, sitting at the kitchen table, going through consecutive cans of soda while correcting papers and reading manuals.

While at his assigned elementary school site, Bill focused on his students and made an effort to establish rapport with parents. Bill did his best to work cooperatively with his host teacher. Because he kept highly engaged in his newly developing profession, Bill missed many of the behind-the-scenes, under-the-table, and out-in-the-parking-lot dynamics that occurred at this school.

During his stay of only a few months, he assumed that all the staff worked with integrity, and he naturally trusted that they operated as mature and whole human beings. Consequently, he had a rude awakening after actually taking his first job at another elementary site. What did

Bill find when he passed the honeymoon stage with his new faculty? How did they appear through the eyes of one newly trained to teach young people in a professional and experienced manner?

Bill and other beginning teachers sometimes give the staff of their first school mixed reviews. Bill and those new to teaching gravitate toward colleagues open to their presence and receptive to their ideas. He and his peers seek out assistance from those who are generous with their time and talents, offering to build on what new teachers know and to exchange ideas with respect and generosity.

These new professionals find satisfaction in the company of those who welcome them and those who are willing to hear out their ideas and respond to their questions with patience and respect. New teachers value a welcome that includes a sharing of experience about methodology, proven tried and true over the decades. Beginners such as Bill also encounter unhealthy personalities whose behavior and actions on the job cause negativity, confusion, uncertainty, and duplicity in staff exchanges and organizational dynamics.

How do such staff members manifest their emotionally unhealthy behavior, and what skills do Bill and other beginners need to survive in such an environment? Is it just new teachers who need to further their social and communication skills? Perhaps seasoned staff benefit from taking stock of how they affect staff dynamics as well.

They, too, may need to pause to determine who challenges their own professional integrity, how they cope with the waves of uncertainty created by unhealthy colleagues, and how to maintain their dignity and stability amid such teachers, staff, and administrators. Examples of emotionally and relationally challenged and challenging peers follow.

They may bring to mind familiar behaviors of staff and similar circumstances that many teachers can relate to. Both new and experienced teachers may find that these examples bring to mind certain sagas and undercurrents from personal experience. Since many teachers are so close to some situations and staff members and have become accustomed to some of their ploys, plotting, and the pathos surrounding their actions, the normal and familiar disguise themselves as healthy simply because they are common and frequent.

Reviewing examples of fictitious faculty offers the opportunity to remember and reflect on challenging coworkers governed by particular dominant emotions, those using counterproductive communication styles and ways of relating, as well as those whose social patterns diminish the cohesiveness of all who work in an educational setting.

STAFF GOVERNED BY DOMINANT EMOTIONS

Irate Kate

Anger released inappropriately or "shoved under the carpet" causes discord, disruption, and disturbances among the adults in a school. It even reverberates outward to students and families in unidentified ways. Irate Kate brings unaddressed anger from her past, perhaps even rightfully attached to a teacher from her school experience, from her family life, her marriage, or previous work experiences. Wherever its source, Kate has not addressed her anger, and consequently she fails to manage the new triggers that she encounters.

Were Kate to uncover her background through reflective time in a journal or with the assistance of a good friend or relative, she could begin to verify her pain. If she opted to take an anger workshop or address it with a mental health professional or clergyperson, she could begin to get on top of the internal flares of feeling that accompany her to her job.

As it stands, Kate readily reacts to circumstances that bring her dissatisfaction whether they originate with administration, coworkers, parents, or students. She freely makes harsh comments without consideration for the reaction and feelings of others. Kate finds herself wondering why people avoid working with her on her favorite committees, why some parents ask that their children not be in her classes, why students tense up as she demands an answer to a question that she has posed.

Kate enjoys seeing her principal wince when she comes up with what she considers a clever quip at a staff meeting. Her principal, however, perceives her comments as sarcastic and rude. Secretly, this administrator fantasizes about trading her with another principal, as team managers trade undesirable sports figures, in hopes that someone else will have a better experience.

Because Kate remains locked in to a pattern of behavior that developed earlier in life, she maintains a guard to protect herself from being hurt by others. Consequently, Kate withholds her trust and caring from students and staff. Thus, she wears an armor of defenses as she waits in anticipation for someone to attack her. Her peers, on the other hand, wonder when the next curt remark or expression of frustration and anger will hit them.

Those teachers who relate with Kate and are honest about self-assessment may wonder how to begin to manage their anger. As expressed earlier, there are avenues available through personal relationships and professionals that will enable one to start explaining inner hurts and to air them out honestly. In time, with work, new responses and means to manage anger will replace former patterns of hurtful angry expression. New ways to deal with this human and common emotion will change circumstances and relationships for the better.

Those who work with someone like Irate Kate may struggle with how to deal with the unpredictable eruptions of irritation, even rage. They may sense their sullen resentment and wonder if they have done something to cause the angry teacher distress. When such staff fly off with fury these coworkers may wish they could fly out of the country! Persons like Irate Kate make a team uncomfortable and even put a whole building on edge.

To deal well with the likes of Kate, perhaps it is best to begin at square one—with oneself. All staff experience anger and are susceptible to various triggers for this fluctuating and challenging emotion. Healthy staff who have their own anger brought into the light of under-standing, know its real origin, and take responsibility for these feelings are on the way to dealing effectively with Irate Kate.

Those who can vent this emotion with an understanding friend or trusted colleague who realizes the importance of keeping confidences are heading toward having their own public responses more and more under control. When Kate bumps into bully mode a teacher in her presence has the choice to respond in a calm, rational, and mature manner. If they feel like "hitting back," they may choose to take a deep breath, think first, and react in a way that retains personal dignity.

Staying within the framework of personal emotions, a steady staff person avoids imitating Kate and presents her with a model of someone that she, at some level, may want to become. When a Kate works down the hall, eats during the same lunch shift, or shares responsibility for an upcoming school event, teachers may want to consider rehearsing ways to act when she begins a tirade or cuts someone to the quick.

It may also be helpful to reflect on ways that bring a positive and calm dynamic to the situation. Confidence in one's repertoire of reactions, maturity, and experience as well as a sense for the discomfort of others offers the opportunity for an emotionally healthy teacher to contribute a presence appreciated by others in the school.

Such teachers know that they cannot control Kate's lack of command over her anger, but they can control their own response to it. They choose to remain self-possessed in her presence in spite of any annoyance that they may feel. Teachers who work with Irate Kate do not allow her proximity to diminish their dignity. They continue to treat all faculty, families, and students with respect while maintaining esteem for themselves.

Blue Stu

A continual low mood can secure a teacher in its grip and color the classroom of its victim with dreariness. Teachers who feel sadness on a regular basis appear with faces frozen in joyless and grim expressions. Blue Stu embodies this kind of teacher. He lacks enthusiasm for teaching, makes no effort to communicate a love of learning to students, and offers little support or information to his colleagues. He fades into the woodwork when it comes time to enter into the expected team involvements at his school. Stu prefers not to be noticed.

He goes through each day like the walking dead, anticipating the evening when he can sit in his lounge chair, comfort himself with cookies, and block out memories of his day with the drone of the television in front of him. He views people as impositions in the limited world that he has allowed himself. At times Stu participates in staff meetings and activities, and as a result his peers believe he has come out of his shell.

But his contact is short-lived, as Stu again retreats into the familiar dullness in which he lives. Stu goes through the motions of teaching year after year, using the same manuals, lessons, and approaches. Incorporating new methods requires too much time and effort on his part. When parents telephone, he speaks in a monotone, offering them pat educational answers and succinct standard formulas.

Stu perceives contacting parents, whether to learn more about his students or to report their progress, to be superfluous. He completes the required work, doing each deed devoid of vitality or spark. Stu sings the blues, and he is loyal to his plight. He plans to stick it out until retirement, going through the motions in the same room that he has had for seventeen years. His territory at the end of the hall protects him from any extra interaction with peers, parents, or students. He likes it like that. It is familiar, and he is "fine, thank you."

The temptation toward complacency and routine dullness, as exemplified by Stu, can come to many at some time or another. Perhaps on some days it seems easier to remain at a moderate level of performance. After years of work, it might be an easier option to withdraw from the drama of education and its players and to commit to going it alone, refusing to open to enthusiasm, new ideas, and the uniqueness of each class assigned in the fall.

What do educators do when they see this in peers? How does one relate with a colleague such as Stu, who prefers to shrug off the positive part of teaching? The temptation is there to try to be Miss Cheer in his presence, hoping that it will rub off. However, to convert a teacher like Stu into becoming a full participant in the school community may be daunting and nearly impossible. To continue to try may be an exercise in futility and an ultimate defeat. Stu is going to be the way he is going to be.

Being Mr. Chipper when Stu is at a committee meeting will not bring him on board. He has carved out his parameters. Can a colleague help Stu and those in his camp? Those who spend work time with Stu may choose to pass on falling into the fix-it trap, and instead behave with genuine interest in him and his educational efforts. They decide to use eye contact and speak directly to him. They reach out in a matter-of-fact manner, assuming that he is wholeheartedly involved like everyone on the staff. It will be up to Stu to respond to such invitations to job fulfillment.

Another temptation may be to try to do things for Stu, to pick up the slack with families and students that Stu does not reach. Unless individual staff members have fully covered their own territory, it is best they not attempt to build the bridges that Stu must build for himself. Warmth and kindness to his students and families are workable and doable, but to try to go beyond that invites frustration and depletion for well-meaning educators.

Eventually, Stu will have to determine if he is alive and present in his own life and at his own job. Each teacher has his or her own path to follow and his or her own student and family relationships to develop and maintain. At some point Stu and those like him will have to decide, as all teachers do, to live a life of low spirits and limited options or to choose vitality and presence in the careers that they have selected.

Juvenile Judy

Somehow it seems that certain teachers blend in developmentally with their students. It might be that they have chosen to work with children or adolescents because their own development has not at some level exceeded that of their students or because full adulthood has not come to fruition within them. Maybe some staff members have failed to develop strong-enough adult personalities to withstand the modeling of the young people with whom they spend their days.

Consequently, they sometimes act like elementary students or teenagers when adult behavior is warranted. Such a teacher can be called Juvenile Judy. Teachers falling into this category, conjured up to explain additional emotionally unhealthy behavior, slip easily into whispers and snickers during a faculty meeting. When an outside speaker is present or when a required in-service class is being conducted, Judy and her pals grab the back row. There they entertain themselves writing notes to each other, sharing mints, and rolling their eyes with boredom.

It is as if they are taking the opportunity to act out the behaviors for which they reprimand their own students. When with her peers in social situations, Judy enjoys the spotlight. She freely tells her colleagues the details of her divorce and her current prospects on the dating scene. She giggles excitedly as she previews her weekend plans, making others privy to events beyond the scope of their interest or curiosity. Judy maintains limited boundaries between the events of her professional life and social activities.

Once Judy gets the attention of other faculty, she complains about a child with special needs who has been placed in her class. It is easy for her to share a family's private circumstances after hearing the details during a confidential conference. It does not occur to her to respect the privacy of others, as she has no sense of her own boundaries.

While having a conference with her principal, Judy throws an adult tantrum when asked to make academic accommodations for a certain student. She sees the world her way and has no room for adults telling her what to do and when to do it. She believes that she knows what is best for her class and wonders why an outsider would want to tamper with her domain.

Judy enjoys chewing gum at work in spite of the rules that explicitly say students must not do this. She dresses in "cool" clothes in the fashion of the day as defined by the youth culture. Judy believes that if she can blend in with her class, they will like her. She is certain that if they think she is really "with it," then she will have achieved success.

Teachers may find that they have had a Judy phase at some point in their career, even for a passing moment. It is important to be fun-filled and to "let the hair down" with others on the job. However, when professionalism and competence are sacrificed for immaturity, teachers must draw the line. There is a world bigger than one defined by an emotionally immature teacher.

For some, this may be a phase equivalent with age. For others, it is a permanent state chosen by personalities such as Judy, who do not want to grow up. They believe that they can avoid adulthood by hanging out and hiding out in a school setting. How does an adult professional tolerate Juvenile Judy? Not easily, perhaps. When Judy and her group begin their shenanigans in the back row, the look reserved for students using the same inappropriate behavior may be fitting.

When Judy models her lack of boundaries and blurs the details of her personal life with social communication at school, it is best to change the subject and steer the conversation toward topics appropriate among professionals. When she chatters on about confidences of students and families, she needs to be told that she has crossed a line both professionally and legally. Adults at the school will have to take charge to protect those whom she has harmed by her lack of respect for the privacy to which they are entitled.

Administrators and team members will have a challenge in supervising and working with Judy. Direct, clear, and consistent expression of expectations and desires, just as to a child, is the means to attempt to reach the part of her that strives for developmental appropriateness. Official and unofficial mentoring will be of direct benefit to those who fall into the Juvenile Judy category, not only for the teacher's advantage, but also for the benefit of students and families.

Jealous Ellis

Among the staff members of any school are those who strive to develop themselves to the fullest. They might do this by perfecting a lesson until they believe it to be optimally effective for students. Maybe they express their desire for reaching their professional potential by going to graduate school, aiming for a deeper working knowledge of their chosen subject area. Some may decide to pursue additional studies to change their educational role to that of school psychologist or administrator.

Also working among these high performers are those content with their levels of function. When a colleague demonstrates a desire to exceed the status quo, some teachers respond to feelings of jealousy by behaving in a negative and destructive manner toward those whom they perceive as a threat. Such a teacher is Jealous Ellis. When Ellis finds out that the teacher next door is spending more time after school than he is, Ellis scoffs and finds a way to belittle her for her efforts.

When he gets word that a teacher in his department has decided to pursue graduate studies, Ellis recalls their first year of teaching together. Somehow he feels abandoned in his complacency and comments about the arrogance of any teacher choosing to do this. Ellis expresses how expensive it will be to pay for all of those classes.

When he learns that a teacher in his school has administrative aspirations, Ellis launches a smear campaign with the words "Who does she think she is?" Yes, it is natural for educators to experience jealous feelings when noticing the ambition and excellence of others.

However, this feeling does not often overwhelm those teachers with healthy personalities who are willing to write a note of encouragement and congratulations acknowledging the efforts of others. They understand that the growth and advancement of individual teachers enhances the entire teaching profession. When they see the achievements of their peers, they offer their proud support and take others' successes as motivation to put effort into their own professional development.

TEACHERS CAUGHT IN UNHEALTHY COMMUNICATION STYLES

B. Z. Body

The job of any teacher comprises many facets, and to do the job effectively, a professional must remain focused and on target. Organizational skills and efficiency come from personal discipline and prioritization of duties. Some teachers, however, are unable to move through their day in a focused manner. Instead, they are easily distracted by minor occurrences that take place in the domains of other teachers.

They easily go off task and become overly involved in events irrelevant to their role. Gossip and small talk take precedence over the needs of students in their charge. They easily slip from consideration of their own responsibilities in exchange for retaining a juicy tidbit of news to share at noon. A teacher representing this aspect of unhealthy communication is B. Z. Body. She gains her energy from fixating outward in anticipation of the next newsworthy happening in her hallway.

If another teacher leaves to see the principal, she finds an excuse to go to the office, ever hopeful of hearing a request for a transfer or private information about a parent. If B. Z., who checks her front window regularly, sees a challenging parent pull up in the parking lot, she manages to excuse herself for the restroom in order to find out where Ms. Troublemaker is headed. B. Z. enjoys district-wide meetings and after-school get-togethers, where she is sure to hear the latest from other schools.

Though she complains about not having enough time for her own work, B. Z. manages to cover all bases and keep her sources groomed through regular contact. She never knows what conversation will enable her to learn the latest and spread it to her next willing listener. B. Z. does not wait to determine if her information is factual or not. Bedrock truth, hearsay, rumor, and innuendo are all the same to her. This teacher enjoys playing the telephone game, and as information passes her way, she embellishes and adds emotional tones to tales as they transpire.

When student papers pile up, B. Z. grabs her red pen and positions herself in her favorite spot in the staff lounge. Her trained ears perk up when the intonations of her colleagues' voices indicate when a tantalizing topic comes next on their agenda. She readily notices subdued or highly emotional levels of language. It is then that she puts her correcting on autopilot and detours in the direction of the conversation of current interest. For B. Z. and those in her network, education remains an exhilarating and exciting profession indeed.

When working in the close company of others, it is natural to want to know about interesting events that have occurred. Human nature is such that there is a place in all staff that resembles B. Z. to some degree. However, when one becomes obsessed with knowing the news and using that news as a device for social communication, one demonstrates limited ability to interact with others. Teachers like B. Z. have settled for the sensationalism of the moment at the expense of developing adult communication skills.

They unknowingly restrict themselves from speaking about matters requiring warmth, social ability, and genuine caring for others. When working with B. Z., avoiding her insatiable quest for personal information about the lives of others can be difficult. Staff in her proximity could become her next headline after she pumps them for information about events occurring in their classrooms.

Defending against her incessant spreading of information about other faculty may make her peers wary of being near her. Obviously, no one can control what she says about them or anyone else. However, her coworkers can control what they say to her. When in B. Z.'s presence, it is wise to choose words carefully, with particular awareness of the privacy rights of students and parents.

When B. Z. corners a coworker for a consultation and provides unwelcome information or gossip about others, it is sometimes necessary to curtail the conversation by changing the subject or choosing to go back to one's classroom or move on to one's duty elsewhere. Eventually, B. Z. will get the message that those who move away either verbally or physically are not her takers and have no news to give her.

Antagonistic Agnes

Some teams work together in harmony. Each person in the group demonstrates that she or he has learned the art of give-and-take. When communicating among themselves, group members are sensitive to the concerns, hesitations, motives, and goals of others in the group or on the committee. Achieving staff harmony comes from the efforts of emotionally mature people who understand the principles of sharing, involved listening, and negotiating. They are able to forgo their own desires when it becomes apparent that to do so serves the greater good.

Others on the staff remain adamant that their way is the only way to go. They believe that their ideas are best in all circumstances. Their self-centeredness translates into a communication style breeding animosity instead of harmony. When things do not go their way, they are willing to engage in hostility and hold out to the end to secure what they believe to be the best outcome for a project. They do not understand cooperative communication skills and often position themselves in the opposite corner of progress in their school.

Such a teacher, Antagonistic Agnes, knows with cement certainty what she believes and what she wants. Her ilk, like spoiled children who have been indulged with their own ways for all of their young lives, remain tenacious in their views, bedrock solid in their desires, and immovable in their perspectives. Consequently, it is not uncommon to hear the Agneses on staff pipe up when they do not agree with the plans unfolding at a staff meeting. Immediately, they insert an opposite position into the discussion.

They harshly throw rocks into the still pool of harmony so desired by a staff working toward legitimate consensus. Typical ploys used by teachers in the Antagonistic Agnes category are criticism, sarcasm, and ridicule. From their position of arrogance, they quickly interject such opening lines as "Don't you understand that . . . ?" "If we do it your way, then . . . will happen because . . ." "I cannot believe you are going to try . . ." They turn phrases with a tart tongue as they lash out at new ways of doing things that they refuse to attempt.

The Agnes contingent appears angry and tough, but at some level they are more afraid of their own failure if called on to participate. They feel uncomfortable contributing time and effort to a project when they believe that they have a better idea. When tired and weary, any staff person may want to snap at the group or create an opposing position for group members to consider. However, the purpose and regularity of this response put a teacher in the Antagonistic Agnes category.

A few oppositional slips are forgivable on a team, but a steady and aggressive animosity causes disruption in a building's communication pattern. A teacher like Antagonistic Agnes is particularly difficult to have in a school. Teachers and administrators feel like they are walking in a minefield when Agnes participates in a discussion or planning session.

Yet those who seek results and work to try something new will continue to move ahead with their plans in spite of Agnes's attempts to thwart their efforts. They may behave in a calm, gentle manner, yet next to her abrasive and loud clamor they bear strength and hold determination. Maintaining personal poise and integrity, teachers learn to work around Agnes.

By not giving in to her unrealistic demands, they build an emotional fence around her objections and carry on anyway. Emotionally mature and healthy teachers internally shake their heads and find it within themselves to pity someone who occupies space among them who has no intention to participate. They politely thank her for her input, stick together, and refuse to follow. If new to a school where Agnes and her ilk have created a coalition, administrators and teachers must selectively seek out those with the desire to be constructive and courageous.

And in spite of all odds, they must maintain unity and confidence as they progress toward creating a school culture free from the grip of educational tyrants. Patience and the ability to take deep breaths, alone or in the company of others who are truly interested, will prove stronger than the means used by the insecure and frightened staff who choose to align with Antagonistic Agnes.

Two-Faced Grace

At least Antagonistic Agnes tells others exactly where she stands. However, those on staff who strive for communication styles commensurate with an emotionally healthy person are clear on where they stand as well. They part company with Agnes in tone and purpose. They choose to express what they believe to be constructive, and they do so in front of the group in a sincere and respectful manner.

Others operate a parallel culture from that of the rest of the staff. They give their nod to group consensus only to reverse direction in word or action when they desire to express their true feelings. Two-Faced Grace behaves in such a manner. She sets up her official office in the school parking lot. After attending a meeting, smiling and nodding her approval of what has transpired, or sitting stone-faced without indicating her position on an issue, Grace leaves the meeting and goes directly to this second "office."

There she leads a huddle of faculty who lack the assertiveness, directness, and respect for their administration and peers to express how they truly feel. Without courage of conviction, they sit through a staff meeting and watch the dynamics, making mental notes of whom to criticize. They set their agenda for the week ahead, knowing just when to smile and nod and when to speak behind the backs of others.

Trust is a concept that Two-Faced Grace does not understand. She continues to look others in the eye and make statements of agreement. When she finds a "safe" person, she reveals her true perspective on the current events in her district. When teachers are tempted to behave like Grace they may resort to duplicity when uncertain of the response they will receive if they speak out on a topic.

They may use an alternative communication pattern when unsure of themselves with a larger group. They may decide that withholding their opinions provides temporary protection from any potential criticism they are unwilling to face. When the crowd gathers in the parking lot after school, staff members may wonder if they should join in with them. They ask themselves if they should assume that such members cluster together to express what they did not say at the meeting.

They may gather their courage, get involved in the discussion and suggest that those in the cluster participate in the official staff meeting next time. Or they may prefer to pass them by, in a hurry to get home to prepare dinner, pick up a child at day care, or meet a spouse to go to the mall. Maintaining communication integrity requires practice and persistence. When looking another in the eye, expressing thoughts in a direct and clear manner, an educator walks the path of integrity.

Eventually, consistent behavior sends the message of belief in personal convictions. Educators who conduct themselves in a consistent manner send the message that they are trustworthy employees and colleagues. Unlike Two-Faced Grace, they know themselves, live a life based on principle, and communicate clearly and consistently in all circumstances.

Martha the Martyr

Schools function better when staff are willing to verbally show honest support to their leaders and speak out to come to consensus regarding an upcoming school-wide event. Successful staff members see the positive aspects of plans and attach themselves to that energy. They willingly compliment others who put time and effort into their classroom teaching. When they notice that a student's performance or behavior has improved due to the involvement of another teacher, they are the first to publicly give credit where credit is due.

Unfortunately, others see the negative side of the exact same circumstances. When they hear about a parent picnic, they complain that it has been scheduled on the wrong date. When someone in their department receives recognition for bringing their debate team all the way to the division competition, they grumble that the event took the students away from their social studies classes and that the makeup work slowed their grading system.

No matter what good occurs, teachers who focus on negative energy look only at how circumstances cause them inconvenience or difficulty. They position themselves in the role of one who is continually suffering with no end in sight. Such a teacher can be called Martha the Martyr. Martha finds disturbing events everywhere.

In spite of other staff members' enthusiasm for an event or project, she complains that it is somehow disrupting her teaching day. When asked to serve on a committee, Martha agrees because she knows she is required to participate. As she consents to stay an extra hour for the meeting, Martha explains to others in the group how much more this will cost her for day care, how the traffic on her route home will be heavier later in the afternoon, and how much she must do in the evening because she could not complete it at her desk after school.

When she returns the next morning, Martha may retell her woes about child care expenses, her longer commute, and extra work, adding that she had to come in earlier to prepare for the day ahead. When the committee meets again and peers express their appreciation for her willingness to get involved with the project, Martha will note how her classroom has suffered. She will lament that because she has not been able to enhance her lessons to the degree that she would have wished, her committee involvement has indeed impaired her classroom effectiveness.

Out of the corner of her eye, Martha examines the daily duties of others on the staff. She readily mentions how much easier it would have been for her if she had gone into another field, such as school psychology or speech and language pathology, so that she could work shorter hours. What Martha fails to notice is the amount of paperwork these people in such professions have to complete and the conferences they need to attend in their other buildings.

She lacks respect for the professionalism of others and does not trust that her colleagues will do their jobs in a proficient manner. Martha wastes her energy fussing and fuming about how tough she has it. Martha manages to contribute complaint and negativity to conversations and meetings. Her presence lends a downward drift to the moods of those assigned to work with her. All teachers have down days and discouraging moments, yet many manage to take charge of their attitudes and find the good and purposeful in their jobs.

When tempted to take on the Martha persona, healthy teachers catch themselves before they tarnish the atmosphere of a staff gathering. How does a teacher manage when working closely on a daily basis with Martha the Martyr? It takes resolve to emotionally edit her comments from the conversation. It requires determination to keep an upbeat atmosphere in a group instead of engaging in response to her negativity.

It takes conscious determination to avoid being hooked into her pattern of complaint and self-pity. It takes perseverance to remain positive when Martha continues to poison the atmosphere of the staff lounge with her complaints and whining. To healthy teachers, the change of Martha's facial expression and tone of voice signals that she is morphing into a martyr. With this recognition, they realize that it is time to mentally decide to dismiss the content of her speech, change the subject, or exit her space to work elsewhere.

Their emotional distancing is wise and may even indicate to her that they place no value on what she is saying. Through their lack of interest, they send Martha the message to curtail her negative remarks. Their choice to not expend energy in unhealthy communication gives them the ticket to continue their day on a positive course.

WORK RELATIONSHIPS DIMINISHED BY UNHEALTHY BEHAVIOR

Distrustful Russell

Many teachers extend themselves to develop professional relationships with their peers. They build respect and trust by sharing teaching tips, working as a team to produce a successful spring music festival, or offering suggestions for themes for a graduate paper. Unfortunately, others keep their best ideas to themselves, certain that their colleagues cannot be trusted to credit them or offer them something in return.

Teachers who behave in this manner fear that others will pass them on the path to pedagogical success. Teachers who view their peers through the lens of mistrust block the flow of sharing that builds staff rapport. Due to a limited vision of camaraderie, they shut down the enthusiasm that could occur when individuals interact with openness and trust.

Teachers whose actions originate from a sense of distrust shut down their own abilities to help create an educational climate that reaches its fullest capacity because they refuse to give from the heart. Teachers operating with excessive caution limit staff cohesiveness. They live in continual fear of being found out, turned in, and trampled on by others.

They decide to climb the ladder of professional development by themselves, certain that they have their own best interest to think of first and foremost. Due to this withholding of sincerity and trust in the workplace, a teacher who holds back confidence in others and exchanges openness for doubt and suspicion can be known as Distrustful Russell. Russell dodges the opportunity to contribute his ideas at faculty meetings. When an educational leader scans the group for ideas during a brainstorming session, Russell lowers his eyes, keeping his thoughts to himself.

Perhaps he could have come up with five ideas to promote the school fund-raising efforts, but if he stated them in front of the group, they would get lost on the flip chart. Someone else would surely claim credit for his contributions. When the teachers in Russell's grade area approach him to join them for an after-school popcorn and unit-planning session, he feigns interest while explaining that he has an appointment.

Wishing them well in their planning, Distrustful Russell has no intention of participating. He has his own ideas about how to teach electricity. Why should he be part of a group who will drain him dry of energy? Who knows how things will turn out if he has to rely on others to write a section of the unit? What if he is put into a position of having to teach something that lacks his stamp of approval?

Russell has been working long hours to complete a master's degree in order to increase his salary. However, he has not told the other teachers in his grade area about this. When they ask about how he spent his evening or his weekend, Russell is vague and says little. He does not think it is any of their business how he spends his time or what classes he is taking. After all, someone might encroach on his time upon learning about his developing area of expertise— cooperative learning.

Russell arrives at school feeling sad because of the death of his golden retriever, Max. On a human level, he desires very much to tell Elaine, the teacher across the hall, about his loss. Elaine is an animal lover who keeps a hamster, rabbit, and guinea pig for her class to enjoy. Would she understand his void since Max died? Maybe she would.

But maybe she would tell the entire staff about this, and they in turn might talk about him behind his back. Even worse, they might watch to see if they can catch him slipping up on the job due to his preoccupation with this unfortunate loss. Russell concludes that some things are better left unsaid. He will handle his hurt by himself.

Distrustful Russell moves through each day, consistently imposing rigid parameters on his relationship with other staff members. It is easy to do because his emotional walls help him to keep a regular and firm distance. There are areas in him to which no other human being is allowed access, especially people at school. He does not comprehend the nuances of healthy professional boundaries that vary among teachers.

He cannot detect those who would keep his confidences, support his ideas, credit him sincerely, and hear out his plans for tomorrow's lessons. With consistent and solid barriers around his teaching and personal life, Russell knows exactly where others stand at all times. To him, each teacher is an equal threat to his equanimity, and he resolves to continue his standoff with trust.

Where Russell could have made a contribution for the betterment of all, he supplies missed opportunities in exchange for a potential offering. When Russell could have forged bonds of collegial support, he instead chooses to keep his own counsel. When he could have given his insights to a new, struggling staff member, Russell returns a blank and unfeeling glance, choosing to send the message that he will pass on this exchange. His legacy to his peers is a void because he has chosen to avoid the risk of relationships.

When things get busy, when a streak of insecurity or selfishness rises within, one's own strains of mistrust surface. It is only human for such to occur. However, having a temporary phase of distrust is far different from surrendering totally to its constraints. It is also different from having unhealthy boundaries that allow the inappropriate description of private emotions and personal experiences with colleagues at school.

Dealing with transient times of mistrust can lead to growth in discerning what to share and determining how to develop healthy, balanced, and open relationships with peers who deserve reasonable trustworthiness and interest. Trust also offers the freedom to follow personal instincts when they signal caution, suggesting limiting trust in those known to abuse confidences.

When trying to relate to a "mannequin," a peer refusing to engage in professional dialogue and debate, a teacher may reach a point of frustration. Personal perceptions might indicate that a distrustful teacher has potential. There may be an inner impetus to tap such a coworker as a resource when working on a unit or committee. However, no one can force another to break a long-standing pattern very easily.

Patient affirmation, gentle invitation, and consistent reassurance may eventually conquer hardened social positions. In the meantime, the primary use of energy would be best directed into relationships with adults who understand the reciprocity of professional teamwork and the benefits of sharing their gifts and talents with others.

Petty Betty

When working with others, day in and day out over months and years, there are bound to be times when conflict arises. When it does, skills in listening, objectivity, and constructive dialogue help to get a school-based relationship over this temporary hurdle. Some teachers, however, lack the ability to see the big picture—to stop, step back, and take a breath.

They do not understand the concept of letting go, nor do they realize how to prioritize problems. Such teachers cannot forgive and forget. They let small things pile up, and they put minor scuffles on an equal plane with major differences. It seems that they are continually tangling over small matters. Worrying and fretting from one petty problem to the next, such a staff person can be called Petty Betty.

When the supplies are handed out in the fall, Betty notices that the teacher across the hall has been allotted one more box of dry erase markers than was registered on the check sheet. Not only does Betty spot this, but she also spends time wondering why this occurred, when others in her circumstances would have thought nothing of it. She controls her world by staying on top of every detail. When one does not match her calculations, her whole world tilts in the wrong direction. Petty Betty makes constant comparisons between her situation and that of her peers.

To Betty, everyone must be treated equally according to her perception. She will be quick to tell other teachers on her team how many times this month she has had recess duty in comparison with their assigned number of days. Betty notices when someone brought only a plate of brownies for the weekly staff treat as opposed to her cake, bag of chocolates, and plate of petit fours. Also important to Betty is the fact that her carpet has not been designated for replacement until the following year. Yet the carpet in the room across the hall is scheduled for replacement next month.

Not only that, but the building custodian failed to clean the corners of her whiteboard after she left on Wednesday. When she discovered this on Thursday morning, Betty gave in to her impulse to check this detail in the room next door before her colleague arrived. She just had to know that she was being treated just like everyone else. To top it off, when inspecting that whiteboard, she noticed the extra two feet of space on the south end of the room and wondered how the architects could have possibly slighted her in that way.

When a turf war occurs, Betty will for sure be a prime instigator. Betty once put in her claim for the work area farthest away from the music room for prep time use. When the principal decided in favor of another teacher, Betty chose to maintain a grudge for years. The fact that she lost the spot that she requested fueled a feud among teachers on her hall in future fall scheduling sessions.

Because Betty brought pettiness to the relationships among the staff in her school, she introduced several snags in the communication flow. When small matters could have been overlooked and dismissed and when colleagues wanted to move on, they could not because Betty readily threw in a reason for division. In the course of any school day, there are many details to remember, many minor matters to negotiate, and small bumps to climb over. Anyone can get snagged into having a petty perspective once in a while.

Yet maturity includes the ability to sort what is a big deal and what is irrelevant in the grand scheme of things. When working with Petty Betty, colleagues get their cue when she is about to move into her petty mode. When they see Betty's face tighten and her nostrils contract, they know this is the signal that she is attempting to minimize their world. They understand that she is poised to amplify an argument that could easily be put to rest with a brief airing out. They sense when she is about to magnify a minimal matter not worth belaboring.

Betty may insist that her students have three more inches of space on the hall coatrack, and the teacher next door will have to decide if quibbling with her is worth the trouble. Mature teachers who work with the Petty Betty types know the difference between important issues and those that deserve only a deep breath and a quick exit from her presence. They sort this out daily and move forward in spite of her attempts to set them back with her petty perspective on an incident.

When something is really important and worth the fight, they decide to take her on with reason and logic. They cluster in support of one another and face her head-on with direct and clear communication skills. They paint the big picture and point out the natural conclusion of one alternative as opposed to another. When her narrow-minded views jeopardize the welfare of their students and families in any way, colleagues pick their battles with wisdom and prudence. They fully realize why they are engaging with her when they do push their point.

Brown Nose Rose

Administrators most often know a genuinely good teacher when they work with one. They hear comments from parents, see test scores, and watch classes develop into educated and well-mannered young people. They notice the small steps of progress that students make and realize a lot of what is happening in a classroom by frequent visits, conversations with teachers, or just passing in the hall day after day and year after year.

Some teachers work hard to position themselves to gain favor with administration. They strategically plan out what they will say when they see their principal, careful to mention their agreement with something said at a staff meeting. They are never at a loss for flattering comments to make, whether sincere or not. They persistently put out a word of praise for the principal for the purpose of shining up the communication lines between them. Just as certain students put in their time to do some "apple polishing," so too do these teachers follow suit on an adult level.

The term Brown Nose Rose covers a multitude of teacher behaviors. Those in her category know how important it is to flatter an administrator in front of a parent. Brown Nose Rose rehearses the words and puts on a false smile to ensure the success of her performance. She publicly proclaims how much better the school has become now that the current administrator is at the helm. Rose never fails to notice a new suit, haircut, or purse worn by the principal.

With a voice as sweet as honey, using just the right intonations and inflections, she affirms the greatness of every administrator whom she encounters. Her possibilities for public praise are endless. Rose also knows how to advantageously direct her adulation in private as well. She times a note or a phone call to the office to coincide with her need for remaining in the administrator's good graces. Rose makes a complimentary comment about her principal to the school office staff when she is certain that her words will be expeditiously shared with the boss.

Rose uses others to make a good impression. She parades her class by the office, making sure that they walk lockstep in a straight line at just the right time. She works her public relations strategy by staying in close contact with the other favorites in the building. After all, she reasons, if one runs with those who have made a positive impression on the principal, one will be considered favorably as well.

Staff members who work with Brown Nose Rose quickly catch on to her agenda of gaining administrative favor and attention. The temptation is there to play the game and compete with her constant conniving. They see through her scheming and realize that administrators will likely figure out quite quickly when Rose is on a roll. They figure that their energy is more productively spent developing relationships with students, parents, and staff around concerns and curriculum.

They also know when, why, and how to initiate effective and purposeful communication with their principal or director. All staff members desire to have positive rapport with administration. It makes for good communication and supportive ongoing collegiality to put one's best foot forward when with the director or principal.

The behavioral difference between acting like a mature teacher is behaving in a consistent and affirming manner and showing genuineness of purpose in all settings, particularly in the company of administrators. Rose acts from an established baseline of service to self. Really good teachers do not need to do that. They know why they are at school, and they perform their jobs with interest and sincerity. Top-of-the-line teachers engage in conversations with administration to better the lives of students and families in their care.

When they communicate, they naturally make a positive impression on their administrators. In that context, if they share well-deserved recognition mentioned in a note from a parent or election to the presidency of an educational organization, administrators resonate with the reality of what they already know in their hearts—that these teachers deserve the honor that they have received.

Inspector Hector

Teachers working to better the lives of students and families and to maintain open and effective communication with other staff members have nothing to hide. They have their professional priorities straight, use their time efficiently and appropriately, and give their district its due through hard work on a regular basis. Unfortunately, some administrators fall prey to teachers seeking their favor as minions who offer their ears and eyes as spies for them.

These weak individuals partner to meet one another's unhealthy needs. The administrator wants to know what is going on in the building and seeks assistance in doing supervision on the sly. Teachers who sell out their peers by reporting unfavorable behavior among colleagues behave adversely themselves. Teachers catch on to the game and realize who works as a roving reporter for the principal.

They know that the label Inspector Hector fits well with those who eavesdrop on their peers. An Inspector Hector type knows where to spend time to learn the news. He positions himself behind a newspaper and monitors lounge conversation. When data comes past his highly attuned ear, he files it in his head, in the slot marked "confidential," and he keeps it for his next unofficial debriefing with the principal. Certainly, juicy tidbits about how the new teacher spent her weekend will be worth a few points.

When Hector goes to his mailbox, which is more often than necessary, he scans the other boxes for material that may not relate to education. After all, the principal will want to know why teachers are passing around a decorator or clothing catalogue. Wouldn't the boss want to know the contents of a message being passed among union leaders?

When Hector has the chance, he notices the content on computer screens of his peers, hoping to catch them on social media instead of media for educational purposes. Even when he goes to a local Internet café, he hopes to catch peers spending too much time online instead of being home doing schoolwork. This would be ideal to pass on to administration.

Hector keeps his eyes and ears open when he walks down the hall, taking particular notice of student behavior, teacher use of time, and parent visits. When he sees a parent and teacher engaged in intense discussion at the far end of the hallway, Hector changes his route. He believes that something is up and that, if he passes by, slowing slightly as he slinks behind the teacher's back, he will pick up on the topic of mutual interest.

Even when Hector is out in the community, he takes his role of watchdog seriously. Behind the shelves of the grocery store or while pumping gas, he has heard parents make comments about certain teachers and what they have told students. Also interesting is what parents say on parallel treadmills at the health club. He perks up immediately when they begin to discuss what their children tell them about what goes on at school.

Teachers who become victims of Hector's avocation of roving reporter have no defense against when or where he takes his operation. Because they cannot control what he hears and when he hears it, they are vulnerable to his underground operation. Yet, they also realize that they have something on him that he cannot take away—their self-respect.

Working with Hector can be irritating, annoying, and potentially demeaning. However, teachers with full ownership of their integrity learn to ride with the operation because their truth is stronger than Hector's partial stories, half truths, and innuendos. They also know when and how to counter any damage to their reputations brought on by Hector's subterfuge.

Teachers who choose to confront their administrator relative to reinforcement of such behavior do so behind closed doors with the support of another person of integrity, perhaps a parent or union advocate. They understand that not only are their personal dignity and professional reputation at stake, but the healthy communication of the school organization is compromised.

They make an effort to improve the school climate when they call others on behavior that is dishonest, cowardly, and unbecoming of an educator. They refuse to reinforce collusions that discredit school personnel and their efforts to carry out the mission of the school. They do not accept betrayal in the building or out in the community. In doing so, they provide a strong message that professional behavior extends beyond school property.

SOCIAL PATTERNS DIMINISHING STAFF COHESIVENESS

Minimum Minnie

Parents express gratitude to teachers who give their all to helping their child grow academically, socially, and emotionally in the school setting. Administrators realize the benefits to the entire school organization when teachers offer constructive ideas at meetings and planning sessions. Colleagues appreciate the give-and-take that comes from working closely with others who freely and willingly offer their time and experience to support the educational efforts of other staff members.

Unfortunately, some teachers do not relate to the concept of giving one's fullest on the job. They instead calculate how to keep things going in the classroom while putting in the least amount of time and effort possible. Teachers who begrudge their students of their best can be labeled Minimum Minnie. Not only does Minnie deprive her class of her full effort, but she also holds back contributions to her team.

A social system is nurtured forward when each person contributes fully to the daily operations of the organization. In a school, teachers, administrators, and support staff who reach out to one another in respect, offering their sincere suggestions, work as social partners. Such partnerships can be demanding and challenging. To those who are enlivened by the give-and-take reflected by such systems, working in these circumstances can be rewarding.

Minnie, however, does not seek the gratification and fulfillment of cooperation and collegiality. Her truncated style sends the message that she cannot and will not contribute to the positive social flow of the school. Instead, Minnie keeps a low profile. She does not appreciate attention. If no one comes into her classroom, no one will notice what is not happening there. At staff meetings, she sits on the sidelines and withholds ideas and contributions. She makes no effort to volunteer for any staff committees beyond what is required of her.

She affects social situations by applying her attitude to staff events. When the holiday party comes around, Minnie sourly signs up to bring a jar of pickles. Why would she want to bake for all of these people anyway? She avoids participating in picnics, TGIF stops, baby showers, parties where she would be expected to buy something, and breakfast gatherings.

Minnie sees only the externals of the event and places no value on the social benefit of spending time with colleagues after school hours. Why would she want to be put into a position of having to spend money to be with people she can see five days a week? Minnie excludes herself from the fun and fringes of school life. While there, she is all business.

When teachers gather in the hall after school for a few minutes of stress release, joke exchange, and laughter, Minnie ducks back into her dull classroom, gathers her thermos and handbag, ready to bolt for the door the minute that she is officially free for the day. What would be the point of wasting time talking about nothing? As she leaves the building, she notices three teachers gathered by a bulletin board admiring the student art. Why get involved in that? The students are from a different grade.

When tired and overextended, one finds it easy to fall into the Minnie mind-set. Setting limits certainly is a healthy behavior when one has lots of work to do and deadlines to meet. Minnie lives like she has too much to do, but she does little to contribute to the staff community because she withholds her most important gift—herself.

Teams saddled with Minnie find frustration at every turn. As she shuts down and refuses to participate, staff can easily become discouraged. A team of four with Minnie functions as a team of three, and the group is better off working as a dynamic threesome. Response to her avoidance with avoidance works well in some circumstances.

If required to participate, she will deaden the atmosphere of a group meeting. Enthused and vital teachers do not deserve Minnie's draining presence. Their pie can be cut into three pieces instead of four. Even if they have more work to do without a fourth person, they can be assured that the work done will be quality contributions to the team effort.

Bossy Flossie

Working in a school requires use of adult social skills on a continual basis. Teachers over time develop an awareness of the best ways to approach one another. They become sensitive to the personalities of those around them and know when they have said too little or too much relative to completion of a task. Wise and mature teachers also discern when to give up their outcomes. They realize when relinquishing their visions and personal plans best serves the social whole of the school.

One person, however, does not understand surrendering to the big picture. Called Bossy Flossie, she holds out to the end, promoting her pet projects and ideas. Whether favored or dismissed by the majority, Flossie presses on with her thoughts about student hallway passage patterns, lunch schedules, and detention duties. When the time comes to select a school program for parents, Flossie insists on using a poem that she composed. She presses her plan to the point that her peers nearly lose their composure in trying to discourage her.

When working in a secondary setting, Flossie finds herself tangling with her department head every step of the way. She refuses to follow the syllabus, believing that some activities are unnecessary for her pupils. Flossie demands the attention of this teacher when she needs help with a new computer grading system, yet she refuses to answer an e-mail requesting her input on a new discipline policy due in the main office by the end of the day.

Parents cringe when Flossie tells them how to raise their children, using an arrogant and dismissive tone, as opposed to offering constructive and caring suggestions. After all, she knows from her own upbringing what is best for the youth of today. Flossie finds a way to introduce control in parent conferences held with other staff. She brings her own agenda, written or unwritten, and tries her best to steer the discussion in the direction that works for her timetable and interests.

Administrators look busy when Flossie enters the office with a flurry. What will be her next demand? What area of expertise will she next display for all in the office to see and hear?

Who will she criticize and cut down to make way for her ideas? When will she finally figure out that she has no following and learn to listen?

Everyone wants the upper hand once in a while. Teachers sincerely believe that their viewpoints are worthy of consideration and will go to bat for what they think is best for the big picture. Yet they understand when to relinquish their right to dominate a discussion or smother the thoughts of their colleagues through persistent arguments, no matter how politely made.

Flossie cannot determine the distinction between healthy wrangling and domineering discord. Flossie wants her way, every step of the way. Staff often bristle and feel angry, frustrated, and resentful by her oppositional antics. Healthy teachers understand assertive speaking skills. They know how to communicate with Flossie on matters of meaning and priority to them.

They realize when the greater good is jeopardized by a domineering and dictatorial personality. Their silence sometimes says more than words as they sit back and let Flossie run out of wind, refusing to be trapped in her invitation for contention. Instead, they wait patiently and quietly until a space in the conversation opens into which they can plant a wise and intelligent comment. Flossie may have the last word in a dialogue, but healthy teachers refuse to give her victory over their hearts and minds.

Disloyal Doyle

Emotionally healthy teachers understand loyalty as it applies to students, their school community, and their district as a whole. They know that it is important to share student confidences with a social worker or administrator when there is potential abuse, but they also know that when they have had a heart-to-heart conversation with a student that included information not relevant to the child's safety, mention of it remains between them alone.

The loyalty of a healthy teacher to the school community means expressing grievances to the persons involved in a disagreement, not with a colleague in the grocery store within earshot of the general public. Loyal teachers lend support to the mission of their building and district. They use proper channels to express concerns, and they refrain from airing out private school matters in their neighborhoods and in the marketplace. Disloyal Doyle does not understand that breaching loyalty negatively disturbs social patterns in his school.

When a student seeks to bond with him by sharing her secret dream to be a pediatrician who works in a Third World country, Doyle dribbles her private goal to colleagues during his typical after-school debriefing. In doing so, he has dishonored the loyalty entrusted him by his student. He does not stop there. When he uses his smartphone, he is not being smart as he tells his brother on the West Coast about a student with autism in his class as the neighbor of the family pushes a stroller past him, having heard enough.

For some time Doyle has believed that his building principal has sent too many teachers to workshops, replacing them with substitute teachers. That annoys him because he is more comfortable working with his hall buddies. Instead of discussing this in-house, Doyle "lets it rip" with his pal from another building while selecting hose pieces at the local hardware store. Doyle's pal, on the other hand, feels uncomfortable discussing these matters in a public place. Doyle's disloyalty becomes obvious to the owner, a fishing buddy of his principal. Due to his indiscretion, Doyle damages his social relationships with three people.

During contract negotiations, Doyle wanted badly to return to work. His discomfort with the process escalated when his union chose to go on strike. Doyle felt uncomfortable in the midst of conflict and was not sure what the hubbub was about anyway. He could give or take a few hundred here and there. Also, he did not think that the retired teachers deserved continued health insurance coverage at its present rate. Not only did Doyle think this, but he also told his brother-in-law all about it over a beer at the local burger and tap where they met each Friday.

As the conversation progressed, his voice grew louder, and other customers, also union members on strike whom Doyle had never met, overheard his entire conversation. They pulled Doyle aside at the next district-wide union meeting and explained that loyalty and unity would bring this thing to a swifter end than would complaints aired in a public place. They reminded him that he stood to benefit from the health package when he retired as well.

Moments of indiscretion occur, and teachers err in sharing some information and personal opinions with the wrong people at the wrong time. Mature teachers stop to consider the results of their words, and they determine how to balance loyalty to students, their school community, and district with a need to express their opinions. They take time to release their concerns in a journal and choose their confidants and the location of their sharing carefully.

Working with Disloyal Doyle brings on some complications in the social systems where he operates. To engage in discussion with Doyle reinforces his indiscretions. Removing oneself from his company or changing the subject helps to maintain personal loyalty to the trusting students, families, and employers who expect better. When a colleague directly tells Doyle that he does not want to hear more and that he perceives the discussion as being disloyal, the colleague is offering Doyle a growth opportunity at a teachable moment.

Reclusive Lucy

Social connections enhance work relationships. Healthy teachers take time to find out about the interests, families, and plans of their colleagues. Conversation starters built on personal knowledge of one's peers enhance the bonds of connection among teachers. Taking time out to discuss the success or struggles of a local sports team over coffee and partnering for an after-school walk that includes small talk and personal sharing allows for social time that may help sustain a professional relationship strained the next day by a curricular conflict.

Throughout her career as a teacher, Reclusive Lucy has never understood the value of making social contact with her peers. Lucy does not understand that sharing recipes or listening to a teacher proudly describe her grandchildren's first steps makes for a solid school community. Lucy does not understand the concept of community, nor does she realize the value of her contribution to that aspect of her work life. To Lucy, getting grades in on time, thoroughly completing a science unit, and getting her students to lunch promptly is what really matters.

When a new staff member entered her room when school began in the fall, Lucy crisply cut off the conversation, remarked about how much she had to get done, and directed her eyes to the pile of papers in front of her. The new teacher quickly got the message and redirected her social needs elsewhere. Lucy lost the opportunity to make a connection, gain fresh perspective, and informally mentor a willing recipient of her expertise.

Lucy loves her prep and lunch times the best. She closes her door, shuts the shades, and, after picking up a student's jacket left on the floor, puts order into her life. She loves her solitude and uses the time to not only complete her duties but to also withdraw into daydreams of a summer driving trip to the deserts of the Southwest that she plans to take alone.

When pressure is on and things get busy, social contact with colleagues impinges on the small goals and professional priorities at hand. While still adhering to these deadlines and sharing the reason for being unable to visit at the moment, emotionally healthy teachers explain that they would enjoy continuing the conversation after they have completed grades or parent conferences. They send the message that they feel interest in their colleagues but have to attend to work at the moment.

They convey the importance of building relationships by offering reassurance that there will be opportunities to socialize at a future time. When Lucy cuts off her colleagues, they receive a message that is more about her than it is about them. They eventually realize that Lucy's curtness is about her inability to develop and sustain social relationships. She allows her lack of social skills to overrule her need to spend time with others seeking to create a school community based on human interaction as well as academic excellence.

CONCLUSION

The sixteen fictitious teachers presented in this chapter work among the mature and healthy staff members in many schools. They also serve as means to identify such tendencies within all teachers, who from time to time lose sight of their professionalism and desire for personal growth. When such individuals occupy space on a faculty or reside within the best of staff, they create challenges for all involved.

Unhealthy teachers who are governed by certain dominant emotions, who use counterproductive communication styles and ways of relating, and whose social patterns diminish the cohesiveness of the faculty present negative models for what a professional should be. Their gift to any group is their demonstration of a contrast to the image of a healthy professional. A healthy professional, upon realizing these unwholesome ways of operating, will wisely choose to go in the opposite direction.

ACTION PLAN

1. Educators should assess the general emotional category of challenging coworkers and relate with them in ways appropriate to the way these staff members behave.
2. Educators need to view the behavior of their coworkers with the understanding that it is a choice that they may be able to influence but not necessarily control.
3. Educators may want to begin peer mentoring, officially or unofficially, in order to help bring an immature coworker to a more mature manner of acting in the school setting.
4. Educators should keep the big picture in mind when it comes to viewing the achievements of their peers, realizing that when one succeeds it benefits many.
5. Educators should use judgment about what information they share with certain peers.

6. Educators should work on their own behavior and attitudes and watch to maintain personal integrity in the face of challenging peer attitudes and behaviors.

Chapter Eleven

Advocacy for Children versus Job Security

Advocacy for children is my calling
But some educators find that appalling
I just can't go along
I know I have to be strong
Every day I see what a child needs
I must learn how and to whom I plead
Success for this child depends on me
I must make sure he can be all he can be
But what trouble will I find myself in
Advocating for children around here is like committing a sin
I must learn how to effectively advocate
I can do so if I positively communicate.

Each day, educators work with children who may need more than what those educators can give them. They believe that they should advocate for the needs of their children. While doing that though, they may become unpopular with the building administrator, who is strapped for money and does not believe that the school should provide a specific service.

They attend an IEP planning meeting for a student, and they believe that a child needs more speech/language services, but the administrator says that no additional service is available in the school district. They suspect that a student is being abused; all educators are mandated reporters, but fellow colleagues warn them that they are not supposed to file such a report because the administrator does not want other agencies involved in the school.

How do educators handle standing up for what they believe is needed for the student versus making the building administrator angry and jeopardizing their jobs? Let's look at some of the dilemmas that teachers often face in their role and some suggested methods for dealing with these challenges.

FULLY UNDERSTANDING THE ROLE OF THE EDUCATOR

Educators play an important role in the lives of their students—not only are educators charged with providing their students with an excellent education, but they are also charged with protecting the students that they serve. This is a serious yet difficult role.

Teachers know that they need to protect and educate, but at times this role can become challenged by higher officials. The following depicts this challenge.

Greg was a junior high school special education teacher. One day, when Jonathan, one of his students, arrived at school, Greg noticed that Jonathan had a large bruise on his arm that had not been there before.

He also had a bruise on the left side of his face. Greg was concerned. He pulled Jonathan to an area of the classroom where the other students could not hear and asked Jonathan what had happened. Jonathan lowered his head and said, "I don't know." Greg assured Jonathan that he could tell him what had happened. Jonathan admitted, "Dad got mad at me last night and hit me."

Greg thanked Jonathan for telling him, and he told Jonathan that he had to report it so that Jonathan could get help. Jonathan seemed both sad and relieved. Greg knew that, at his first chance, he needed to go to the office and make a call to the Department of Children and Family Services, the agency in his state that handles cases of abuse and neglect.

When Greg's students went to gym class, Greg went to the office to use the phone. On the way to the office, he ran into his principal, Mrs. Terrance, and told her the story and that he was going to call the department and report the suspected abuse. Mrs. Terrance told him not to make the call—Jonathan's father belonged to an organization that the principal belonged to, and Mrs. Terrance did not want to cause any trouble in the family.

Greg was upset and said that he believed that he had to make the call—especially because Jonathan had told him that his dad hit him. Mrs. Terrance said that Jonathan probably made the whole story up, and, consequently, Mrs. Terrance forbade Greg to call the department.

Greg was very upset—he was torn. He knew that he was a mandated reporter of suspected abuse, yet his boss told him he could not call. Greg decided that he must work to protect Jonathan, and he went to the office and called the Department of Children and Family Services. At the end of the day, Greg was called to the office by Mrs. Terrance.

Mrs. Terrance told him that she was very upset and that Greg had defied her order and caused a great deal of embarrassment for the school. Greg stated that he was doing his job as a mandated reporter. Greg was surprised that Mrs. Terrance did not write him up but then figured that Mrs. Terrance did not want to do that, given that Greg was correct in the action that he took.

Greg documented the call that he made to the Department of Children and Family Services. Separately, he also wrote up the altercation that he had with Mrs. Terrance. Two weeks later, Greg's evaluation conference was scheduled.

Greg had worked in the district for over fifteen years and had never received anything less than an excellent evaluation. This time, Greg received an unsatisfactory evaluation and was told that he would be put on a remediation plan.

Greg was in shock—his career was going down the tube because he did what he was mandated to do. Greg decided that he could not let this happen. Greg went to the teachers' organization, hoping that it would represent him; but he also decided that if it would not do something, he would hire his own attorney. He was not going to let this woman ruin his career.

Fortunately, the teachers' organization in his building did represent him because Greg had documented the entire event and because the secretary in the office, when questioned by the teachers' organization, verified that Greg made the call, witnessed how upset Mrs. Terrance was, and overheard some of the comments that Mrs. Terrance made. Mrs. Terrance had to change the evaluation to satisfactory.

Greg made a decision at the end of the year that he would ask for a transfer, and he did. He left that school building knowing that he could not work for an administrator who would engage in such behavior. The secretary also left the building because she had been appalled at what she had witnessed in the behavior of Mrs. Terrance. After one more year, Mrs. Terrance's contract was not renewed.

Greg understood his role and did what he was legally obliged to do, but he did pay the price for what he did. Greg felt positive about his decision—he knew that he did what he had to do to protect Jonathan from abuse.

In an article entitled "Teachers Resign After Peer Is Fired in Mo. District" (Tonn, 2005), appearing in *Education Week* on June 8, 2005, a group of teachers resigned after a fellow teacher's contract was not renewed because she questioned an administrator over the treatment of a student.

Christa Price, a second-grade teacher, observed the principal who was also the superintendent administering a punishment in September to a fourth-grade girl—the little girl was ordered to use a five-gallon bucket to carry rocks from a former construction site to a wooded area that was near the school. The only supervision that the student was provided was that of a security camera.

Ms. Price asked the principal/superintendent to reconsider the penalty or to let the little girl conduct the activity closer to school. The principal/superintendent refused, so the teacher and some of her colleagues took turns monitoring the child.

In December, the administrator recommended that Ms. Price's contract not be renewed because she failed to support him. This was Ms. Price's fourth year in the school, and she had three previous successful reviews. Six of her colleagues who were nontenured decided to allow their contracts to expire to protest Ms. Price's dismissal, and one teacher who was tenured also resigned. The seven departing teachers issued the following statement:

> If a teacher who advocates on behalf of safety of a student is not fit to be a teacher at East Lynne or anywhere in Missouri according to this administration, then none of us are fit to teach at East Lynne. (p. 3)

Ms. Price stood up for the rights of a student and took action to protect that student from a harsh punishment. She also was concerned about the safety of the child due to the lack of supervision. She tried to work with the administrator to get him to consider a different punishment, but he would not do so. She and other teachers then provided supervision for the child.

What was also admirable in this situation was that some of the teachers joined together to stand up for what was the right thing to do. The good news for Ms. Price is that her initial certificate level was extended for another year, entitling her to gain career certification in one year.

There are several common themes in both of these situations. Both teachers stood up for what they believed was their role—to protect the needs of the student. Both teachers also understood that they answered to their administrator, and they tried to work within the system and report to the administrator first. However, when the administrator told them that he or she did not agree with them, they had to make a hard decision.

The administrator was telling them to do something that they believed was wrong, so they decided that they would do the right thing and suffer the consequences. In the final analysis, both teachers were able to continue teaching.

GAINING AN UNDERSTANDING OF THE LAWS AND REGULATIONS THAT PROTECT STUDENTS

Both of the examples in the previous section point to the importance of knowing the laws and regulations that govern the educational rights of students and the teachers who serve them. Greg knew that he was a mandated reporter of child abuse. He had attended workshops on the topic to gain a clearer understanding of what the law says about child abuse.

Ms. Price knew the laws that require the supervision of students. She also knew the importance of positive behavioral interventions as opposed to harsh punishments to change behavior.

It is critical that teachers stay current on the laws and regulations that protect students and protect them as teachers. Laws and regulations change frequently. No Child Left Behind is a good example of a law whose interpretations change frequently. Teachers must stay abreast of the changes.

No longer can teachers say that they choose not to get involved in legislation. What happens at both the federal and state level affects all teachers, so they must stay informed. They must also try to affect legislation before it passes—teachers have the opportunity to mold legislation that may affect them, and they should try to do so.

Teachers must be advocates for themselves and the students within their classrooms. Many times, educators are quick to criticize legislators for their actions: "They are always doing something to us." Educators may certainly feel that way, however, it should force them to pause to reflect on whether they have communicated with their legislators and conveyed their thoughts about the topic.

Many educators want to stay out of politics because of the dirty connotations that are brought to mind. However, there is no such thing as staying out of politics; all issues are political issues.

If educators are going to be true advocates, they must try to influence the process. When they are asked to communicate on an issue and they have a specific viewpoint, they need to voice that viewpoint to our legislators.

They also need to establish a positive working relationship with key policymakers. Voters elect representatives to our state legislatures and to Congress. They need to get to know those individuals. They need to communicate with them on issues that are of concern.

They must also study how legislators vote on specific issues, and they must voice their pleasure when they vote positively on an issue that is important to educators.

Knowledge is power. This is an old but true statement. When individuals know what the laws and regulations say, they understand better what their rights and responsibilities are. They also feel empowered to influence decision makers.

The following is an example of a teacher's role in advocacy.

Meghan, a special education teacher, is concerned about the Individuals with Disabilities Education Improvement Act and the No Child Left Behind Act. She is worried that the new requirements for highly qualified teachers may result in the loss of her job. She has worked with her professional organization to keep abreast of the changes in the law.

She has heard that there is a hearing that is coming up on the proposed regulations for that law. The hearing is in the summer, in a large city close to her home. She decides to attend the hearing. She is planning to just listen to what other people have to say. She wants to keep abreast of other people's viewpoints.

She sits for over four hours at the hearing—she listens to testimony from her professional organization and from parents, administrators, and teachers' organizations. She notes that no teacher is providing testimony on behalf of his or her situation.

No teacher is communicating what these new highly qualified provisions will mean to him or her personally. She decides then and there that if other people can testify, she can be brave enough to do the same. She signs in to testify and gives testimony based on her personal experience. She talks about what these proposed changes will mean to her within her classroom.

Officials from the U.S. Department of Education pay attention to her comments and ask her questions. She feels empowered. She has taken action and has tried to influence laws and regulations. She has become more knowledgeable and goes back to her colleagues and encourages them to write to the Department of Education to voice their opinions on the "highly qualified teacher" provisions per the Individuals with Disabilities Education Improvement Act and the No Child Left Behind Act.

Not only did she gain knowledge and take action, but she also shared that knowledge and, by doing so, empowered her peers.

JOINING LISTSERVS, E-MAIL NETWORKS, AND ENGAGING IN SOCIAL MEDIA

Educators may ask themselves "How do I really keep abreast of what is going on? How do I know when hearings are happening? How do I find out whether I am the only teacher out there dealing with this situation?"

Educators are at a distinct advantage in today's world with such easy access to other people so quickly. Communication is much easier and quicker for everyone now than it was ten to fifteen years ago. Educators can join a variety of listservs or e-mail networks. These allow them to get information almost instantaneously.

E-mail networks allow educators to gain quick information about what is happening at various levels—within their state or at the federal level. Professional organizations may provide information about various listservs, or educators may find information about legitimate listservs and e-mail networks on reputable websites.

Here is an example of how an effective e-mail network helped many teachers and resulted in teachers being able to advocate for their retirement future.

Over one Memorial Day weekend, the Illinois General Assembly was in session and was in the process of passing legislation that would change the early retirement options for teachers. As soon as the legislation passed, it was critical for teachers to know about it because to be eligible for the benefits for the next two years, the teacher had to notify the school district of his or her intention to retire before the governor signed the legislation.

It was anticipated that the governor might sign the legislation at any time. Consequently, all the teachers' organizations were sending out e-mails over the weekend to notify the teachers of what they needed to do. They were also posting updates on Facebook. If teachers were not members of e-mail networks or Facebook, they did not know the information.

Years ago, organizations did letter-writing campaigns or utilized telephone trees to notify people about what was happening. Letters, however, are delayed, and sometimes by the time that a person gets the information, it is already out of date.

Telephone trees have to rely on people's making telephone calls and catching people at home. If one person fails to call people on the tree, they do not get the information. E-mail or Facebook have become the quickest way to access information because people can communicate any time, day or night, provided they have computer access.

Educators may find that they have a question about something that affects them in their classroom. To be an effective advocate, they must be able to access answers to questions. Sometimes they may not know the answer, but with a quick e-mail, they can get a speedy response.

They may also find that an e-mail network, listserv, or Facebook is a good support system for them. It is good to talk to other people who may be facing the same classroom challenges.

BECOMING INVOLVED IN THE LOCAL TEACHERS' ORGANIZATION

Educators can derive a great deal of satisfaction by being involved in their local teachers' organization. This organization gives a person a feeling of belonging with other educators who share interests, concerns, and frustrations. This is the group through which educators can advocate for better salaries and better working conditions.

If the teacher is concerned about the way he or she has been treated within a school, this organization can be helpful. Some states and locales have stronger teachers' organizations than those in other areas. Regardless of the strength of the organization, it provides educators a mechanism for voicing concerns and advocating for positive change within a school building. Here is a fictitious illustration to show this point.

Julie has worked within her school district for the last five years. She has advocated for safety in her school building. She is concerned that there is no security check-in when people come into the building. She has voiced her concern to the administrator, but nothing has been done.

One day, an angry parent enters the school and goes into the classroom, causes a disturbance, and tries to hit Julie. Luckily, Julie is able to avoid being hit and get the parent out of the classroom. Julie has never been active in her teachers' organization, but she decides at that time that she needs to get involved. She must advocate for the safety of her students and herself.

She attends the next meeting of the teacher organization; of course, every other teacher is also concerned about what happened to Julie in her classroom. Julie is asked to serve on a safety committee.

The committee outlines a plan of action and goes to the administration and requests the development of a plan. Because the teachers' organization has become involved, the administration agrees to put together a task force right away. Julie serves on the task force, and within two months there are new security procedures in the school. She had advocated successfully for safety for her students and the educators who serve the children.

INVOLVEMENT IN NATIONAL AND STATEWIDE PROFESSIONAL ORGANIZATIONS

A sad phenomenon that has been occurring over the last fifteen years is a decrease in membership in professional organizations. Many educators are no longer joiners of organizations anymore—they do not believe that they have the time or the money.

This is really unfortunate because state and national professional organizations can be a wonderful support and informational system for educators. Those organizations are ways that educators can keep current in the field. The dues are well worth it; in return, educators can network with others, advocate for best practices in their field, and make a positive difference for the profession.

Educators also can make lifelong friendships and meet people from across the state or the nation. Those professional relationships can affect lives positively.

As an example, the authors of this book met each other through their national professional organization many years ago and have kept in contact via the organization and e-mail throughout those years. They have collaborated in the writing of several articles and have written books together. This would not have happened if they had not become involved in their professional organization.

Another reason that educators are not joining organizations is that some administrators are not encouraging membership in other groups. They are not allowing teachers to attend conferences outside the school system. Some administrators have done this intentionally—if they do not allow teachers to attend conferences or be part of organizations, then teachers do not know what is happening and can only receive information that is controlled by the school district. Here is a true story.

A teacher learns about a professional conference in her state and is impressed by the program. There are sessions on making adaptations and accommodations for students with special needs, information about the latest on teacher certification, and positive discipline strategies. She is excited about the conference and asks for a professional day to attend the conference. She is turned down. She then offers to pay her own way, so the only expense is for the district to pay for her substitute. The district administrator refuses to allow her to attend.

The teacher learns from other fellow teachers that the administrator will not allow anyone to attend a workshop that is not planned by the school district—he does not want anyone to learn any strategies other than those that are specifically endorsed by him.

The teacher then learns that the conference has sessions on Saturday, so she decides to attend on Saturday. What she learns that Saturday is worthwhile to her—there are practical strategies that she can utilize in her classroom, and she meets some other educators with whom she has interests in common. They exchange e-mails and continue to communicate with each other. She joins the organization.

The next year, she is asked to serve on a committee for the statewide organization. She feels empowered and important in her role. She moves up in the organization; the board meetings are held on the weekend.

The year that she is elected president of the organization is when the principal who had kept her from attending the organization leaves the district. The new administrator does not feel threatened and is pleased that she is so active in an organization.

She then encourages other colleagues in her building to become involved in the organization. She grows professionally and has the opportunity to affect, through her professional organization, state and national policy issues. She is truly being an advocate and becomes a leader in her field because she took that step to devote one Saturday to attend a conference.

Many state and national organizations provide not only conferences and networking opportunities but also advocacy services for their members. As an example, a teacher may be upset because she has an overload of students within her class. She is afraid to complain because her principal might become angry with her. She learns, however, that her organization operates a hotline for teachers where teachers can anonymously report violations of state class-size limits.

She utilizes the hotline. The organization then files a request for the State Department of Education to investigate the class size.

In a 2003 report entitled *Synthesis brief: Supply and demand of special education professionals* (Muller & Markowitz), the authors reported that several studies suggest that teachers with high levels of professional and organizational commitment are likely to remain in the field.

This makes sense—when the going gets rough for some teachers, it is nice to have the collegiality and support of a professional organization. The educator can look forward to attending the next conference of the organization—such a conference can recharge someone who is feeling frustrated or stressed.

ESTABLISHING A POSITIVE WORKING RELATIONSHIP AND COMMUNICATING FREQUENTLY WITH THE BUILDING ADMINISTRATOR

Administrators want to know what is going on within their schools. They want to have the pulse of the building. Teachers may not always agree with some of the decisions that an administrator has to make every day in the building, but it is important to better understand why they make the decisions they do.

Administrators tend to like teachers who keep them informed and ask for their advice and guidance. They certainly prefer that they ask them a question rather than jump into a decision that might not be perceived as correct.

Teachers will certainly get off on the wrong foot when the administrator finds out that they have gone to a school board member and voiced a complaint when they have not told the administrator about their concerns.

If the teacher has approached the administrator about a concern and does not feel that it has adequately been addressed, it is a good idea to follow up again and find out what was or was not done. The administrator may be working on the situation, but a resolution is taking longer than anticipated.

If the teacher still does not believe that the concerns have been addressed, the teacher will want to put the concerns in writing as a follow-up and keep a copy of the letter. As much as possible, the teacher should make sure the follow-up letter or e-mail is worded positively. Here is an example:

April 5, 2012

Dear Ms. Burns:

Thank you so much for meeting with me last week about my request for a new computer for my classroom. According to Nathan's IEP, he is in need of the computer for doing his math.

The problem I am having is that Jeremy, Beth, and Melissa also need to have access to the computer during that time. Since there are only two computers in my classroom, this has presented many problems. As we discussed, I have been having trouble with one of the computers. I will appreciate any assistance you can provide.

Ms. Dorris

In an earlier chapter, we discuss the need that the administrator may have for power and control, so it is critical that the teacher keep the administrator informed and that the teacher recognize that the administrator is responsible for overseeing the activities within the school.

If the teacher decides to go out into the community and ask a local business for a computer and has not told the administrator, the teacher will probably be in a great deal of trouble.

Imagine the administrator who receives a call from the business saying that a computer will or will not be donated to the school, and the administrator did not even know that someone from the school asked for a computer.

Administrators may also want to have access to attention and may like to have positive attention from the teachers in their building. Asking for advice and soliciting administrators' help when dealing with a problem is a boost to their egos.

Will the teacher look like she is just being a principal's pet when she communicates with the administrator? Certainly the teacher may, but communication is key to anyone's success in a school building. The teacher must be sincere in her efforts to seek advice and input.

The teacher must also seek the administrator's assistance when it is truly needed; otherwise, other teachers will view the particular teacher as an individual who runs to the administrator for every little problem. The teacher should seek advice and input when it is needed.

Effective advocacy can be best achieved through communication. If the teacher has established a positive relationship with her administrator and she communicates frequently with him or her, the teacher is more likely to be in a better position to ask for something when she needs it.

GETTING TO KNOW THE RIGHT PEOPLE

The old saying "It's who you know" is certainly true when it comes to advocacy work. Teachers can advocate better for the needs of their students when they have established a network of people who are influential in policymaking.

Too many times, educators choose to not get involved in political issues and do not believe that what happens in their local area, state legislature, and Congress affects them. Au contraire. What happens at the local school-district level—in terms of school board members and their meetings—clearly affects teachers' salaries, budgets for the classroom, and working conditions.

Educators should make a point of learning about the candidates for school board elections and where they stand on issues that are important to classroom life. One wants to think that people run for the school board because they want to improve the education of the children within the school district.

The reality is that that motive is not always present when some people run for the office. They may be running for office because they have a personal vendetta against a school administrator or are interested only in cutting costs in the district because they think that their taxes are too high. To be an effective student advocate, educators must know the platform of each candidate for office and then vote accordingly.

Once school board members are elected, educators should monitor their votes on particular issues. Some teachers' organizations assign educators to attend school board meetings so that their presence is known.

It is important that teachers know the school board members and that they educate them on the issues that are important to them. Teachers do not always have to make a formal presentation to the board; informal conversations can make a big difference.

It is also critical to know other key policymakers and leaders within the community. When teachers know those people and talk with them about educational issues, they are educating them on the needs that teachers face.

When the school administrator asks for volunteers to serve on a local chamber of commerce committee, teachers should do it, if at all possible. They will have an opportunity to share positive ideas about the school setting with members in the business world.

Teachers should make it a point to be active in local social organizations—oftentimes those organizations may provide assistance to the schools. A student may need a coat, yet you cannot afford to buy the student a coat; however, an organization might have the purchase of clothing as a service project for its organization.

People in today's society are so busy that they are joining fewer groups and are not being as active in volunteer work as people were twenty-five years ago. This is unfortunate because the personal and professional benefits of expanding horizons and helping others are many and are long lasting.

JOINING THOSE WHO SHARE SIMILAR CONCERNS

There is power in numbers. Teachers may be concerned about specific working conditions in their building but do not want to say anything. However, in the school, they hear other teachers with the same concerns.

There are many advantages to working with people who share the same concerns. They can serve as a sounding board—to advocate effectively, teachers will find it useless to just gripe about something, but will find it helpful to have others who share their concerns listen. In the process of talking with others, they are able to brainstorm with them for ideas on how to solve a problem.

Teachers may also decide, as a group, to present their case to the administrator and to propose some workable solutions to the problem. The old saying "There is safety in numbers" does hold true in some of these situations. One teacher may not be brave enough to approach the administrator on his own, but he will feel reassured to go with another person or with a group.

IDENTIFYING THE KEY POLICYMAKERS IN THE SCHOOL

We know that in the reality of today's schools, it is not always the administrator who is really in charge of the school building. There may be teachers who have been within the school for many years, and they have more power and control than what the administrator has.

The administrator may be new to the school or may not be a strong individual and therefore does not really set the unwritten policies of the school. To be an effective advocate for students or for better working conditions, each teacher needs to know these people and where they stand on specific issues.

Although the teacher may not choose to become friends with them or they may not want that teacher as a friend (as discussed in the chapter about ostracism, Chapter 13), the teacher stills needs to know their viewpoints and their beliefs about what is important in the school.

The teacher may be able to network with one of them on an issue. The teacher may ask for their advice on a particular issue, always, however, being careful about how much information is divulged. The teacher needs to know them well enough to know that they will not break a confidence. They may be flattered that the teacher has come to them to seek advice and may be able to give some assistance.

WORKING EFFECTIVELY WITH PARENTS AS ADVOCATES FOR THEIR CHILDREN

Some parents are effective advocates for their children, whereas others may not have the knowledge or the willingness to advocate for their children. Some parents may be so overwhelmed with their parenting career that they cannot stand up for the needs of their children. Other parents may be too demanding, in your eyes.

The key is to work proactively with parents to assist them in effective advocacy for their children. Chapter 8 deals with maintaining professional behavior with parents. This section deals with how to work together with parents in advocacy issues.

Think about this often-faced challenge: a parent may ask the teacher a question about whether his or her child is getting enough of the services that he or she needs. The teacher may believe that the child is not getting those services—she believes that the child needs more Title I services or more speech/language services.

The teacher tells the parent that the child is not getting enough services. The parent goes to the administrator and says, "Mrs. Johns says that my child is not getting what he needs, and I want to know why." Later the administrator comes to Mrs. Johns and "chews her out" for making such a statement to the parent. Mrs. Johns was just being honest. Is there another way that she could have dealt with this situation?

The parent came to Mrs. Johns, and Mrs. Johns agreed with the parent that the child was not getting enough services; what Mrs. Johns could have done would have been to say, "Why don't I talk with the principal and see if we can set up a meeting about your concerns." Mrs. Johns would have been advocating yet going through the appropriate channels.

Parents can be effective advocates if they have accurate information. When a parent asks a question about a particular situation, it is critical that the teacher provide accurate information while refraining from incorporating her own bias.

As an example, a parent comes to the teacher and complains that the playground supervisor is not watching the students well enough. The teacher may agree with that statement, but to bad-mouth the playground supervisor would not be wise. Instead, the teacher may say, "I hear what you are saying, and I will talk to the playground supervisor to see if we can come up with a solution."

The parent may come in and report that the bus driver is too negative with her child. Instead of saying that the teacher has heard a lot of negative comments about the bus driver, the teacher can say, "Why don't I meet with the bus driver and see if together we can work out a positive behavior management system."

Let's take this example of how Ms. Herder effectively provided information to a parent, and the parent utilized the information for the betterment of the teacher and the students in her class. Mrs. Johns is one of the parents of a student in Ms. Herder's class. Mrs. Johns is upset about the large class size that Ms. Herder has. Mrs. Johns comes to Ms. Herder and asks about the class size.

Ms. Herder provides her with the information about the number of students in her class. Mrs. Johns also wants to know whether Ms. Herder has any help in her class. Ms. Herder shares with her that there is one parent volunteer, who comes in three days a week. Ms. Herder urges Mrs. Johns to talk with the building principal.

She lets the building principal know about her conversation with Mrs. Johns and that she has requested that she meet with the principal. Mrs. Johns goes to the school board meeting and requests an aide for Ms. Herder's class. The school board approves the request.

Educators can also provide information to parents about support groups or other educational meetings where parents can receive information. Parents can be encouraged to become active in PTOs, and within those settings parents can network with other parents about common issues for which advocacy is needed.

KNOWING HOW TO ASK THE RIGHT QUESTIONS

Advocating through questioning can be an effective technique. Perhaps the teacher is sitting in a meeting, and the administrator makes a comment about an action that is going to occur. Rather than become negative and complain, the teacher might ask, "Are there any other options?" "Is this a final decision?" "Can we discuss this more?"

These questions let the administrator know that the teacher has concerns, yet they do not make the teacher look unreasonable and may cause the administrator to be less defensive and cause him or her to think thoroughly about the statement. Here is a fictitious example.

Mary has an IEP planning meeting coming up for a student, Jeremy, who is in her general education fifth-grade classroom over 70 percent of the time. She is concerned that he is in need of more special education services, but Beth, the special education teacher, has told her ahead of time that she does not have any more time to see the student.

At the IEP meeting, Beth reports that the student is not doing well but that she simply cannot provide any more services to the student because she does not have enough time. It appears that the other IEP members are going along with Beth. Mary is upset and believes that she must advocate for Jeremy's need for service.

She decides to ask these questions: "Can we review Jeremy's goals to see whether we are able to meet the goals with his current program?" This causes the group to reflect on whether Jeremy's goals are being met within the given time frame—the special education placement is supposed to be designed to meet Jeremy's goals.

Another question she asks is, "Are there other options we might consider in providing services to Jeremy?" Mary is advocating for the student without being offensive; instead, she is asking questions that cause the group to focus on the child's needs.

FILING MINORITY REPORTS

Both general and special educators may find themselves in IEP meetings for students with disabilities. One of the educators may feel strongly about what a student needs educationally. The educator has worked with the student and believes that she has a thorough knowledge of her or him. However, within that meeting she may find herself in a disagreement with some of the other people in that meeting.

Perhaps the administrator has decided that a specific placement will be recommended, and the educator does not agree. There are no unilateral actions in special education—the team is supposed to make the decision through the process of consensus.

It may also be that five of the team members agree with a decision about the needs of the child, but two do not agree. There is a process by which those who do not agree with the decision of the majority of the group can voice their disagreement in writing.

Everyone has the right to file a minority report, which becomes part of the IEP. In terms of advocacy for students, this is each educator's right to voice their beliefs about the needs of a student with a disability. Let's look at this example that one of the authors encountered.

Ms. Johns was scheduled to attend an IEP meeting. Before the meeting, an administrator visited her and said that he wanted the student placed in a particular type of program. Ms. Johns was surprised that the person would provide his opinion before the IEP meeting—before he had a chance to hear all the information about the student.

What was more surprising to her was that the administrator proceeded to tell her that he wanted her to agree with him in the meeting. She replied calmly that she would make her decision when she got to the meeting and heard all of the information about the student.

The administrator was not happy with her. At the meeting, he clearly tried to sway the group—he was successful with most people there. However, Ms. Johns did not believe that the decision was in the best interest of the student. Another team member agreed with Ms. Johns.

There was consensus for the decision that the administrator wanted. However, Ms. Johns calmly stated that she did not agree and that she would file a minority report that would indicate her disagreement and rationale for her decision—she outlined what she believed was the appropriate placement for the student. The other team member signed the minority report along with Ms. Johns. Ms. Johns wanted in the record what she believed was in the best interest of the child—she engaged in advocacy for that child.

CONCLUSION

To advocate is to plead in favor of another person. You as an educator must advocate for the needs of your students; this certainly may be easier said than done. Every day, we must do what is right for the children. We have to decide what we are willing to do and how we can best achieve our goal of advocacy. Through this chapter, we provide educators with the tools that they need to advocate positively on behalf of children.

ACTION PLAN

1. Educators should join networks that keep them abreast of the latest laws and regulations that impact them.
2. Educators should stay current with the status of laws and regulations that impact them.
3. Educators should be active in their professional organizations.
4. Educators should establish a positive and open communication system with the building administration.

5. Educators should get to know and establish a positive rapport with influential individuals within the community.

6. Educators should establish a positive partnership with parents.

REFERENCES

Muller, E., & Markowitz, J. (2003). *Synthesis brief: Supply and demand of special education professionals.* Washington, DC: Project Forum at National Association of State Directors of Special Education.

Tonn, J. (2005). Teachers resign after peer is fired in Mo. district. *Education Week, 24*(39), 3.

Chapter Twelve

Ways to Open Avenues to Acceptance

It's a common expression
"All things being equal"
Inserted casually into a sentence
But are they equal?
In education
Across the nation
Maybe more needs to happen to bring this about.

Sara is a third-grade teacher and has been teaching for the past five years. She finished her teacher preparation program from Michigan and completed her master's degree before she got her first job. She has always been concerned with the issues of equal access to opportunities for students with disabilities. She got involved with students with special needs because she has a brother with autism and her family has been actively involved in his education. She wants to ensure he receives the best possible services.

Despite the tremendous emphasis on social acceptance of students with disabilities, these students are marginalized from the mainstream society. Sara believes that her brother may have developed strategies for academic learning but he still lacks social skills that are necessary for effective social functioning. He also shows difficulty in developing relationships with peers and adults. She is concerned that he may face a bleak future in the real world if he does not improve his social behavior. He can't read the social cues emanating from his contexts. He really does not know how to recognize a social issue and fails to generate solutions to social problems.

Even in her courses that she took from college, Sara always looked for innovative pathways for students with autism. She sought input from her instructors and colleagues. She went over and beyond in meeting the course objectives and expectations. She really wanted to contribute to the future of these children. She did her internships and student teaching in the schools that were serving children with autism and learning disabilities.

Now as a teacher, Sara integrates social skills and social problem-solving strategies in her instruction. She attends to the social functioning of her students as much as she attends to their academic needs. She encourages her third-grade resource students to participate in the general education curricular activities as much as possible. She ensures that her students have access to equal opportunity and advantage for participation in experiences as do their normative peers.

She has learned from her personal life, her training, and her professional context how important it is to accept students with disabilities and to promote them in all possible aspects of life. She sees her students beyond their disability, as people with dignity and desire to grow. Besides knowing the causes of their disabilities, she focuses on possibilities and opportunities that may enable them to lead the best lives that they can.

Mike, the school psychologist in Sara's school, sometimes thinks that Sara is too involved with her students, and he keeps telling her that she needs to loosen up, be more detached and less concerned about her students' progress. He continuously reminds her that many of her students do not have the capacity to learn; therefore, she should not expect too much from them. She disagrees with his opinion and keeps doing what she is doing. Is she doing the right thing? Should she pay attention to what Mike is saying? Is she overindulged in seeking true success for students with disabilities?

Many beginning teachers face this dilemma and struggle with these issues. As they get out of the teacher preparation programs, they believe that the world out there is going to be fair toward students with special needs. They get a shock when they find themselves in situations like Sara's. Those teachers who are strong advocates of students with special needs keep doing the right things; others tend to give up.

ISSUES OF EQUITY IN RESEARCH AND PRACTICE

Teachers have to be concerned about the issues of equity in opportunities if they want to work with students with special needs. They have to be interested in the success of these students. They have to go beyond solely holding a professional career of a teacher in order to create situations that are likely to produce successful outcomes for students with special needs.

Although many social scientists and researchers have been conducting "disability" research since the 1950s and have drawn attention to the economic and social inequalities encountered by people with disabilities, a few have questioned the underlying cause of these problems (Barnes, 2003). The simplest explanation that they can provide is that impairment or disability is the main reason why people with disabilities are disadvantaged. Oftentimes, they forget to see how much a person with a disability can do or accomplish.

Perceptions around disability can incapacitate growth and learning opportunities for many of these students. Research that is based on a medical approach could only suggest cure or care as an option for the individuals with disabilities. The idea of capacity building and growth is not suggested. Professionals guided by a medical approach find themselves unsuccessful if they cannot come up with interventions that provide a cure for the disability. This perspective does not allow for examining the role of social, cultural, and environmental factors that serve as additional barriers and prevent access and participation in educational and social contexts. Thus, this further adds to the disadvantage of individuals with disabilities.

In recent years, however, the emancipatory disability research has assisted in providing a clearer focus on the economic, environmental, and cultural barriers encountered by people having some form of disability (Barton, 2005). Some of these barriers include lack of access to meaningful education systems; inadequate working environments; inequity in employment and disability benefits; discriminatory health and social support services; and lack of transportation, housing, and insurance facilities. Others include promoting negative or apprehensive opinions about strengths of students who have disabilities. The greatest impediment to acceptance of disabilities is the negative perception of disabilities continually presented in the media—films, television, and newspapers.

Perceptions of others about disability oftentimes play a significant role in how people with disabilities respond to their social contexts. If Sara will see disabilities in her students first, she will overlook their strengths, and then she may not be able to assist them in their learning. She does not subject herself to the biases promoted by the media; rather, she searches for scientifically based approaches and attempts to apply them in her classroom. She creates a congenial context around her students that allows them to display their strengths. While she accepts their disability, she also provides them with an opportunity for growth.

If the cultural environment only promotes biases where people see impairment as being unattractive and unwanted, the individual with a disability is likely to develop additional issues of inadequate self-esteem, pessimism, and depression. The job of an educator is to create opportunities of growth for these individuals.

Along with that, an educator must understand how students with disabilities learn, how a student who is in a wheelchair and has speech impairment can apply the augmentative device for communication. A student who has no physical ability to use his arms or legs can tour the school independently with a powered chair. Perhaps a success story of how such a person helps others in a similar situation teaches a child to learn about his or her strengths and capacities.

Oftentimes, parents do not know how to bring up a child who is born with disability, since they have never encountered a similar experience. It is a brand-new experience for them to raise this child, so they treat this child based on what they have learned about disability from the world around them.

People who became disabled later in life also rely on what others have gone through in similar situations. If their contexts are filled with bias and negativity, they are likely to have uncertainty about the possibility of growth. It is not surprising that many people do not know how to respond when they encounter disability and fail to get included in the lives of the other people.

Promotion of negative outcomes are seen when a disability interacts with a lack of interpersonal support, with discrimination, and/or with exclusion. People must understand the strengths within the disability. It is imperative that success stories be brought to light in order to change the perceptions of people about disabilities.

Sara believes that as an educator she must fully involve students with disabilities in her teaching process. She also keeps herself actively involved in their learning process from beginning to end. She keeps herself opened to procedures and practices that are beneficial for her students. Her greatest strength is that she is committed to creating a better position for each of her students by confronting their disabling barriers and by not submitting to them.

Emancipatory disability research produces knowledge that has some meaningful practical outcomes for individuals with disabilities, their strengths, and their struggles. Sara attends those conferences where people with disabilities share their insights. In addition to reading the articles in the refereed journals, she tries to attend the forums where individuals with disabilities share their experiences and success stories. A society that is increasingly organized around the needs of a comfortable majority tends to develop a disabling attitude toward individuals with special needs. Sara thinks it is important to get the firsthand information by participating in the lives of people with a disability.

Disability should not merely meet with empathy or concern; it needs to reach out for opportunities and preparation for success in life. To reach this goal, educators need to create situations that lead to this path. They need to provide full access to interventions that prepare students for challenges in life and provide them resources that enable lifelong support.

ACCESSIBILITY TO INTERVENTIONS THAT MEET STUDENT NEEDS

Accessibility means creating opportunities for participation in various life situations that have been repeatedly shown to contribute to healthy adjustments of individuals. A consistent finding is that students with disabilities participate in effective social situations less often than do children without disabilities. Sara is aware that developing meaningful activities for her students will help them participate in general education environments. At the same time, she understands the value of specialized interventions that her students may need, such as anger management, self-control strategies, and social problem solving.

Students with disabilities cannot be put in one-size-fits-all-type programs. Specialized interventions are based on the premise that students need individualized and differentiated learning opportunities in order to be successful. Many students need intensive instruction and individualized approaches in order to achieve academically and also to grow socially and emotionally. Others may need more time in least restrictive environments, which often leads them to interact with their normative peers. Some may still need self-contained settings because they function better when they are within a secure and predictable environment.

Sara uses the whole continuum of options, and her students achieve success when such approaches are utilized to meet their individual needs. Sara has noticed that her students often learn best with direct instructional practices and strategies. Oftentimes they need more prompting, cueing, and repetition, which may interfere with the instructional approaches that general educators like to adopt. Sara keeps in mind the evidence of effectiveness of these practices, and she uses them for each student's individual needs.

As important as academic success may be, the emotional well-being of students with disabilities is just as important. Special education classrooms provide the opportunities for teaching self-efficacy along with functional and social skills. Many students with disabilities find success in the smaller, supportive environment of the resource room. They find themselves lost in general education primarily due to a lack of support in the environment. Educators should not be placing all students with special needs in inclusive environments without specialized resources and supports that they need for differentiated programming.

The authors have accumulated approximately seventy-five years of experience total and have had the opportunity to learn from many teachers who worked with students with emotional and behavioral disorders. They have known instances in which students with emotional and behavioral disorders have sabotaged reentry into general education classes by engaging in inappropriate behavior.

For instance, Michael deliberately engages in vocal vulgarity within the general education classroom when asked to do math. The reason for this behavior is that Michael has difficulty completing math tasks and adopts escape tactics in order to avoid the situation. Students like Michael think that they are not allowed to learn in a context that is more productive for them. He probably needs additional supports to be successful in the general education environment. These supports are only available in his self-contained environment.

Another issue that seems to be interfering in providing the continuum of options is that many educators do not perceive special education as a service; they view it as placement. The purpose of special education is to provide enrichment in learning to all students with special needs. The concept of continuum contains in itself the essential fluidity in the processes and the notion that one can go back and forth in providing these specialized services and supports according to their needs. It is important to understand various learning styles of students with special needs and align instructional strategies accordingly.

USING COMMUNICATION THAT REFLECTS ACCEPTANCE

Special educators need to share information with parents, administrators, and other service providers. They should seek information on the types of activities that allow for creative individual programs for children with special needs. Special educators should keep themselves aware of the emerging research that shows the best practices for children with disabilities.

Special educators must keep themselves abreast with the instructional practices and preferences of students who come from various cultural backgrounds. They should discuss new strategies with colleagues who are working with students without disabilities. This may increase the general educators' understanding of the needs of students with disabilities and the resources available to support them.

Sara always keeps in mind that she needs to be an effective communicator. She must view the social environment (family, peer group, school, local neighborhood, culture) as a major source of influence on the overall development of young people. Sara makes an effort to understand the nature of the relationship between environmental factors (e.g., family, school culture, peer relationships) and person-oriented mechanisms (e.g., social skills deficits, low self-esteem) by which students with disabilities are affected.

She organizes a family night when all the parents, guardians, and grandparents of her students come to meet with her and one another. She asks them if they have any specific interests that they can share with the whole class, such as their careers on the career day, the art masterpiece and the work of an artist, whether they can help in any school events, and so forth. Parents seem to be pleased with Sara; they find her truly interested in student learning and growth.

PROVIDING CRISIS INTERVENTIONS WHEN NEEDED

Susan starts her day as any other day. Some students gather in the hallways; some are talking on the playground; some are slamming lockers; others begin to enter into the cafeteria; and some go to their classrooms. School starts. No one expects that something would go wrong that day. Four periods have gone by. All of a sudden a student collapses in the cafeteria with his peers all around. Shauna screams, "Blood." A distraught paraprofessional rushes into the cafeteria and asks someone to call the nurse. Susan takes her students from the resource classroom for lunch. She is uncertain about what she should do now and how she should help the students. She needs to remind herself that she needs to stay calm.

She knows that in crisis, she has a tendency to become anxious and overactive, and it is important for her to assess her own feelings and whether she can model a calm, appropriate response. She also needs to evaluate whether the situation is dangerous for her students, who have already begun to show the symptoms of anxiety and panic. Heidi screams, "Oh my! I think he is dead." Tara starts crying. Nancy starts asking if she can call her mom and go home.

Susan decides to figure out the accuracy of the information. She sees the nurse coming, and she goes toward the location where the situation emerged and asks her what has happened. The nurse calls 911 and asks for a paramedic to rush to the cafeteria. George, a twelve-year-old, had a seizure and collapsed, which caused a fracture in his skull.

Susan reassures her students that George is being taken to the hospital and doctors will take care of him. She takes her students back to their classroom; however, the students are not ready for their class work. She asks them to do what they feel like doing and assures them that she will stay with them for as long as needed. She provides them with paper and asks them to draw their feelings. She informs the parents by sending a letter providing updated information about the incident. She also seeks assistance from her school psychologist and adds his contact information to further provide information to them about community supports and counseling resources.

Students have started questioning about how George is doing at the hospital. Is he in the emergency room? Is he going to be alright? There has not been any news. It is important for Susan to take care of herself and her feelings. She decides to take her students to the library, where they will feel more peaceful. She is also worried about what is going to happen to George. In the meantime, she sees the principal coming to her class. The principal tells her that "George is in critical condition."

After coming back from the library, she tells her students about George's condition. She helps them in gathering their thoughts about what they would like to say to George at this time and asks them to put those thoughts in their papers. She takes those papers to the principal's office because the principal plans to visit the family to share the feelings of George's peers. Susan also finds out that the principal is going to send a letter describing this incident to parents.

A few days later the school was notified that George's fracture would heal within six weeks; however, he would not be able to attend school during that time. Susan finds this as an opportunity for her students to expand their situational realms. She talks to the principal about visiting George in the hospital. The principal asks the parents, who gave permission for them to visit after a couple of weeks. She informs her students that they would all make a field trip to the hospital to visit George after a couple of weeks.

Prior to visiting, she coaches the students on what to expect (so that the hospital does not bring unexpected anxiety to any students) while visiting George. Along with them, they brought a big poster board saying "Get Well Soon, George!" with additional commentary from each individual student plus Susan.

Despite the perfect arrangements in school life, a crisis can happen that may warrant teacher attention. It is important to develop skills for providing effective crisis intervention. Teachers should encourage students to communicate their feelings not only in discussions or conversations but also through display of poems, pictures, and drawings.

PROMOTING PREVENTION

Before a crisis happens, it is important that students be taught conflict-resolution strategies and skills for coping with difficult situations, disappointments, and struggles. When students are prepared with choices in potentially difficult situations, they are more likely to face them effectively. Teachers can use scenarios, role-plays, and simulated situations to provide them practice for generating solutions that are safe and effective.

Sara uses a suggestion box for students to report their concerns anonymously. This provides Sara with the knowledge she needs about some situations that may be brewing and warrants her attention to prevent further escalation.

Sara continually engages in discussions with her students that help them see possibilities in the future. Some of her students are unable to see their future or are confused about it. Therefore, they engage in disruptive behaviors to get her attention. To provide them with positive attention, she encourages her students to share their interests, hobbies, and talents and celebrate their success in these activities.

Teachers like Sara and Susan examine the context of the school and the needs of students. Threats to safety are promoted when students in a school have not learned adaptive responses to social situations. Social skills training may also assist in developing specific, prosocial, and desirable responses among these students.

In addition, teachers may want to teach basic social problem-solving skills to their students. They should teach them how to identify a problem, how to generate solutions, and how to evaluate solutions and consequences. Some students may need anger management and self-control training. Teachers should provide them with opportunities for learning these skills.

PROMOTING A SENSE OF ACCEPTANCE

It is important that all children—those who have special needs, those who do not always fall within the traditional format of the family, those who come from households that have suffered the strains of civil war, those who are affected by HIV/AIDS, and so on—are accepted in the teacher's classroom.

The teacher's primary job is to teach and not to judge why a student has a specific condition and why it has occurred in the student's life. They need to prepare themselves for what they can do for the student, how they can support the student academically, behaviorally, and emotionally. Teachers should not attribute student situations to their deficits.

Another example is students who are HIV-positive. The first thing to keep in mind is their confidentiality. Any medical documentation submitted to school becomes a record that must be treated with confidentiality. Schools are committed to nondiscrimination against those who are HIV-positive. Teachers should also exercise confidentiality while dealing with such cases and try to gain more accurate information about HIV.

To prevent unnecessary concerns, appropriate information and education on HIV infection and AIDS, including how the virus is transmitted, should be made available to staff, students, and their parents. Teachers should be aware that when students with such conditions have to take a leave of absence for their medical condition, they need to be considerate and should maintain confidentiality about these events. Counseling and medical support should be available for these students on a regular basis.

RESPECTING DIVERSITY

Students benefit from an environment that appreciates and respects diversity. The teacher who shows regard for the cultures represented in the classroom builds a respectful and trusting climate. The teachers who treat the various cultures and languages that their students represent in their classrooms as assets, not as weaknesses, are likely to create opportunities for success for their students. At this point in educational history, teachers would do a great disservice to the future generations if they encourage people to think that knowing only one culture and speaking only one language is enough.

It is not going to serve the future generations of students with disabilities well if they are not encouraged to use technology and the Internet, when it is apparent that they have brought the whole world closer together. Teachers must examine their own cultural backgrounds and their biases. They should develop understanding of the effects their biases can have when they interact with students of diverse linguistic and cultural backgrounds.

PROMOTING HIGHER EDUCATION GOALS

The image and traditional profile that individuals with disabilities are older, poorer, less educated, and less likely to be employed have started to change. There has been a significant increase in the number of students with disabilities seeking higher education. This increase in numbers has been due partly to enhanced technology, expanded support services, and higher expectations of what students with disabilities can accomplish.

It also has changed because people around them have begun to see them as individuals first. The federal laws mandating services for students with special needs have assisted in reaching this level of accomplishment. General education and special education teachers have employed accommodations to support the learning processes of these students. The colleges and schools have developed attitudes of inclusion and acceptance, which have shaped the disability programs. Students with disabilities are fulfilling their academic and social aspirations.

Indeed, it is this acceptance of students with disabilities that has shaped various disability programs to change the outcomes for students with disabilities. The following are a few simple suggestions that may enhance teachers' ability to show acceptance for students with disabilities.

Engaging in Active Listening

Teachers should know that they may not be able to solve all problems of all students. When they develop trust and listen to students to truly understand their needs, they present a rare gift: they give the young people the trust and understanding that they have the ability to express their concerns. It is not up to the teacher to solve all the students' problems or to know all the possible solutions. A simple way to start is by just asking them how they are doing.

Throwing Biases out the Window

If the teacher knows a child and family with special needs, then they know only one student or a family. They should not compare them to other students with special needs or their families because the uniqueness of that child and family is incomparable. Each child with special needs has gone through his or her unique part of the journey. Each case is idiosyncratic; its characteristics may be distinctive to its own case.

Offering Positive Help

The greatest help the teacher can offer to a student with special needs is to provide the best possible instruction, assistance, and support in the learning processes and opportunities for social success. They should always remember, success in life is largely determined by the degree of social acceptance that one can achieve. A challenge for students with special needs is to promote their functional and social competence in their overall growth and development. A teacher should become an advocate for his or her students and their needs.

Promoting Adoption of Best Practice

Teachers need to have awareness about universal accessibility and usability of products and services that benefit students with special needs. They should raise awareness and promote the knowledge of other stakeholders about how students with disabilities need to be accepted in the process of success.

ACTION PLAN

1. Educators should become active listeners to serve as advocates for students with disabilities.
2. Teachers should be aware of the issues of equity and open various avenues of acceptance for their students with special needs.
3. Teachers should expose students with special needs to a full range of interventions and supports that prepare them for challenges in life.

4. Educators need to maintain confidentiality about students' personal and medical documentation.

5. Educators should develop understanding of the effects that their biases may have when they interact with students of diverse linguistic and cultural backgrounds.

6. Educators should make themselves aware of best practices for universal accessibility that benefit students with special needs.

REFERENCES

Barnes, C. (2003). What a difference a decade makes: reflections on doing 'emancipatory' disability research. *Disability and Society*, 18(1), 3–17.

Barton, L. (2005). Emancipatory research and disabled people: some observations and questions. *Educational Review*, 57, 317–327.

Chapter Thirteen

Dealing with Ostracism:
From Other Teachers and Colleagues

You don't seem to care
It just isn't fair
To parties, you don't invite me
My feelings hurt, can't you see
In this school, I am so left out
The anger in me makes me want to shout.

Sarah is excited about her recent transfer for this school year to Lincoln Elementary School. After all, it is closer to her home and it is a newer school. Sarah had specifically asked for this transfer even though it had been a hard decision because she really liked the teaching staff at her previous school.

She had made many friends in the five years in which she was there. Her friends had celebrated with her and vowed that they would all still get together once a month for dinner; jokingly though, they said that Sarah might forget about them because of the friends that she would make at Lincoln.

Sarah is looking forward to making more friends but knows that she will continue her friendships with her colleagues at her previous school. They have supported her through the trials and tribulations of being a new teacher in a new locale. Sarah is sure that the staff at Lincoln will welcome her and treat her well.

Before the start of the school year, Sarah goes to school to get her classroom at Lincoln ready; she eagerly checks in at the office, and the secretary smiles and immediately lets Sarah know that she is the only new teacher at the school this year. She proudly announces that all of the staff at this school have been there at least five years and some have been at the school for over fifteen years.

Sarah replies that she is eager to meet all of them. She walks through the halls of the school, and as she sees people, she greets them with a friendly "Hi." They return her greeting and move on to where they are going. At the opening staff meeting, Sarah is friendly, and her new colleagues smile but continue in their discussions while ignoring her.

The school year begins; Sarah overhears conversations about the staff getting together for happy hour on Friday, but she is not invited. She hears discussions about a baby shower for one of the teachers in the building; she is looking forward to attending and thinks about what she will give as a gift. Sarah waits for the invitation that never comes.

Before the holiday break, she overhears conversations that one of the staff members is having a party and everyone else seems to be going. Sarah plans to go home for the holidays but will rearrange her schedule to return in time for the party. Once again, no invitation comes. Sarah is so upset. What has she done wrong? Why doesn't anyone like her?

She is deliberately being excluded but cannot figure out why. She no longer likes Lincoln School and feels like an outcast. She starts thinking about asking for a transfer back to her old school.

After the holidays, Sarah hopes that things will be better, but they are not. She continues to go out of her way to be friendly, but not much changes. In the spring, she decides that she will make one more last-ditch effort to make friends.

She plans a St. Patrick's Day party open house at her apartment and invites all of the staff to come. She gives invitations to everyone and asks them whether they will be able to attend. She gets similar responses—staff say they will try to come.

At the close of school on Friday, she goes around the building and tells everyone she is looking forward to seeing them at the party that night. Some of her colleagues let her know that they will not be able to come; some are noncommittal. The bottom line—she is ready for the party, and no one comes.

Sarah has experienced the ultimate in ostracism. She has tried her best, but the staff just does not want to accept her. More than nonacceptance, Sarah is in fact being alienated.

Ideally, such extreme scenarios do not happen often in schools, but incidents of ostracism in some form certainly happen on a daily basis in schools and often cause teachers to leave a particular setting. Teachers fear the terrible feeling that comes from being excluded from a group.

Recently, while attending a high school reunion, one of the authors was thrilled to see an old-time friend with whom she had lost contact. The friend had not attended several reunions. As the two reminisced and caught up with each other's life, the classmate admitted that this was the first time that she could make herself come to a reunion. She had longtime hurt feelings because of the way that she was treated by some classmates who were part of a high school clique.

That encounter revealed the long-term emotional damage that is done when children and young adults are ostracized by their peers. All educators can probably remember instances when they were excluded from a group, whether it was long ago when they were a child or today as an adult in the workplace. They can also remember how hurt they felt and how they may have suffered some loss of confidence in their ability to handle a social situation.

In today's society, it is natural that people have certain friends with whom they have interests in common, and those friendships are important; but deliberate ostracism is another story.

It is normal that certain people invite others to parties and lunch, but to deliberately exclude another person by words or actions so that the individual knows that he or she is being excluded is ostracism and is cruel to those who endure such behaviors.

This high school classmate recalled how some of the girls in the clique would look at her clothes or shoes, frown, and look away from her with their disgust that she did not have the clothes that were as nice as their clothes. Bullying by ostracism had long-lasting consequences and resulted in low self-esteem and lack of confidence in this colleague's ability.

Many school personnel have taken action to prevent overt physical, verbal, and sexual bullying by students, but some school personnel must look closely at what they may be doing inadvertently to allow this form of emotional bullying to occur within the schools.

Signs of bullying by ostracism may not be easily observed by school personnel or, if seen, may not be viewed as being important. School personnel may address this issue when it is seen by students, but they do not deal with this issue when it occurs among staff. Because staff are role models for students, it is unfortunate that ostracism is allowed to continue in schools.

If educators are to stop forms of ostracism within the schools, they must start with themselves. This chapter looks at what can be done when staff are ostracized or observe others being ostracized. It sends a strong message to all readers that educators must lead by example; they must not engage in ostracism but rather be inclusive in their involvement of others within the schools.

An article appearing in *Educational Leadership* in 2005 used the term *hazed* to describe poor working conditions for new teachers as opposed to conditions for their veteran colleagues. Author Mary Patterson (2005) discussed the new teacher who has no parking spot even though he has the longest commute or the new teacher who is teaching "in a dirty bungalow with no desks, no chalkboard, and the discarded teaching materials of someone else's 30-year career" (p. 20).

In this article, hazing is defined as harassment. Such hazing or harassment can also be described as ostracism—people engage in exclusionary behaviors to the new staff member. This is a phenomenon that must be explored if the educational system is going to retain new teachers and, in fact, all teachers in the field of education.

DEFINING OSTRACISM

Ostracism can be defined as the deliberate isolation of an individual from an activity or a group. Goldstein (1999) referred to ostracism as a form of low-level aggression and one of four types of verbal abuse: teasing, cursing, gossip, and shunning. "Being isolated, ignored, avoided, excluded, rejected, shunned, exiled, banished, cut off, frozen out, made invisible—all are experiences that give the sense of ostracism" (p. 61).

He stressed that ostracism can vary in degree, from coolness of tone and the denial of eye contact to total ignoring, when the person is not spoken to, looked at, or paid attention to. The impact of ostracism can be devastating and long lasting to the victims.

Williams (1997) found that ostracism deprives individuals of a feeling of belonging, threatens their self-concept, robs them of a feeling of control, and reminds the victims of the fragility of their sense of worth. In our opening example, the teacher had a good sense of worth in the previous school but lost that sense of worth within the new school building.

TYPES OF OSTRACISM

Ostracism can be obvious or subtle. A teacher may have made a comment in a faculty meeting and had someone roll his or her eyes. A teacher may have attended a faculty dinner and sat at a table and the other people then sit at a different table.

A teacher may have made a comment in the teachers' lounge about something, only to have her colleagues ignore her and immediately change the subject. A teacher may have learned that there was a baby or wedding shower and almost everyone in the building was invited except for her.

Some of these examples are subtle—rolling the eyes, changing the subject. Others are obvious—most people are invited to the shower, but one teacher is not. Some may be obvious to a particular teacher but may not have been designed to be ostracism by the others.

Others may be so oblivious to their own ostracizing behavior that they do not realize what they are doing to the person being ostracized. Ostracism may be viewed differently by different people, but one thing is certain—what really is important to the individual is whether he or she feels ostracized.

The following is an example of a faculty dinner and whether an action was really ostracism. People are going through the food line and looking for a table at which to sit. Many of the tables are full, but there are three empty tables left. One of the teachers starts another table. The colleagues after that teacher are in a group of six. Because the table holds only six people, if the group sits with the one teacher, a person in their group will need to be excluded. They then start another table. The group was excluding the teacher but was not doing so deliberately.

It certainly would have been helpful if they would have explained the reason that they were not sitting with that teacher, or it would have been even better if they would have just pulled up an extra chair so that everyone could have sat together.

In the viewpoint of the teacher being excluded, this was ostracism—that teacher perceived it as being obvious. She was ostracized and left to sit alone in front of many people. On the other hand, the group might have argued that it was not ostracizing her. It was simply making sure that each group member got to eat with the others.

Other people would argue that they were engaging in cliquish behavior from the beginning when they decided that only their six group members were to sit together. Those who witnessed the episode look at the individual sitting by himself or herself and wonder why no one wants to sit with him or her. The individual who is excluded is embarrassed, feels alone, and has a miserable time at the dinner. That person feels ostracized.

FEAR OF OSTRACISM

Many educators fear ostracism, and their actions within a school are driven by that fear. They are afraid that they will do something that will offend someone and they will thus be alienated, or they are afraid to take a stand for fear of being different and therefore alone within the school. Kidder (2005) argued that courage is one of the core virtues of humanity and that it takes courage to stand up for what one believes is the right thing to do.

Educators must find ways to express that courage, support it, and teach it. It takes courage to stand up for what one believes is right, but only if more educators do that within the school environment will we ever eliminate or even decrease the climate of ostracism within the schools. Kidder outlined the attributes of moral courage: greater confidence in principles than in personalities; high tolerance for ambiguity, exposure, and personal loss; acceptance of deferred gratification and simple rewards; independence of thought; formidable persistence and determination (p. 18).

Some fellow teachers in a building may have chosen to ignore a particular teacher of whom they are jealous. One of the teachers knows the person who is being ignored and finds that she is a kind and compassionate individual. She is torn—she wants to be accepted by the group of fellow teachers but is afraid that she will make them angry if she includes the colleague. She may then be ostracized by the group of fellow teachers.

That teacher must be confident enough to stand up for the right thing to do and befriend the teacher who is being ostracized. She knows that her actions may result in personal loss for her, but she is determined that she will not condone the exclusionary actions of the others. When educators are strong enough to refuse to participate in acts of ostracism, they are doing their part in stopping it in the schools.

The following is another example. Teachers are resentful about a new teacher who is coming into the building. They decide that at the opening-day breakfast, no one will sit with the new teacher. One of the educators is faced with a decision—he can sit with the new teacher and make her feel welcome within the school, or he can go along with the crowd and decide to ignore her.

He decides that he will think independently and not be swayed by the group. He knows that he is taking a big risk and may be ostracized himself, but he knows that he must suffer the consequence to be kind to another individual who has done nothing wrong except come to work at the school.

All educators have feared ostracism at one time during their careers. It is normal to want to be a part of the group rather than be apart from the group. People generally fear that they will be excluded, and sometimes that fear overshadows their courage. They may become weak and timid in certain situations—afraid to take a stand. However, they should make decisions based on their sense of kindness and fairness.

The following is another variation recently experienced by a colleague. Barbara was asked to serve on the nominating committee for the teachers' union in her building. She was excited to serve on the committee because she firmly believed that her building needed strong leadership.

She attended each of the nominating committee meetings that were held; each meeting turned out to be contentious. One of the members had specific people that she wanted as officers; they were her friends. Barbara and two of the other members of the committee agreed on their recommendations on the board. Cathy, the member who came in with a specific agenda, got one of the other members to go along with her. Cathy played on that individual's fear of being ostracized by Cathy and her colleagues.

When the final decisions were made, there was a split vote of three to two in favor of the slate. The three people who were not afraid to stand up to Cathy did so. Cathy and the other individual were upset. Cathy had been appointed, before the contention, to prepare the ballot from the slate and to send it out to members of the union.

When Barbara received her ballot, she was in shock. Cathy had changed the ballot and put one of her friends on the ballot instead of the individual who was determined by the committee to be on the ballot. Barbara could not believe what she saw.

She approached the other members of the committee, thinking that there must have been some mistake. They could not believe it either but felt that they should just let it go because they were afraid of what Cathy would do to them. Barbara tried to talk them into joining her to bring it out into the open; what Cathy had done was not ethical.

Barbara knew that she had to take a stand but learned that she would be alone in doing so. She then approached the president of the teachers' union and reported it to her. The president did not want to rock the boat because she was afraid of retaliation from Cathy. Consequently, Barbara let the members know via a memo that the ballot that was presented was not the ballot that was recommended by the nominating committee.

Yes, Barbara did fear retaliation and ostracism, but she knew that she had to do the right thing. In the final analysis, the membership voted that the ballot had to be redone to reflect the work of the nominating committee. Barbara found that she gained a higher level of respect because she was not afraid to take a stand to do the right thing.

An editorial in the *Chicago Tribune* ("Tattling for Dollars," 2005) dealt with the sad topic of the school shooting in Red Lake, Minnesota. After the incident, it was reported that some students had some knowledge of what the student was going to do, but they were afraid to come forward. They were afraid that they would be known as snitches, and they feared that they would be picked on or teased. They feared alienation from their peers.

This fear seems to begin in people at an early age and continues into adulthood. If these students would have come forward and done the right thing, a number of people would be alive today. As the article stated, "It often takes tremendous courage to come forward" (p. 10).

The more educators take a stand in favor of the right thing to do, the more it becomes a habit. Once it is a habit, it is easier to maintain, and they then decrease their feelings of any fear.

REASONS FOR OSTRACISM WITHIN SCHOOLS—FACTORS OUTSIDE YOUR CONTROL

Ostracism in schools may be related to something that a person has done, or some impetus out of a teacher's control may have precipitated the ostracism. Maybe the educator did not ask for it but got a bigger or better classroom than what some of the other teachers got, or she got a bigger budget for her materials this year. Educators are alienated by others who are angry that the one educator was treated differently. In their eyes, she was treated better than they were treated.

In a sad example in a school where a colleague worked at one time, a teacher received a well-deserved statewide award for her excellence in teaching. One of the other teachers in the building, who was not an excellent teacher, was so jealous that she organized a group of teachers to ostracize the teacher who received the award.

The ostracism was so cruel that the teacher who received the award finally left the school building and went to work elsewhere. Unfortunately, the ostracizing teacher continued her bullying efforts against anyone who she perceived was a better teacher than she was, and she continues those efforts today because she works within a building where the administrator not only condones her tactics but utilizes information from her to keep staff in turmoil.

In those instances, it is difficult to combat the ostracism other than by being open with people to let them know that the educator did nothing to cause their anger toward him. Although it takes a strong person to confront those who are doing the ostracizing, it is important to consider doing so rather than spend a miserable year within the environment.

It may be difficult and uncomfortable to confront colleagues with one's feelings. Educators must decide whether they are comfortable with this option. If an educator does this, she should proceed cautiously. If she has been able to determine the one person who seems to be leading the pack of those who are ostracizing her, she may want to consider approaching that person to gain information.

The educator should give the person the benefit of the doubt—believing that she or he did it unknowingly and not deliberately. The less confrontational that the educator is, the better— if she becomes angry and confrontational, this will probably lead to more resentment and retaliation on their part. She then may be ostracized even more.

The educator may wish to open the conversation utilizing "I" statements—"I sense that I have done something that offended you," "I would like to talk with you about your reaction to what I said in the teachers' lounge," or "I was disappointed when I wasn't invited to the shower for Meghan." Such statements are less likely to evoke a defensive response than are those such as "You have really hurt my feelings" or "You really make me angry."

FOCUSING ON KINDNESS AND INCLUSION, NOT ALIENATION

Another option is to focus on kindness. It is easy when confronted with the reality of being ostracized to succumb to similar tactics. The educator may be angry that he has been excluded from events, and he becomes resentful toward others and begins to engage in ostracism. This becomes a vicious cycle and adds to a negative climate among school staff; students see what is occurring, and staff have set a bad example.

Educators have been in situations where they were ostracized, and they have learned the importance of remaining kind and compassionate to their colleagues. Although this is certainly difficult, it is indeed the high road to take. It is more difficult for people to continue to ostracize them when they are being kind and thoughtful to them.

Here is an example: there has been a death of a close relative in one of the teachers' family. The teacher feels certain that most of her colleagues will either attend the funeral or send a card. Much to her surprise, several people do nothing to console her. She is hurt that they did not think enough of her to be kind in her time of need.

It would be easy and understandable to engage in the same behavior if one of them loses a loved one. Although that might be an understandably justified option, it will probably make the educator feel worse because she would have resorted to their tactics.

In life, it is important that in those situations people put their feelings aside and do the right thing—focusing their efforts on kindness, not alienation. In this situation, educators need to say to themselves that they will be there when they are needed by others. When they do that, there may be unintended consequences—the other person may learn from the example and work to change their negative behavior.

Anger and resentment toward others can consume some people, causing them to focus their efforts on that bitterness. The bitterness can make them feel miserable. For an educator, those feelings can be projected onto the children whom they serve. They might inadvertently take out anger on them. They know the satisfied feeling that they get when they have done something nice for someone else—those acts of kindness reap many benefits for the sense of well-being.

Although it is difficult, it is critical that educators vow not to resort to the same tactics as those who ostracize them. Otherwise, educators contribute to the vicious cycle of ostracism. They will not stop this behavior with unkindness but with kindness and a vow that they will continue their kindness in the face of adversity; although it may be easier said than done, positive behavior will go a long way in stopping ostracism within today's schools.

EXPLORING THE EDUCATOR'S OWN BEHAVIOR WHEN HE OR SHE IS BEING OSTRACIZED—FACTORS WITHIN THE EDUCATOR'S CONTROL

When a teacher is being ostracized by others, it is important that the teacher explore his or her own behavior to try to determine whether he or she has done something that has provoked the ostracism. Although ostracism should not be an excuse for people's engaging in inappropriate behavior, the individual being ostracized still needs to explore whether he or she has engaged in provocative behavior that has resulted in the ostracism.

In the earlier section of the chapter, teachers learned that some people may ostracize others because of professional jealousy. Although there is not a whole lot that one can do to prevent this, one can investigate her own behavior to make sure that she is being kind to those people and is personally recognizing their strengths and any help that they provide her. She can also monitor her behavior to make sure that she is not bragging too much and making the situation worse.

One of the reasons that an individual may be ostracized is that he or she is not a good listener. She may like to talk a lot about her classroom, her personal situation, or her illnesses. Others may get tired of her continual focus on herself. They may be looking for friends who will listen or assist them.

Colleagues want to be with others who show an interest in them. They get tired of hearing about someone's aches and pains, or they get tired of someone's bragging about his or her situation or accomplishments. Although it is expected that people will share their good news with their friends, one must be cautious that he or she is not bragging too much.

People also prefer to be around those who have a positive attitude and provide them with words of encouragement and praise them for their efforts—those people build up their colleagues.

The educator may be ostracized because she has engaged in similar behavior earlier. She may have planned a baby shower for a faculty member. Because the faculty member was not friends with some of the staff, she chose not to invite those people. Those not invited are angry with her; they remember the event, and when they plan a later activity, she is on the exclusion list.

She may certainly be able to justify what she did—she did not have a great deal of space in her home; she cannot afford refreshments for so many people. The bottom line, however, is that the other people do not know the reasons, or, even if they know the reasons, they do not understand them and are hurt by her behavior.

What could she have done in that instance? Many people become upset by this type of situation. The easiest thing to do is to try to invite everyone who works with the individual—have the event at a neutral site or keep refreshments simple—but avoid excluding anyone.

DEALING WITH BEING OSTRACIZED

Several pointers should assist the educator when confronted with ostracism:

1. As discussed, educators should continually monitor their own behavior to determine whether they are engaging in actions that are causing ostracism.
2. Educators should not engage in ostracism themselves. It is easy to succumb to the issues that are confronting them, but they need to keep saying to themselves that they must be the one that can make a difference in changing the behavior patterns of others.
3. One of the ways to do so is to practice appropriate and inclusive behaviors that do not deliberately exclude others. Much of the research on children who bully others shows that those who are bullied also engage in similar behavior. If educators are being bullied through ostracism, the way to break the cycle of this aggression is to begin with themselves.
4. Educators should find common interests with people within their building. This is a way to engage in inclusive behavior. Perhaps there is a person who shares an interest in books that they like to read; they can form a bond with that person on that topic. There may be another person who shares their love of knitting or sports or travel; they can form a positive relationship with that person. By focusing on those common interests, they can become involved with a wide circle of friends.
5. Educators should form partnerships or groups with those who share common interests. Groups work together to include others; cliques exclude others and are detrimental to the establishment of a positive climate. Ideally, educators will be in a building whose leader focuses on team building rather than exclusion. However, if they are not fortunate enough to be in such a building, they must do their own part to build those partnership bridges.

WHEN EDUCATORS OBSERVE OTHERS BEING OSTRACIZED

Educators may find that a new teacher in the school is being treated poorly by other staff; the path of least resistance in that case is to stay out of the situation. Another bothersome path is to join the others in their ostracism of the new teacher. Neither of these methods is a productive solution to a problem.

Educators must accept a role that fosters positive relationships with others. How can they do so?

1. Model inclusive behavior. Educators must vow that they will set an example for others and that they will demonstrate the need to be inclusive in their behavior.
2. Avoid cliques that exclude specific individuals. Join groups that include others and capitalize on individual strengths.
3. Practice frequent acts of kindness. When the educators see a person who is being ostracized by others, they should go out of their way to be kind to that someone. Send her or him a congratulatory note or e-mail on a recent success or a thank-you note for something kind that she or he did. This will make a big difference in one's positive feelings within a school.

   Probably all educators are familiar with the practice of people kicking someone when he or she is down. Instead of engaging in such devastating behavior that the person being kicked will never forget, educators must take the compassionate role and pick that person up rather than tearing him or her down.

   Some people may not be comfortable building someone up publicly, especially when he or she is being terminated from a position or is disliked by the administration. However, there is no reason that a colleague should not provide private verbal or written words of encouragement to that person.

   People who are at low points in their careers need that support. One of the authors can remember a person who was fired from an educational job on the same day that she learned that she had breast cancer. She needed friends then more than ever, and several people sent her words of encouragement to keep her going. Some years later, she overcame the cancer and now has an important position—she reported that she has never forgotten the words of encouragement from those who were true friends, not fair-weather friends.

4. People who engage in collegiality, not exclusion, should be reinforced by all of us. If educators want to ensure a school building that promotes kindness, all educators need to take responsibility for reinforcing those who encourage others rather than exclude others.
5. When educators see deliberate exclusion of others through cliques, they need to work to encourage those who are ostracizing to include everyone. They need to point out the strengths of each person.
6. All educators must vow to be sensitive to the needs of others.

The movement to ban ostracism within our school settings must begin within each of us. Educators should vow to practice acts of kindness that promote inclusion, not exclusion of our peers.

ACTION PLAN

1. Educators should go that extra mile to make colleagues in the building feel welcome and part of the team.
2. Educators should monitor their own behavior to ensure that they are not engaging in behaviors that are hurtful to others.
3. Educators should not allow themselves to become part of any ostracizing activities.
4. Educators should take a stand on the right and ethical thing to do.
5. Educators should engage in kind and compassionate acts toward their colleagues.
6. Educators must explore their own behavior to ensure that they are not engaging in provocative behavior that may be resulting in ostracism to themselves.

REFERENCES

Goldstein, A. (1999). *Low level aggression: First steps on the ladder to violence.* Champaign, IL: Research Press.

Kidder, R. (2005). *Moral courage.* New York: HarperCollins.

Patterson, M. (2005). Hazed. *Educational Leadership, 62*(8), 20–23.

Tattling for dollars. (2005, May 21). *Chicago Tribune*, p. 10.

Williams, K. D. (1997). Social ostracism. In R. M. Kowalski (Ed.), *Aversive interpersonal behaviors* (pp. 133–170). New York: Plenum.

Chapter Fourteen

The Politics of Technology

Blogs, Facebook, texting, wikis
Many new communication systems have become sticky
Professional use of electronics must be the rule
For anyone working in our school.

Since the first edition of this book, technology has exploded and permeates our everyday school life. E-mails, Facebook, Twitter, LinkedIn, and a variety of websites are at the fingertips of teachers. While advances in technology were supposed to make everyone's life easier, they in fact have complicated our existence. There are individuals who have become experts in hacking into systems.

The term "cyber-bullying" is commonly used for the phenomenon that exists where individuals are bullying others via the Internet. A lot of hours are wasted in surfing the Net or checking Facebook or responding to hundreds of e-mails. Responses are expected instantaneously. The world has become impatient with the ability to register for conferences online, bank online, check everyone out online, and more. Text messages are exchanged during meals, in meetings, and in the car.

Does technology present specific political issues? It most certainly does. Educators are even more in the public eye because anyone, including students, can access a great deal of information about their backgrounds. How does one separate their personal use of electronics and communication over the Net from their professional use? What do educators do when they know that their colleagues are abusing technology?

Carrie has been teaching English for two years at a high school with 1,200 students. Carrie loves to write and has several hundred Facebook friends and a blog that she updates frequently. She received positive evaluations during her first year of teaching but was recently called into the principal's office as a result of parental complaints about some of the comments she made on Facebook.

She made some statements about the lack of motivation of her students and even wrote a piece about the lack of motivation that her students show in class on her blog. In her postings, she mentioned that today's parents don't seem to care about their children. The principal explains to her that if any further postings that are negative toward her students or their parents are reported on Facebook, she will be asked to resign immediately.

Since Carrie is now in the public eye as an educator, she must be very careful with what she posts. She has to learn that she can't post anything that she doesn't want the world to see because anyone can see what she has written.

This chapter will discuss a variety of political issues that are the result of technology.

TEXTING

Texting has become a way of life for many individuals, and its increase has resulted in lots of questions about appropriate social behavior, attempts to multitask, driving while texting, and etiquette about its use in general. Educators have found themselves sitting in a boring faculty meeting or even an IEP for a child, and they are found texting others in the room rather than devoting their attention to the meeting. This is not appropriate.

Many individuals have found themselves in a social situation where they have met a friend for lunch and the friend spends a portion of the time texting other people. This is inappropriate social behavior unless an emergency has occurred. The message that the texter is sending to the friend is that they have other individuals that they prefer to communicate with.

We live in a time when people think they can multitask, but we all know that this is very difficult. In a 2012 book entitled *iDisorder: Understanding Our Obsession with Technology and Overcoming Its Hold on Us* (Rosen, 2012), the author writes that thirteen-to-eighteen-year-olds use more than six types of media at one time when they are not in school. He attributes this to the fact that there is so much technology and social media and that some individuals are afraid that they are missing out on something. He argues that these individuals are paying partial attention but really cannot concentrate deeply on one thing (Sparks, 2012).

There has been a misconception that younger people find that they can multitask, but Rosen has argued that this is not the case (Rosen, 2012).

Adults are trying to multitask as well and are also only providing partial attention to any one task. Teachers may attend a workshop and are texting while attending the workshop. Speakers who see teachers doing this find it insulting; they are not giving the speaker their attention, and the speaker is wondering whether he or she is boring. This is certainly a question of etiquette.

Those who text must ask themselves whether they are being rude to colleagues, speakers, or their administrators when they choose to text. They should understand when they are supposed to be giving face-to-face attention to other individuals instead of to their virtual friends.

PERSONAL VERSUS PROFESSIONAL USE OF ELECTRONIC COMMUNICATION—SEPARATING THE TWO

All schools have policies about the appropriate and inappropriate use of technology within the district. In many districts, individuals are asked to sign a statement that they will only use the technology for professional reasons and not for personal reasons. Yet some teachers are faced with dilemmas. They want to order some new clothes or they want to order a book for enjoyment. They may argue that they only have time to do this during the day and some of the new clothes they are ordering are for school and they are going to read the book they are ordering during their break. The safest action for teachers to take is to not order such items using the school's computer system.

Another dilemma that occurs is what e-mails can be sent and received from a school e-mail address. A number of educators have gotten themselves into trouble because they utilized their school e-mail address to receive and send political action e-mails. This is not appropriate for school use and teachers should not allow themselves to get caught in that trap. They should establish a separate e-mail system for such information. Teachers may also want to send e-mails to relatives during the day. This is not appropriate utilizing the school's system. Again, the teacher should have a separate e-mail system for such purposes.

Educators must follow all laws of confidentiality when utilizing e-mail. Jordan has had a rough day with one of his students. He sends out an e-mail to several of his colleagues about all of the inappropriate behavior of one particular student; he uses the student's name and sends it to teachers who don't even work with the student. A teacher to whom he has sent the e-mail is a relative of the disruptive student and is very upset about the e-mail and reports Jordan to the principal. Jordan should not have sent information about a student to teachers who did not need to know this information.

KNOWLEDGE OF OTHERS ABUSING THE INTERNET

Christin is a nontenured teacher and is eager to receive tenure this year as a teacher in the district. She really has enjoyed her class and the camaraderie with her colleagues in the district. However, she has found herself in a real dilemma. She has been receiving very inappropriate e-mail messages from the school superintendent, a married male who has been in the district for a number of years. Some of the messages are pictures of individuals with no clothing.

She knows these are very wrong, especially because the superintendent is utilizing the school computer and his school e-mail to send them. She is torn with what she should do. Should she report this or should she keep quiet and just delete the e-mails as quickly as she gets them? She debates about whether she should tell her colleagues; are they also receiving these e-mails? If she tells her colleagues, will someone say something that would lead to trouble for her? She really wants to get tenure, but at what cost?

Christin has an obligation to report this. If she does not, the school superintendent will continue such behavior at the expense of the children for whom he has been entrusted to provide care. Christin needs to go to her immediate supervisor and let the supervisor know that she is offended by these messages and that they are not appropriate for school. The more factual information that Christin can provide, the better; she should avoid becoming emotional and stick with objective facts.

Tom is the dean at a local high school. He sees himself as the teachers' buddy and hangs out socially with a group of the teachers. One day after school, Anna comes to him to see if he can assist her in deleting the computer record on her system. Anna has been cruising pornographic sites on her school-provided laptop. She knows that the technology director periodically checks each computer, and she does not want the director to find out what she has done. She asks Tom, who has expertise in technology, to delete any record of her use of pornography. Has Tom carried his being her buddy too far? What should he do?

When Tom has knowledge that a teacher is engaging in such behavior, he has an obligation to tell the teacher to stop the behavior right away. Covering up for the teacher makes him an accomplice to an inappropriate school action and could be reason for dismissal.

While many inappropriate sites are blocked within the school district, there are individuals who are able to get around those blocks and get into sites that are not allowable. Anna was certainly able to do that. She knew that what she did was wrong and chose to violate school protocol. She had the audacity to ask Tom to assist her in her wrongdoing. Anna knew what she was doing was wrong and clearly violated school policy.

CYBER-BULLYING

This section discusses the role of educators in preventing cyber-bullying of students and also the practice of educators bullying their colleagues using technology. Cyber-bullying can involve the use of e-mails, cell phones, text messages, videos, web pages, and Facebook.

Knowledge of Cyber-Bullying of Students

With the increasing use of technology, there is an increase in cyber-bullying among students. We read a great deal about bullying of students in schools in the press today. Maag and Katsiyannis (2012) reported that as early as 2007, 4 percent of students stated that they had been cyber-bullied. Educators have a legal responsibility to provide a hostile-free environment for their students. Therefore educators must not only closely observe the actions that their students exhibit in relationships but must also monitor their students' use of technology.

Most schools have policies about when and for what purpose their students can use technology. However, those policies are meaningless if they are not enforced by all staff within the school building. Educators must continually supervise the use of technology within school. They must keep their eyes and ears open and when they hear or see inappropriate behavior, they must report any suspicion of cyber-bullying.

Cyber-Bullying among Colleagues

Educators must never post negative comments about their colleagues on a Facebook page or in an e-mail. Here is an example: Deborah sends a bothersome e-mail to Bonnie telling her she is upset about how she handled her classroom. Bonnie becomes angry and sends a negative e-mail out to Deborah about her poor teaching skills and copies it to all of the staff in the school on the general e-mail list. Deborah is so angry that she posts a negative comment about Bonnie on her Facebook page.

Both Deborah and Bonnie's behavior was very inappropriate and could be reported as cyber-bullying. Both of them felt they were being harassed by the other one.

With the advanced technology now available, individuals can change videotapes or audio-tapes and insert someone's picture into an inappropriate tape and then use that tape against the individual.

It is important that educators be very careful about what they communicate electronically with their peers. Something sent on impulse and with emotion can be an action that cannot be retrieved. Once an e-mail goes out, it is gone and sent. Educators are moving at a fast pace. They are certainly busy and often act in haste. However, hasty actions can also be undoable and regrettable actions.

PUBLIC POSTINGS

A safe rule to follow is to remember that no one should put anything out there in a posting that they don't want the world to see. Therefore inappropriate language, pictures, or statements are not acceptable postings for any educators. Some individuals might respond that they have the right to free speech, which is true, but what individuals say can be used against them.

Charlene is upset about something that happened within her classroom, and she writes a Facebook post that makes a negative statement about a student and her family. This is not appropriate and should not be done.

In a school district, a teacher reprimanded a student for engaging in inappropriate behavior and told the student that he could not play at the upcoming basketball game. The parents became very upset when their son told them what happened. The parents went on the Internet and discovered some very inappropriate pictures that the teacher had posted on her Facebook page.

The parents went immediately to the superintendent and showed the Facebook pages to the superintendent and told the superintendent that if their son did not get to play basketball they were going to disclose the pictures of the teacher to the press. After all, they argued, a teacher who engaged in such behavior should not be correcting their son.

ONLINE FRIENDS

An increasing number of elementary and secondary schools have banned teachers from be-coming friends with their students. Some have banned the use of any Facebook on work time. Yet, other schools allow their teachers to have Facebook pages that provide a network for students to communicate with their teachers. Teachers can post homework projects or commu-nicate with their students about a specific topic.

Schimko (2012) believes that teachers need to find the right balance when using social media. She holds that students and their parents can benefit by going to a Facebook page that is set up for a certain class or content. Such a location can be a place to add information, submit related questions, and learn about classroom events. Since Facebook can be accessed outside school hours, it enhances the use of communication. Schimko does draw the line on friending students on Facebook and believes in keeping contacts focused on educational work (Schimko, 2012).

Willard (2012) suggests that social involvement with students on social media should not happen, believing that the majority of teachers would want to maintain their distinct role. Also, she believes that students may not feel comfortable with teachers engaging in their lives.

Students may wonder if those who are online friends with a teacher would get higher grades and be caught between the need for relating only with peers in this venue and the potential for improved grades. In addition, she warns that teacher engagement in the student online world might have implications for mandated reporting. Online relationships could also confuse emotionally vulnerable students about appropriate boundaries in terms of showing care (Willard, 2012).

Teachers must know what their school district's policy is concerning the use of social networks. Teachers must proceed cautiously when friending students who are in their classrooms. They must also be careful about who their other friends are online because some employers check their teachers' Facebook pages and the friends individuals have can tell a great deal about the individual.

DISCRIMINATING BETWEEN CORRECT AND INCORRECT INFORMATION ONLINE

It is critical that educators utilize reliable and recognized websites and teach their students to do so as well. Sometimes teachers will quote sources that are not accurate or research based when they are utilizing information. If a teacher questions information that appears on the Internet, they should check the reliability of the information. It is too easy for individuals to post incorrect information that continues to get passed on to others when it is not correct.

ACTION PLAN

1. Educators must follow their school district's policies on the appropriate use of technology.
2. Educators must report any inappropriate use of technology on the part of their colleagues.
3. Educators must monitor their students' use of technology.
4. Educators should read over any material sent out electronically before sending to make sure that it does not include negative information about another individual.
5. Educators should never post any material on social media that they don't want everybody to be able to access.
6. Educators should always check out information that they receive electronically to make sure the information is accurate.

REFERENCES

Maag, J. & Katsiyannis, A. (2012). Bullying and students with disabilities: Legal and practical considerations. *Behavioral Disorders, 37*(2), 78–86.

Rosen, L. (2012). *iDisorder: Understanding our obsession with technology and overcoming its hold on us.* New York: Palgrave Macmillan.

Schimko, L. (2012). Should teachers friend their students on Facebook? *American Teacher*, 96(5), 3.
Sparks, S. (2012). New research on multitasking points to role of self-control. *Education Week*, 31(31), 1, 13.
Willard, N. (2012). Teachers can be "friends" with boundaries. *American Teacher*, 96(5), 3.

Chapter Fifteen

Teaching in a Time of Turmoil

A time of turmoil we face
How do we cope with grace?
Legislatures, economics, and negative press
Create a situation for all of high stress
Even though the economic times are bleak
We must refrain from conveying a mean streak
We must build a system that sustains
By working together, a positive direction we'll maintain.

We all find ourselves living in a time of discontent about many factors. The Great Recession, high unemployment rates, home foreclosures, escalating prices, and more contribute to a sense of uncertainty about what the future may hold. Teachers may be holding down two jobs because their spouse has lost his or her job, they may have borrowed money for a home only to find they couldn't afford that home, or they are commuting to work and finding that gas prices have eaten up any raise they received. In some states, teacher pensions are being threatened. Such problems cause unrest and result in less congenial relationships and in more attacks. Everyone wants to blame someone else for the problems we face.

Education has always reflected society's problems and is a common target for public attack. Headlines abound about how public education should be fixed, how teachers aren't doing their jobs, how schools should be run like a business. These attacks are hard for educators to take. They are demoralizing while those teachers go into the classroom every day and do their jobs well even with the limited resources they are provided. With budget cuts, teachers' jobs are continually being threatened. Those teachers who are fortunate enough to keep their jobs have their workloads increased to cover the hole that is left when other teachers are not replaced.

Betsy is a third-grade teacher at Lincoln Elementary School. Her husband recently lost his job and they have two children. She is now the main breadwinner in the family. Betsy and her husband are worried they are going to lose their home because this year Betsy got no raise. Her school district is on the financial warning list in her state and state aid has been reduced for the last two years. Betsy is a conscientious teacher who works long hours and buys many of her own classroom supplies because the district cut her classroom budget. Her dedication and teaching resulted in her being awarded Teacher of the Year in her county. This morning she has picked up the newspaper and sees that the legislature in her state is considering a bill to reduce teachers' rights to bargain for adequate wages. She continues to scan the paper to find a letter to the editor by an individual complaining that teachers make too much money and their salaries should be reduced. She is feeling down as she heads into school.

She stops at her mailbox only to find a memo explaining the new evaluation system for teachers that will be based on student test scores. Betsy asks herself if all this is worth it. Should she consider a different career? Does anyone really appreciate her work? How is she going to walk into her classroom and face her students while keeping a positive attitude? Betsy faces a dilemma that is common for teachers in today's schools.

TURBULENCE IN ECONOMICS

The turbulence in economics is impacting teachers in a number of ways—personal financial issues, issues faced by the parents of their students, and budget cuts within the school districts.

When teachers are worried about their personal finances, including repayment of student loans, rising health care costs, and costs incurred with having children or caring for elderly parents, they become stressed, and it is difficult for them to concentrate on their teaching. More and more, teachers report that their spouses have lost jobs and they are the sole bread-winners in the family. They are trying to support an unemployed spouse while juggling all of the demands of their own job.

Parents of the students within teachers' classrooms face economic hardships. Parents may be working two jobs; as a result, when the teacher sends homework, the student may come back without the work completed because no one was home to assist the child. Teachers then realize that they must be careful about what work they send and may not be able to send any home with some of the children within their class.

Financial hardships within students' homes can result in high levels of anxiety for them. There may be more arguments about money at home, students may be worried that they will be displaced from their home, and they are witnesses to the stress that finances are putting on their parents. Students worry that parents won't be able to buy their needed school supplies or that they won't be able to buy decent clothes to wear at school.

Budget cuts in school districts are a reality in many parts of the country and teachers are worried about whether they will be on the chopping block. A teacher recently reported that he wasn't able to do much copying for his classroom because the district's paper budget had been cut and there was no paper unless he bought it himself. Since he was strapped for cash himself, he hesitated to purchase reams of paper.

Teachers are stressed because they fear that their job will be cut, and the uncertainty and the turmoil that this causes can certainly impact how the teacher does his or her job. The teacher is worried, and the anxiety that is caused makes it hard for the teacher to concentrate on doing his job.

When budgets get tight and jobs are on the line, teachers feel unappreciated for all the work they do. They feel that no one values them.

FACING CHALLENGING ECONOMIC TIMES

There are no easy answers on how to face the bleak economic times. We know the obvious answers about cutting down on expenses and looking for all possible ways to save money. Instead of going to some of the more expensive teacher stores, teachers find themselves frequenting dollar stores that have teaching materials at a much lower cost. Instead of buying new books, teachers check books out of the library or buy used books from Amazon. Instead of getting take-out lunches, teachers pack their own. They wait for sales and bargains at office stores. They find themselves only buying clothes that are on sale and they are asking themselves more the age-old question before buying something: "Do I really need this?"

Teachers are working in schools that are strapped for cash. Educators find themselves keeping a supply of paper in their classroom. They reduce the amount of copying they do for class; instead of copying worksheets, they look for alternatives.

They ask themselves whether it is the time to retire or if they should work longer to build up a better retirement fund. They look at what their health care costs will be to determine whether they can afford to leave the school system. Many teachers cannot afford to just work at their teaching job; they find themselves moonlighting at other jobs.

Teachers who wish to advance their education look for grants that might be available and ask themselves where they can go to school that will provide the best education at the lowest price.

PUBLIC ATTACK ON EDUCATION

An article in the *Kappan* in 2012 described a "legislative contagion" (Underwood & Mead, 2012, p. 51) that swept the Midwest during 2011. Specific states wanted to take away the right of public employees to bargain. A group has identified themselves as ALEC (The American Legislative Exchange Council). This group shares a belief in "limited government, free markets, federalism, and individual liberty" (taken from their website: www.alec.org/about-alec). With their agenda to introduce market factors; increase testing, vouchers, and charters; and reduce the influence of local school districts and school boards (Underwood and Mead, 2012), they are striving to change the look of education as we have known it in the past, and they are becoming a powerful force in an increasing number of states.

On state fronts, there are new types of advocacy groups within the legislatures. Teachers' organizations such as the National Education Association (NEA) and the American Federation of Teachers (AFT) represented the needs of teachers and were their voice at the table in negotiations about state legislation that impacted teacher evaluations and their working conditions. Now such groups as Stand for Children, Democrats for Education Reform, and StudentsFirst are at the tables negotiating for educational issues. They are viewed as a counterweight to the NEA and AFT, and they are financially supporting political candidates who agree with their viewpoints. Their influence seems to be growing. These groups may have very different viewpoints than the traditional organizations (Sawchuk, 2012a). Tensions between the NEA and the AFT and these new groups are increasing. As an example, the founder of StudentsFirst has supported reducing teachers' bargaining rights (Sawchuk, 2012b).

Excellent teachers have no problem with accountability. They are striving hard to do the best job they can do. Many do have problems with the notion that accountability is based on test scores alone. Teachers recognize that they cannot always control all of the variables that may impact a child's test scores and thus become frustrated with such accountability systems. Accountability should be based on a variety of factors, not just one. There is tremendous pressure to teach to the test because the teachers and the principals are being evaluated based on those test scores. When math or reading scores fail to increase, teachers are blamed. Educators are blamed for many of the social problems the children face. The child may not have been fed, may have gotten little sleep, has a parent who is incarcerated—all factors over which the teacher has little control, although schools now provide breakfast and lunch, and some teachers send food home for children to eat in the evening. Some teachers also provide clothing to the children in their classrooms; yet the general public does not recognize all of these factors and continues to increase criticism of the teachers. The public may not always recognize that some teachers face large class sizes, lack of enough books for all the students in their classes, interruptions throughout the day that keep them from teaching, and other issues.

MAINTAINING PROFESSIONALISM WHILE BEING ATTACKED

Because teachers are facing attacks from the press, from the legislature, and from the general public, it is easy to become very negative and hostile. However, educators must recognize that they are public servants and professionals and must maintain that stature. Even when being attacked, rather than becoming angry and feeding in to the behavior of the individuals who are bad-mouthing the educators, educators must present the facts about what they do and the challenges they face.

Educators must present their beliefs about the importance of accountability and should be part of the discussions about what accountability should look like. They should make every effort to be proactive rather than reactive.

At times educators become very frustrated about what legislators are saying about them or about what anti-teacher groups are saying. This is very understandable—what they are saying is angering. However, it is not productive to make negative comments publicly about those individuals or to post derogatory comments on Facebook about what is happening. Instead, educators must spread the good news about what they are doing.

Educators have to work to create a positive morale within their individual school buildings. They must remember their purpose to provide the most appropriate education that they can for the students they serve.

EDUCATING THE PUBLIC ABOUT WHAT EDUCATORS DO
AND THE RESOURCES THEY NEED

It is the educators' job to educate the public on the situations in today's schools; yet the reality of the situation is that the teachers are busy doing the best job they can and don't always have the time to network with the public about the challenges they face. In some states, legislators try to cut teacher benefits knowing full well that teachers are busy in the classroom and don't know what is happening.

As in other parts of this book, we have stressed the importance of belonging to professional organizations. There is strength in numbers, and organizations should be representing the needs of their members in state capitols and in Washington, D.C. It is, however, not enough to just belong; educators must become active in those organizations and accept the realization that they each must do their jobs—whether it be to send letters or make phone calls when requested, to testify at hearings, to read alerts that are sent, and to keep informed and updated. If members find they are not getting updates from their organization, they need to voice their opinion to the organization rather than just complaining.

A teacher, Lorna, was feeling very frustrated at the state's situation. She worked very hard with the resources she had. The principal in her school was ineffective; he had been reassigned to her school after being unsuccessful at other schools, and he was planning to retire at the end of the school year. The budget cuts in her school had been drastic and with her class enroll-ment at thirty-nine, she did not have enough books for the two students who had moved into her classroom midway through the year. She also was short a desk for one of the students. Even though her own financial situation was not good, she herself bought a set of books for each of her new students, and she gave up her own desk to make room for the two students.

The legislature in Lorna's state was still meeting after school was out and her professional organization contacted all the teachers to see if they would come to the state capitol and testify at a hearing about the low test scores within the state. Lorna decided that she could do that. She would overcome her fear of speaking because she realized the importance of telling legislators the sad state of affairs in her school. She prepared a written statement that she would read aloud. When she was called to testify, she told how she worked hard to improve the test scores for the children within her classroom. She shared briefly the innovative prac-tices she used, and then she told the legislators about her lack of books and desks for her students. The legislators at the hearing looked shocked that a teacher didn't even have books for her students. Needless to say, she had an impact. They were not so quick to bad-mouth this dedicated teacher.

Through this experience, Lorna had the realization that indeed she could make a difference and became more involved with her teachers' organization.

Facing the pressures of school and family commitments, some individuals feel that they don't have the time to devote to their professional organization. Yet they can and should at least belong and support the work of the organization. When asked to write letters or pick up the phone or send an e-mail or sign a petition, they should take the few minutes it takes to do so.

THE CRITICAL ROLE OF SUPPORT TO FELLOW EDUCATORS

Educators must support each other and not allow legislatures to "divide and conquer," a common ploy that is used by some to get what they want. If they are allowed to divide the field, then educators are busy arguing among themselves, and legislatures use that as an opportunity to pass unacceptable legislation. Educators may have worked with administrators who are very good at dividing and conquering. They deliberately use this as a ploy to get any negative attention away from themselves.

Mrs. Jamers approaches one teacher and says that another teacher has made a negative comment about her and she just thought she should know. She then goes to the other teacher and makes another negative statement *about* what the first teacher said. The two teachers then become very angry at each other and don't speak, and both of them think that Mrs. Jamers is their friend when she really is anything but their friend.

New teachers may make negative statements about their more experienced colleagues, and the more experienced colleagues may resent new teachers and what they may perceive as their naïve ideas. Both sets of teachers should recognize that they can all learn from each other and should not allow themselves to get into an "us versus them" situation. New teachers must recognize the talent of their more mature colleagues and ask them for advice. More experienced teachers should recognize the novel ideas that their new colleagues bring to the school. More experienced teachers need to understand that newer teachers may be more skilled at technology and are much more used to texting and using social media than they are and should learn to integrate more technology and to communicate using texting and social media. New teachers should recognize the wealth of experience that their colleagues have about curriculum and instruction and managing behavior. Everyone can benefit from others' expertise.

New teachers may be hesitant to join professional organizations; they see no need to work together through organizations. They utilize social media. Therefore, they may not be joining, and therefore numbers in such organizations are decreasing. Experienced teachers are insulted by such action and believe that they don't want to work with them, when in reality the new teachers don't see the need or don't believe it is time well spent. Experienced teachers must work together with them to explain the importance of working together through professional organizations. At the same time, professional organizations have to regroup and spend less time in meetings that may be perceived as time wasters and more time providing information electronically and using face-to-face meetings for very important information that can't be conveyed in any other fashion.

When a teacher is struggling in a building and is working hard to do the right thing, colleagues should use this as an opportunity to help and support that teacher. Lending an ear or providing some resources to that teacher can go a long way in establishing a healthy school environment.

ACTION PLAN

1. Educators should recognize colleagues and parents facing economic struggles.
2. Educators should work to create positive morale within their school.
3. Educators should work together to provide a united front within the field.
4. Educators should do their part in painting a positive picture about what schools are doing.
5. Educators should keep abreast of what is happening in the field of education.
6. Educators should be proactive in their professional organizations.

REFERENCES

Sawchuk, S. (2012a, May 16). New breed of advocacy groups shakes up education field. *Education Week*, 31(31), 1, 16–19.

Sawchuk, S. (2012b, May 23). Advocacy groups target local politics. *Education Week*, 31(32), 1, 14–15.

Underwood, J., & Mead, J. (2012). A smart ALEC threatens public education. *Phi Delta Kappan*, 93(6), 51–55.

Chapter Sixteen

Making That Final Decision:
Can I Stay, or Do I Need to Move On?

You did not plan to feel this way
When you began it was almost like play
Then as time moved on
You felt you were done
With the pressure
With the stress, sure
With the routine
Perhaps the whole scene
You chose to step back
Check if you were on track
You needed small change
Or had to big-time rearrange
Your career
But the fear
Of the unknown
Trust you will be shown
The path that is best
If you stop, look, and rest
Your new future will come clear
Your path will appear
In education or toward another career.

What is the chemistry between the teacher, the school, and the teaching profession? It is crucial that the teacher reflects and makes a conscious decision about the costs and benefits of the choices that he or she makes regarding his or her professional career of teaching.

It is imperative that teachers review their decisions from time to time. If they discover that they have engaged in this reflection process and find themselves faced with barriers and misunderstandings that repeatedly crop up between them and the principal, parents, peers, and students, then they are probably facing some soft signs or triggers that are indicating that they may be better off changing their jobs.

Although making decisions about career change seems difficult, it is not the making of the decision that presents the problem. The reason why people do not make decisions is that they do not engage in the conscious deliberations of costs and benefits or are unaware of the steps involved in the process of decision making.

It is not the decision that is grueling; what is more difficult is getting the information on which the decision is based and having certainty that the information that one has collected about himself or herself is correct, meaningful, and complete. Only by taking an honest look at strengths, weaknesses, and commitments is one able to make a better decision for himself or herself.

People make several decisions in their lives—social, academic, personal, and professional. Sometimes they make decisions on the spur of the moment, and other times they have to deliberate and ponder various choices to evaluate a better choice for themselves. They know they can make better decisions with relevant information.

Here is an example of Pat's decision-making process. Pat, a special education director, came up with an idea of using computerized IEPs in her district. She wanted to explore various softwares to support her idea. She needed information about details, such as how much would it cost to train the teachers, if the district adopted the computerized process.

Well, it took her about a year to collect the relevant details about online IEPs. As she got closer to getting the information about the software that supported the online IEP processes, she found that she was getting closer to the solutions of the issues. In about a year, she identified two sites to field-test the use of computerized IEPs, and then she collected data, addressed the technical support issues, and became more knowledgeable in that process. Now, after hearing her success story, the whole district decided to adopt this method.

The decision making involved a systematic process of trying out an idea, engaging in periodic reflection of issues, and establishing teams to work on various facets of the process and data collection. Only after collecting and analyzing the results that supported the benefits for the full-fledged application at the district level did the superintendent decide to move on to a systemic application of electronic IEPs for the district.

Another example is the route that the teachers may have followed when they had to make their career decision. Their first assessment of their career preferences occurred when they thought that they had the disposition and attributes to get admission to the initial teacher preparation program of their choice; they decided that they wanted to be an elementary teacher with a double major or a special education teacher in learning disabilities. They looked at their strengths and matched them with the available programs in various states that seemed to meet their needs.

No one had told them in their teacher preparation programs that after five years of working as a teacher, they might begin to feel disenchanted or bored with their current jobs. They might feel burned out and stressed; they might develop an apathetic attitude toward the teaching profession that they once loved; or they might need a complete career change because they feel they need to grow in a different direction. Many professionals experience this change in their lives; however, they do not know what to do when they find themselves at this juncture.

Beth has encountered a turn in her professional career when she begins to find herself exhausted, disengaged, and somewhat negative toward her work and profession. The same children who had once driven her to excel in her current position are now causing a feeling of anxiety and fatigue in her. Her irritability has increased. First, she started to blame her principal for not giving her enough support and for increasing the class size this year, but then she recalled that about five years ago she had taught more students in the same class.

She had to sit down and create a complete, detailed landscape of her career, her priorities, her personal life goals, her health, her desire to continue with the same job, and so forth. She needed to evaluate her experience and expertise that she had gained over time and reevaluate whether doing the same thing that she has been doing for the past ten years was a good choice for her.

She figured there is no need to continue with the same routine if her heart is telling her that she needs to adopt a different pathway or explore a different option. Then she needs to assess whether she needs to change the pathway or the environment.

Once teachers begin to feel a bit detached and unmotivated, they need to explore the current school environment and their personal factors. They need to identify if they are experiencing these changes because they are getting ready for a new opportunity for meeting new evolving goals. Sometimes teachers may just need to teach in a different school or at a different level, leading to them not needing a career change.

This chapter helps teachers in developing a process for career change—how they need to attend to the soft signs that they experience as they grow in their career paths. There is no reason to deny a change when they know in their heart that they need to pursue that. They are doing a disservice to themselves and others by continuing with the same situation and feeling bad about that situation.

Teachers do not want to be in a situation with similar problems. Before teachers begin to look for the change in job, they need to find the reasons for dissatisfaction with the current job. Teachers need to answer that before starting a search for a change in career. To help them understand the extent of dissatisfaction with their current job, teachers need to ask the following questions:

- Do they feel challenged or bored at work?
- Is there an opportunity for them to advance?
- Do they have a positive relationship with their administrator, the parents, and students?
- How do they feel about schedule, office location, driving distance, and colleagues' attitude toward them?
- Do they find their job to be too stressful or too easy?
- Do they think that they can do something to contribute to the solution?
- Could they negotiate with their principal to realign some of their duties?
- Do they think that they may benefit from a class at a community college to give them new ways to think about their job?
- Do they need to take a vacation to rejuvenate themselves?

These questions may assist teachers in identifying what other questions they need to ask of themselves and others. If they end up responding to these questions negatively, they may be getting pessimistic about their job. They need to figure out if they need a break for a short time, a vacation to recollect themselves, or a complete change in their work surroundings.

TEACHERS NEED TO READ THE SOFT SIGNS

Sally started her job as an elementary school teacher, and after working for more than five years in the same setting, she finds out that she contributed as well as she could in this setting and would like to explore her competencies with middle school children. Some of the changes that she has experienced in her life are related to her own personal growth: she is a mother of two children who are five and seven years old. She has started to feel that she has to maintain a routine at home for them. She finds that her life at home and at school has become similar. She wants to experience some change and still be able to utilize her teaching skills. She seems to get along with teens, and they seem to respond to her better, as compared to some other professionals at the same school.

She has completed the certification requirements to teach the secondary grades and feels trapped in an elementary school. The first time that she worked in a peer-tutoring program in her school, where students from a nearby junior high school came and served as peer tutors in her classroom, she mentored them on how to teach math and reading to students who were struggling. She really liked those days when they came to work with her. Her interactions with them were productive, and she found out that she became more creative when she had them around her.

When Sally first made a decision to be a teacher, she enjoyed using word games and interactive activities to further enhance children's verbal skills and vocabulary development. She used storytelling, sight words, rhyming games, and role-plays with children. To further improve their social skills, she used scenarios and simulated plays and encouraged them to use social skills of sharing and asking for help. By using manipulative tools, she taught them scientific and mathematical concepts. As students engaged in activities of balancing blocks, building a bridge, or mixing paint colors, they learned the scientific principles behind them.

She went to Europe during summer vacation and took a professional development course in how to integrate social studies and language arts for intermediate elementary grades and junior high students. She also has been working in a team with a career counselor and has enjoyed the experience of conversing with area employers who provide input into the curriculum and offer internships to students. It is clear that she has developed additional competencies and preferences for teaching in a junior high school.

There is nothing wrong with her entertaining the thought of making a move to a different setting, where she can employ her newly developed skills. Learning the new roles and ways of teaching has been her interest ever since she was hired. She has always carved out time that allows her to continue learning and refining her teaching skills, and now she wants to apply them in a different setting.

Different reasons challenge a teacher's decision to remain in the same career for a long period of time, ranging from lack of motivation to dealing with a difficult administrator. Here is a list of situations that may indicate to a teacher that she may need a change in her professional environment or career.

REACHING THE "KNOW IT ALL" PHASE IN LIFE

Michelle has come to an erroneous conclusion that she is a finished product. She believes she knows it all and has done it all. She has now begun to feel like she does not need to learn anymore. She reflects a narcissistic explanatory style in her conversation in faculty meetings. Her colleagues have begun to notice that she has lost her listening skills and has stopped showing interest in anyone else except herself.

When someone begins to share ideas, she shuns that person away with her yawning. Her conversations are full of "She (Michelle) did this . . . ," "In her teaching she does this . . . ," and "All this research is useless." If things do not work out the way she wants, she begins to engage in a process of blaming others. Michelle has stopped appreciating the success of others, has become overcritical of other people's performance, and does not value new ideas and new learning.

Having interest in oneself and sharing one's success story is healthy; however, when Michelle developed a glowing vision of the future for only herself and began to become selfish, she changed the core beliefs about herself. She began to doubt others; she doubted their worthiness for success, and she blamed them for past failures. Every conversation is about her and nothing else. She focuses too much on herself, which is getting to be irritating for others.

It is time for her to reexamine her skills and see which of these skills need further refinement. If she is so bored with what she is currently doing, she needs to check her attitude toward life because every person can benefit from new learning. Her "know it all" attitude prevents her from finding new and exciting interests in her life. Not only that, she has developed a negative attitude toward learning, which is unhealthy for her and for others. She cannot serve as a trigger or a stimulus that prevents others from learning more.

EXPERIENCING LACK OF MOTIVATION

There may be a time in a teacher's career when she develops a self-defeating attitude and increases reliance on motivation from other colleagues, teammates, friends, and so on. She has no desire to be active, to expend excess energy, to engage in self-fulfillment, to do something creative, or to take risks. Nothing raises her curiosity, and it seems that she has lost her adventurous spirit and that lethargy is creeping in. She has stopped feeling successful.

It is time for her to look at her successes and engage in a routine that provides her with some structure in her life and includes fun activities. She may need to engage in self-instruction and self-prompting to do some fun things.

By engaging in a fun routine, she may regain focus and get her motivation back. She may need to take a vacation to rejuvenate, and she may have to give herself permission to enjoy other parts of her life, her family, and her friends. She needs to identify and engage in her hobbies that she had once enjoyed, or develop new interests. Some type of physical exercise and relaxation activities also assist in reducing pessimistic tendencies.

CHECKING EFFORTS FOR SUCCESS

The true test of a teacher's success is not only the success itself but also how well she has prepared herself for it. She does not have to develop a self-defeating attitude or demand perfection from herself. She needs to learn to do things the way that she enjoys them and to do her best. She needs to connect herself with efforts and not with outcomes.

Teachers will be surprised to see how quickly they can get out of self-defeating behaviors. They need to focus on what is happening, not on fears or hopes of what will happen. They do not have to win; they just have to give it a try. They need to get in a mode where the effort is effortless and go full force but without criticizing themselves. If they choose to change their profession, they should leave it feeling that they have given their best to it.

WATCHING FOR A PESSIMISTIC EXPLANATORY STYLE

Sally was a happy-go-lucky secondary education teacher. She has been in the profession of teaching for about fifteen years. Lately, she has started looking at the worst side of a situation and always takes opposing points of view in meetings. She always feels that she is being betrayed and finds herself overwhelmed by the daily social, economic, and political pressures. She has become snappy and brusque with others on a couple different occasions. She knows that there is no justification for mistreating others but finds herself negative toward them.

Susie decided to take the time to find out why Sally is reacting in professional situations the way she is and asks her if she needs a colleague to discuss her concerns with. She asks her to go out for lunch, and they spend a couple of hours in a nice Italian restaurant away from the school environment. Susie finds out that Sally is experiencing some personal issues and that school-related factors were merely serving as triggers.

One of the issues that Sally wanted to resolve immediately was the driving distance from her school to home. She has a son who was identified with a terminal illness, and she needed to find a job closer to the hospital where she could visit him more frequently. Clearly, Sally needs to change her career, not because of school-related issues, but for her own personal reasons. In fact, Susie was able to guide her toward seeking professional help, and she gave her information about a therapist in the local area.

After a couple of weeks, Susie found out that Sally had found a job as a residential teacher within that hospital where her son was receiving treatment. Sally shared this news with Susie, and Susie was delighted to see how Sally was finding her way to spend more time with her son and was able to maintain her job.

SEEKING PROFESSIONAL ADVICE

In teaching careers, teachers encounter many situations that warrant unbiased and objective advice. They may be in the process of choosing a career, going for further education, reentering the workforce, or recovering from a job loss or a personal trauma, and they may develop emotional stress.

Changing a career can become an overwhelming process, and they may need help and advice. They may need to contact career-counseling offices in their local areas and seek their guidance. They need to get to know other people who may have gone through similar stages in their career changes or transitions. They may like to find out how they can have direct access to a coach who is a specialist in career transitions.

MAKING A CHANGE

After making a decision that they really need to change their job, they need to find out if they want to remain in a related field or would like to consider a complete change in career. If they still want to be within the education field, they may consider several options, such as moving to administration or college teaching.

From Teaching to Administration

Teachers who have mentally checked out from their professional obligations but have continued to stay in their classrooms with students without having an ongoing desire of becoming better and highly effective are more negative than those who are seeking new career opportunities. They are doing more damage as an educator by holding themselves back from doing other things that may be more productive.

For example, if a classroom teacher aspires to become an administrator, she does not have to apologize for that. She needs to make a decision as to when she will start a new career as an administrator, and she needs to sharpen her leadership skills and decision-making processes. When a school administrator makes a decision, good or bad, the school's community is impacted significantly.

Anytime a principal decides to implement a rule or a policy that yields negative outcomes, there is a spillover effect. A poor decision contributes to disservice—not only to the teacher but also to his or her students and their families. As a principal, when she forgets, even for a moment, what years of teaching experience should have taught her, she may not be making sound decisions.

So, the best thing is to make the decision that she will be an effective administrator who will make a significant change in the lives of students and their families. If she is effective, she is able to transform a school organization into a nurturing community of professionals, where teachers feel supported, children enjoy learning, and parents are involved.

From Teaching Young Children to Teaching Adults

Susan had taught in an elementary school for about ten years. In the meantime, she had completed several graduate hours in instructional strategies for reading. She was called in for staff development opportunities in her district and was regarded as an expert in reading instruction. She began to enjoy the independent thinking and self-directedness as she taught adults. She also began to enjoy how adult learners accumulate a reservoir of experiences that could be used as a basis on which she could build new learning.

Her peers liked to acquire information that helped them in becoming successful in their roles. One of her friends, Billy, asked Susan if she would consider teaching a foundational course at a state university. Susan decided to try it out for a semester, and she found out that she totally loved this experience of adult teaching.

Boredom in one's profession is often bolstered by a combination of factors, such as little or no professional growth, a lack of emphasis on collaboration and innovation, task repetition, a lack of upward and lateral mobility, and a growing disinterest in students. Teachers need to get out of this feeling of worthlessness. They need to have an opportunity to explore options of adult teaching. They may find that their teaching experience in the classroom may make them a better college instructor. Students in college also benefit from the real-life experiences that teachers accumulate in their classrooms.

Adopting a Different Career Pathway

John had the experience of teaching in a middle school for about fifteen years. He was an effective, successful teacher who took pride in producing positive outcomes for students in his school. He had implemented a reading program for students with learning disabilities and had received an award for being an outstanding teacher of the year.

After spending twelve years of teaching in a classroom, he was asked to assume the position of an assistant principal in the same school. Two years later, he became an interim principal because the principal had to take early retirement due to a medical emergency.

John enjoyed working as the principal for one year. He was considered to be an effective administrator. He increased parent involvement in school, was able to get additional funds for assistive technology for students with autism, and created several opportunities for staff development. The school community had great faith in him. But now, he is feeling tired. There is something telling John that he needs to try different things. He really wants to go into real estate.

The economy has started to interest him, and he is getting excited about the changes in interest rates. He believes that he has put too many late nights into finding new information about the economy. With increasing responsibilities, he wants more flexibility for family responsibilities. Using any of his professional networks and connections, he might land a job that provides him with the satisfaction that he needs.

He knows that in certain areas of real estate, there is a decline in job availability. He knows that he needs to gather as much information as possible regarding his new profession before making a final decision, including which qualifications are needed and how he can gain the qualifications and relevant work experience. He is seeking job coaching to get a better sense of the new expectations of himself. After working with a career counselor, he realizes that he needs to place limits on the time and emotional energy that he spends on others; otherwise, he will not be able to balance his career in real estate with his personal commitments.

Career decision making requires a lot of effort, networking, and soul-searching. Re-careering may become essential to maximize the likelihood of being satisfied with one's career. People tend to spend a lot of time deciding where they want to live, who they will marry, what car they want to buy, where they will go for vacation, what kinds of clothes they like to wear, and what kind of furniture to keep in their home, but they spend less time on determining what career best fits them in terms of their beliefs, interests, personality, and skills.

They do not take the time to find out about their strengths and weaknesses, and oftentimes they do not know how to work with their continually evolving skills and competencies. It is important that teachers learn to develop resiliency to fight against stress and increase their coping skills, aspirations for success, and personal and professional growth. They may need to develop mentoring structures around themselves and raise expectations of success for themselves.

Career changes are expected in professional lives but should provide teachers with satisfaction and success. If a teacher's initial career choice was not so satisfying, that means that they need to understand themselves more intimately and deeply. They need to know the source of their decision-making process. Are they making decisions out of fear, impulse, or control? They do not want to see themselves in a similar situation again. They do not accept a job out of fear or impulse rather than passion. The most imperative factor is that they ultimately strive for their passion.

Making a change in a teaching career may not be easy, and it may require determination and a willingness to explore new ideas. But when teachers take the lead and initiate the search for a career that will truly satisfy them, they will have more control over the process. Rather than waiting for an opportunity to arise by surprise, they will be deliberate about their choice.

Other times, they may find that they are fairly successful during their career, and the reason that they want to change their career is that they did not feel passionate about what they were doing. They may also like to seek professional help in getting at their genuine interests and aptitudes. They may have to work on their limiting beliefs and reframe those beliefs to be destined to success.

When teachers feel that they are at an impasse on whether to stay in the current job, they need to try to identify elements that are unsatisfying. If they find that changing the environment is not going to yield satisfaction, they should change their pathway. They can rearrange their life to gain the greatest degree of satisfaction, meaning, and fulfillment. They must remember that an effective career choice relies on finding out their values and gifts from an inside-out basis, and moving toward living them fully.

ACTION PLAN

1. Educators should take a look at their strengths, weaknesses, and commitments to evaluate the need for career change.
2. Educators may need a complete career change because they feel they need to grow in a different direction.
3. Educators should monitor if they have a negative attitude toward learning, because such an attitude may create an unhealthy environment for them and others.
4. Educators should explore other options such as administration and college teaching as potential choices for career growth.

5. When educators see signs of boredom in their current career, they must engage in a process of reevaluating their true passion.
6. Educators should view career change as a viable, positive, and professional option.

Conclusion

This book is meant to serve educators who may need to revitalize their energy levels and self-esteem, who may have started to feel less enthusiastic about their jobs and need to rejuvenate, or who may be just entering the profession with a lot of energy and enthusiasm and need to preserve themselves so that they can prevent burnout. If readers fall into any of these categories, they may find this book on basic coping strategies of surviving within the political arena of the school setting extremely beneficial.

There is no such thing as staying out of politics; all issues are political. Educators' success, in some ways, is also political. The chapters in this book have provided readers with practical strategies so that they can become effective in their school and profession.

The authors hope that readers have enjoyed the additions to the book in this second edition. As readers have noticed, the chapters have been written by educators who have collectively worked within the school setting for over seventy-five years—the voices of experience share some helpful survival skills.

No matter how well prepared or experienced, the teacher who lacks self-respect is not going to survive in the midst of indignities such as listening to ceaseless interruptions by daily announcements, dealing with difficult parents and students, being ordered by the principal or the state to "teach to the test," dealing with difficult peers, and confronting a host of other factors.

One-third of our new teachers stay in the profession fewer than five years, and more than half of those in special education settings decide to leave within three years. It is obvious that something goes wrong after these teachers have invested their time to prepare themselves for the profession. Clearly, the climates of their jobs prevent them from thriving.

Now, either educators can blame this on the preparation of these teachers and bicker about the universities and institutions for higher education, or they can examine the contextual factors in which these teachers have to work and provide them with some strategies and tools for success.

The purpose of this book is to enable teachers to gain the due respect that a true professional should expect. The authors hope that by reading the book, the new enthusiastic teachers will not get fumbled with an attitude of disenchantment from their veteran peers in their schools.

New teachers will find ways to deal with administrators who wear blindfolds and neglect to see the good for their own schoolchildren.

It is sad to see that teaching is not viewed as a lifetime career anymore. Changes are beneficial, but to have such an influx of people coming and going so quickly in and out of the profession weakens it immeasurably.

It is important that the field of education builds the capacity of new teachers to face daily challenges effectively, to have a voice in the workplace for issues such as the choice of curricula and materials, the types of tests to use to evaluate instruction, and access to instructional resources.

The authors also want to build the stamina of our veteran teachers to cope with the ever-changing school challenges. Teachers should be able to exert some control over their profession as a whole and to build their self-esteem and professionalism so that they can offer productivity and commitment to the workplace and their own teaching capabilities.

New teachers should not leave the profession during or at the end of their first year—frustrated, disillusioned, or self-doubting. Teachers want to know that they have had the opporunity to serve before they decide to leave.

The authors hope that readers find this book resourceful in providing strategies for how to work effectively with building administrators, colleagues, and parents. Oftentimes, the new teachers find themselves in emotionally charged situations created by veteran teachers, or they may worry about politics involved in the decision-making process, or they fear being ostracized by their peers.

Veteran teachers may also find themselves in such situations created by their colleagues, and they fear repercussions and ostracism. As stated in Chapter 10, they, too, may need to pause in order to determine who challenges their own professional integrity, how they cope with the waves of uncertainty created by unhealthy colleagues, and how to maintain their dignity and stability amid such teachers, staff, and administrators.

Professional success depends not only on how effectively teachers teach their students but also on how teachers deal with these situations.

About the Authors

Beverley H. Johns has over thirty-five years of experience in the public schools, working with students with significant behavioral disorders and learning disabilities. She is the author or co-author of sixteen books, an active member in a number of state and international organizations, and the 2000 recipient of the Outstanding Leadership Award of the International Council for Exceptional Children.

Mary Z. McGrath taught both general and special education for thirty-one years. She is a professional speaker to educators, parents, and other groups, and has authored/coauthored seven other books.

Sarup Mathur is associate professor and program coordinator of the special education program at Arizona State University. She has over twenty years of experience in research and programming for students with emotional and behavioral disorders. She has co-authored and co-edited eight books and published more than fifty articles and chapters.